Praise for *African Europeans*

"Superbly researched. . . . This richly layered history brims with stories of how African Europeans contributed to the culture, politics, and language in the countries they lived in."

—Prospect (UK)

"A fascinating history, with a memorable cast of characters, of Africans who had a vital presence in European life. . . . Though this is a work of synthesis, it's an unusually generous and densely layered one. Otele is not just concerned to tell the life stories of her protagonists, but also to follow their changing portrayals after death—as well as explaining how and why they've been differently interpreted by generations of previous scholars."

—Guardian (UK)

"A brilliant telling of a story that's been too long overlooked."

—New European (UK)

"As well as demystifying the longstanding and complicated presence of African people in Europe, this book . . . explains the role that complex intersections of class, skin colour, nationality, and gender played in the nuanced experiences of African individuals."

—BBC History Magazine

"A thrilling, informative read."

—LSE Review of Books

"Rich in storytelling, discovery, question-making and a way forward, *African Europeans* covers no old ground. This is new—and European history itself is not complete without this book."

—Bonnie Greer, playwright, novelist, and broadcaster

"This is a book I have been waiting for my whole life. It goes beyond the numerous individual Black people in Europe over millennia, to show us the history of the very ideas of blackness, community, and identity on the continent that has forgotten its own past. A necessary and exciting read."

—Afua Hirsch, author of Brit(ish)

"Yoking together the 'African' and the 'European,' too often treated as entirely separate categories, Otele skillfully invites her reader to navigate the multiple intersecting worlds inhabited by her characters. This is fundamentally reparative writing that undoes the cultivated ignorance around race and blackness in Europe and shows us what is irrefutably true—that Black history is European history, indeed, world history."

—Priyamvada Gopal, author of Insurgent Empire

"A magisterial book—brilliant, humane, and gripping, and a call to arms for an end to violence and subjugation. Otele explores the individual lives of African Europeans against great shifts of history, and the result is a masterpiece."
—Kate Williams, historian and broadcaster

"This is a book that all must read—now. This story has been lived not just for centuries but for millennia, all the while being consistently suppressed, denied, or untold. Searing scholarship and heightened humanity combine to illuminate, appall, explore, and ultimately inspire."
—Bettany Hughes, historian and broadcaster

"The scope of Otele's research is awesome, as is her unflinching analysis of the shifting prisms through which African Europeans—particularly women—have had to contest their identities. Full of powerful stories with deep roots and livid scars, *African Europeans* is scholarly, revelatory, and important."
—Jessie Childs, author of *God's Traitors* and *Henry VIII's Last Victim*

"Fascinating. Otele reconnects us with the men and women who came from Africa to shape European history: rulers, diplomats, slaves, and soldiers—above all, our ancestors."
—Dan Snow, historian and broadcaster

"The first survey this century of the fascinating 2,000-year-long history of Africans in Europe. Otele's masterful narrative weaves together the lives of prominent figures—St Maurice, Jacobus Capitein, Manga Bell, Paulette and Jane Nardal—with those of everyday people."
—Hakim Adi, author of *Pan-Africanism: A History*

"A nuanced, thoughtful retelling of the stories of African Europeans, with extraordinary scope. Otele triumphs in her commitment to countering the experiences of the privileged with those of the enslaved. This is a learned, impassioned, and searingly important history."
—Suzannah Lipscomb, historian and broadcaster

"Important, exciting, and illuminating. Otele takes us through centuries of history we think we know but shifts the lens onto those who have been deliberately excluded from traditional historical narratives. This book will change how you look at the past and introduce you to wonderful characters with rich and revealing lives."
—Janina Ramirez, historian and broadcaster

AFRICAN EUROPEANS

AFRICAN EUROPEANS

AN UNTOLD HISTORY

OLIVETTE OTELE

BASIC BOOKS

New York

Basic Books
Hachette Book Group
1290 Avenue of the Americas, New York, NY 10104
www.basicbooks.com

Printed in the United States of America

Originally published in the United Kingdom in 2020 by C. Hurst & Co. (Publishers) Ltd.

First Edition: May 2021

Published by Basic Books, an imprint of Perseus Books, LLC, a subsidiary of Hachette Book Group, Inc. The Basic Books name and logo is a trademark of the Hachette Book Group.

The Hachette Speakers Bureau provides a wide range of authors for speaking events. To find out more, go to www.hachettespeakersbureau.com or call (866) 376-6591.

The publisher is not responsible for websites (or their content) that are not owned by the publisher.

Library of Congress Control Number: 2020946300

ISBNs: 978-1-5416-1967-8 (hardcover), 978-1-5416-1993-7 (ebook)

LSC-C

Printing 1, 2021

ACKNOWLEDGEMENTS

A huge thanks to Hurst Publishers, and in particular to Michael Dwyer and Farhaana Arefin for their immense patience and commitment to this book. I also want to thank the generous colleagues and friends who provided me with crucial sources: Josephine Quinn, now that the door to ancient History has been opened, there's no turning back! I'm indebted to Emmanuel Karagiannis for starting a conversation about Afro-Greeks years ago in Brussels and enriching it with wonderful details and sources. Guillaume Cingal, Brandenburg was an important addition, thank you. Karwan Fatah-Black, I am incredibly grateful to you for the bulk of information about the Netherlands. Cheryl Morgan, you are wonderful, and so was Le Chevalier D'Éon. Michael McEachrane, thank you so very much for all the material about racism and Scandinavia, and for your commitment to social justice. Camilla Hawthorne and Tiffany Florvil, you are such outstanding thinkers, you both inspire me.

A few people have kept me going, encouraging me and pushing me when it was needed: my Ore Umoja Welsh-Trinis, Zimbabwean, Nigerian and Jamaican sisters, Maria, Ru, Victoria, Charlene and Marisa. Others have relentlessly fought my corner elsewhere, thus allowing me the brain space to keep on writing: Sadiah Qureshi and Estelle Paranque, your kindness moves me beyond words. Speaking of unique women, a bear hug to my

ACKNOWLEDGEMENTS

agent Georgina Capel, a warrior queen with a heart. I am indebted to my wonderfully protective brother—Bob—and my Divas and sisters—Roseline, Chantal and Chris.

I had the urge to write this book because of the trajectories of three clans: Kono-Onana, Mengue and Otele-Kriker. This book is dedicated to all their descendants, and in particular to my sons Idris and Affan. A final thanks to my kids' dad and dearest partner in life, JLK.

INTRODUCTION

A great many valuable books have been written about black lives and experiences in very different geographical contexts.[1] However, a relatively low number deal specifically with the experiences of people of African descent in Europe before the world wars. A handful of individual stories have been marginally integrated into European history, but most of these relate to the history of enslavement or to colonial encounters from the fifteenth century onwards. Published work often pairs the term 'black presence' with a specific geographical area. From 'black presence in Europe' to 'black presence in Wales', these volumes map out the lives of people of African descent in the named places.[2] The kinds of books that are readily available are also often about known men and women. Of course, such individuals are worth examining, and these biographies provide interesting interpretations and bring new light to their life stories. For example, over the last few decades, several volumes have been dedicated to former enslaved people. From Olaudah Equiano to Mary Prince, both of whom lived in Britain, the focus seems to be on eighteenth-century abolitionists and their connections to various groups of people.

Black abolitionists and other black men and women have been looked at in relation to their roles as models in well-known paintings or as servants who feature in travel writings and other artistic productions. When examined as individuals, these men and women are generally perceived as exceptional characters whose lives were transformed by complex encounters with Europeans. In such accounts, the notion of exceptionalism is used as a plausible reason for their fame. Some of their stories are believed to have survived because of the extraordinary nature of their contributions to European societies. Little, however, has been published about further aspects of their lives, such as the close connection they might have had with other people of African descent. Some histories have been forgotten or their importance underestimated. For example, African resistance to enslavement on African coasts or the fight against the transatlantic slave trade in Africa are scarcely mentioned in volumes about enslavement in European colonial history. Yet resistance was not uncommon, with examples including the powerful story of Queen Nzinga in the seventeenth century, the numerous slave revolts aboard ships along African coasts, and the disruption of plantation lives by Maroons and enslaved people living in proximity to masters. There is a continuum in the history of black resistance to enslavement that forms part of what Cedric J. Robinson saw as the 'roots of black radicalism'.[3] According to Robinson, the West got hold of black bodies through violence to produce wealth, but that also signalled the end of capitalist states. In fact, the seeds of destruction were embedded in the means of acquiring wealth.

The black figures who are remembered are only part of the broader story of a fight against exploitation. The connections between these various stories have been forgotten, because physical subjugation was accompanied not only by a rewriting of the oppressor's history but also by a shaping of the story of the oppressed. Robinson examines the way certain stories have been overlooked—even those that were uncovered by respected scholars long before transatlantic slavery. The renowned historian

INTRODUCTION

Herodotus, for example, recalled encounters with Ethiopians and with the Colchians, who he thought were descended from the Egyptians.[4] Those encounters, in Robinson's analysis, are missing pieces that although recorded by historians have remained largely untold in the modern and contemporary Global North. Using the example of American slavery, Robinson also demonstrates how early European travellers recorded the social, cultural and agricultural systems they saw in areas in West Africa; nevertheless, by the eighteenth century the narrative of unsophisticated 'Negroes' was shaping colonists' ideology. Robinson notes that 'the destruction of the African past' was a process that went through various stages.[5] For example, naming played a crucial role in the process of erasure. 'The construct of Negro, unlike the terms "African," "Moor," or "Ethiope" suggested no situatedness in time, that is history, or space, that is ethno- or politico-geography. The Negro had no civilization, no cultures, no religions, no history, no place, and finally no humanity that might command consideration.'[6] Robinson remarks that 'the creation of the Negro, the fiction of a dumb beast of burden fit only for slavery, was closely associated with the economic, technical, and financial requirements of Western development from the sixteenth century on'.[7] Africans who were valuable enough to be remembered were those who had been deemed exceptional.

The notion of exceptionalism is an interesting tool with which to understand history. It is used in history writing to shed light on histories that intersect with class, gender, religion, race and so on. A pitfall of the term is its suggestion that one story, circumstance or character is better than another. Yet as Philippa Levine contends, these comparisons can make room for transnational and cross-cultural analyses that may help to build bridges between different stories and countries, bringing contradictory ideas together.[8] The problem lies instead in the universalising aspects accompanying many comparative studies, which imply that we draw lessons from stories because of the guiding principles that are supposedly shared by all of us. Levine argues that exceptionalism sometimes attempts to 'humanise' a story, a context or a character, as exemplified by Niall Ferguson's accounts of the British Empire. It can also 'demonise' a story, as shown through studies of dictators such as Hitler.[9] Nonetheless, the appeal of the exceptional is undeniable if we are to believe the high number of books presenting their stories as unique accounts of specific regional, national or global aspects of history.

Exceptionalism is also a notion that plays an important role in studies of race, racism and race relations. Dienke Hondius has argued that exceptionalism was the last of the five patterns that shaped the European history of race and race relations. Hondius contends that Europe has shifted between 'infantilization, exoticism, bestialization, distancing and exclusion, and exceptionalism'.[10] While infantilisation posited that Africans and Asians were, in essence, children, it also brought with it the highly disputed idea of 'paternalism', whereby Africans needed to be taken care of or even saved from themselves and their peers—as exemplified by the justification of slavery by its supporters in Europe in the eighteenth and nineteenth centuries.[11] Exoticism, on the other hand, related to the European fascination with difference and with black and brown bodies, minds and cultures. Equally important in the history of European hierarchisation of extra-European communities was the notion of bestiality, which worked in conjunction with the two previous alleged traits. Both the appeal of the perceived exotic body and the fear it inspired were intertwined with the question of bestiality. The African was equated with a wild animal, untamed and prone to violence. Associated with evil, Africans needed to be 'domesticated' if Europeans in contact with them were to feel and be safe. Undomesticated, they needed to be kept at a safe distance, preferably away from Europe.

INTRODUCTION

Exceptionalism in this context needs to be envisaged alongside other aspects, such as the relationship between Africans and Europeans and the European gaze imposed upon Africans. Exceptionalism raises several questions about whose views have shaped one group's trajectories and whose position with regards to race and racism determined the social status of certain African Europeans. Citing the African American novelist Richard Wright, Hondius notes that 'racism is primarily a white problem because whites governed the conditions through which the discourse of race emerged and endures'.[12]

Grouping the lives of certain populations in one carefully packaged and recognisable word such as the term 'Empire', or resting one's case study on the life of an individual, also helps us understand that exceptionalism encompasses specific and complex contexts. The recognition of these contexts allows for a rich analysis of crossroads and ruptures in historical accounts, as well as making room for the study of local and international trajectories. Exceptionalism can lead to a thorough analysis of the tensions between what has been forgotten and lurks on the outskirts of the discourse (those forgotten or untold histories), and how history is presented and transmitted for various social, cultural and, of course, political reasons.

Exceptional stories serve a purpose in the construction of identities. In the case of the histories of African Europeans presented in this volume, they are exceptional because they have defied obscurity to be included in European accounts. However, many of these stories already existed outside of European hagiographies. Some have been at the heart of accounts from Hebrew, Arabic, and Aramaic civilisations. A vast number of those stories inform us about the nature and legacy of encounters between various worlds. The following chapters move from well-known individuals who are often considered to have been exceptional, to contexts that have provided the opportunity for their recognition and even celebration. These stories follow a chronological order at times, but at others the narrative explores modern and contemporary experiences in a certain place before considering previous histories of people of African descent in the same country or city. The chronological approach helps us to understand historical changes across Europe and their impact on African Europeans at the time, or how these groups of people may have contributed to shaping later mentalities. The choice to focus on specific places, individuals or groups was dictated by the availability of sources and the relevance of these stories to contemporary questions about intercultural collaboration, identity and so on. The stories span from the third century to the twenty-first century. This volume is based on the scholarship of those who have been working on various aspects of the histories of people of African and European descent, and brings these studies together in a comprehensive and unique way that moves beyond a mapping of black presence in Europe to delve into questions such as identity, citizenship, resilience and human rights. African Europeans are defined and perceived as travellers. They are citizens of the world, which would lead some people to accuse them of being 'citizens of nowhere'.[13]

Human rights and citizenship seem to be, at first glance, modern concepts. The rights of men and, later, women have been dependent on certain conditions from time immemorial. In Europe, the history of rights is heavily linked to political, economic and philosophical histories. From Ancient Greece to the Reconquista, the question of rights has shaped European history. But from the fifteenth century onwards it became a pressing matter as Europe slowly moved away from feudalism. With the Declaration of the Rights of Man and of the Citizen in 1789, France was forced to acknowledge the shift that had taken place and the demands of the population for more rights and freedoms, and the rest of Europe rapidly followed. Particularly relevant in this history of human rights and citizenship is the question of the rights of extra-European peoples whose bodies had been deemed relevant only as wealth-building tools. Enslaved and African bodies, barely tolerated in European cities, brought to the surface the question of belonging, identity and freedom, as we will see in the next chapters. Africans enjoying a certain degree of freedom in Europe were considered to have earned or been granted their rights and privileges, and were therefore rendered exceptional, able to enjoy exclusive rights. Exclusivity in some instances required that they were welcomed by the majority group, but in other cases the acknowledgement of their existence did not ensure the acceptance of those African Europeans by all. Acceptance was sometimes achieved through a process that required them to renounce their heritage, or one of their parents. This, however, did not always lead to inclusion, as the experiences of numerous African Europeans in France demonstrated.

Questions of inclusion and acceptance are also linked to issues of citizenship and integration models for minority groups in Europe. France's assimilationist model, for example, does not eradicate institutionalised racism, neither does it change the mentalities of racists at an individual level. In fact, the French assimilation model is based on anti-racialist views. David T. Goldberg suggested that:

> Antiracism requires historical memory, recalling the conditions of racial degradation and relating contemporary to historical and local to global conditions. If antiracist commitment requires remembering and recalling, antiracialism suggests forgetting, getting over, moving on, wiping away the terms of reference, at best (or worst) a commercial memorializing rather than a recounting and redressing of the terms of humiliation and devaluation.[14]

The experiences of African Europeans regarding the question of citizenship and human rights vary greatly and are informed by diverse historical, social, political and economic contexts. Linked to these ideas is a notion of identity that depends on variances across time and space in other notions such as race, heritage and culture. As a result, the terminology employed in this book varies too. It will use and quote terms such as Africans, Negroes, African Americans, African Europeans, mixed race, dual heritage, and so on, not as interchangeable and atemporal categories but as words that have significance in particular places and at specific times in history.

The term 'African European' is therefore a provocation for those who deny that one can have multiple identities and even citizenships, as well as those who claim that they do not 'see colour'. It is also a daring invitation to rethink the way we use and read European and African histories and define terms, such as citizenship, social cohesion and fraternity, that have been the basis of contemporary European societal values. In addition, it challenges the use of such terms against various groups as exclusionary tools. African Europeans living in Europe are at the crossroads of several intersecting identities. It would have been equally adequate to use the term 'European Africans' to refer to people of African descent born in Europe, but most of them are defined by other groups or define themselves firstly through their connection with the African continent. That connection and identification will be further explored in these chapters. The aims of this volume are to understand connections across time and space, to debunk persistent myths, and to revive and celebrate the lives of African Europeans.

Chapter One establishes the connections between past and present through the story of encounters in the Mediterranean regions between the Romans and the Meroites, Egyptians and Ethiopians. These connections bring to the forefront the views of Christendom on Arab Muslim worlds and the dynamics at play in identity construction along religious and ethno-racial lines from 20 BCE to the seventeenth century. These dynamics allowed African Europeans such as Saint Maurice, the Queen of Sheba, Emperor Septimius Severus and other lesser-known individuals to navigate several worlds.

In Chapter Two we continue to travel in time along the Mediterranean, and discover that by the sixteenth century Southern Europe was characterised by a sizeable black population. Some of them, such as the first Duke of Florence Alessandro de Medici, reached prominence, while others lived their lives in subjugation. Although select individuals were free, the vast majority were enslaved and worked in rural areas of Italy and Spain or as house servants in wealthy households. Analysing the way various groups interacted in Renaissance Europe through the lives of Juan Latino and other, often unnamed, enslaved men and women allows us to understand how notions such as racism and racialism were constructed.

Chapter Three examines the lives of African Europeans in Western and Central Europe. Sixteenth- and seventeenth-century Europe continued to thrive through trade, and Western Europe's involvement in the transatlantic slave trade and plantation slavery further shaped the relationship between Africa, Europe, and America. By the eighteenth century European competition for commodities and slave markets had shifted the nature of the relationship between Europe and Africa, as exemplified by the life of the Afro-Dutch minister Jacobus Capitein. The eighteenth century was a time at which black presence was severely controlled, and scientific classification of various species was employed in a bid to establish a racial hierarchy. It was also the era in which key figures such as Joseph Boulogne, Chevalier de Saint-Georges, emerged and challenged those classifications.

In Chapter Four, we turn our attention to those born in Africa with both African and European parents, and the role of black women in shaping identities. This chapter looks at gender roles and trading interests in coastal towns. It studies how several European merchants settled, made a fortune and left behind children of African European dual heritage. It also analyses the blurring of racial hierarchies and boundaries in places where European descent offered great economic and social advantages, as typified by the lives of the Signares in Gorée and Saint Louis in Senegal, and of Ga women in Ghana. In addition, the chapter examines the legacies of these histories in contemporary Danish societies.

Chapter Five takes the territories of Brandenburg as an example of historical amnesia and looks at the processes that have led to the remembering and then forgetting of the region's past and have thus allowed Germany to portray itself as 'unblemished' by the slave trade. The German colonisation of Africa and Cameroon is, however, well documented, and these links provide us with the opportunity to assess the histories of African Europeans such as Manga Bell. African European histories are transcontinental, and it is important to see how they are intertwined with the stories of key African American and Caribbean-, Senegalese- and German-born individuals.

Chapter Six assesses the journeys of African Europeans in the twentieth and twenty-first centuries by comparing the experiences of Afro-Italians and the Afro-Swedish, particularly regarding the question of citizenship. The chapter continues its exploration of the stories of African Europeans by considering well-known individuals, such as Abram Petrovich Hannibal and Aleksandr Pushkin in Russia, and demonstrating that connections with Africa did not bring about a positive societal outlook on the question of race and interracial collaborations. The chapter ends with an example of resistance and resilience by African Europeans in the twentieth and twenty-first centuries through Afro-Dutch scholarly and grassroots activism.

Chapter Seven reflects on the way identities and identity markers function in contemporary Europe. The chapter brings together several notions, such as race, racism, racialism, citizenship, black radical liberation and activism. It looks at how gender, and Afrofeminism in particular, plays a crucial role in shaping African European identities. It also highlights the creation of organising spaces for healing and strategising in order to fight against social inequalities. This chapter sheds light on discrepancies in tackling discrimination within the European Union, as demonstrated by stop-and-search practice in Spain or the experiences of Afro-Greeks. It then recognises the extensive work done in Britain on the subject of African Europeans and the different ways twenty-first-century Black Britons fight against racial discrimination, inequality and marginalisation. The chapter ends by considering commonalities in the histories of African Europeans, and showing the ways in which they are embedded in transnational, European, African and American histories.

Just as they recover stories from the past of encounters, experiences and identity formation, these histories also inform us about the swift and creative ways various communities respond to negative perceptions about people of African descent in the Global North in the twenty-first century. Today, African Europeans continue to build transnational and transcontinental alliances that are powerfully inclusive. African Europeans from Generation Z have shown an appetite for reviving the empowering stories of their ancestors. They are actively seeking these pockets of knowledge by engaging with virtual learning, online debates, social media, and so on. They are also generating new narratives of resilience and diving into activism, from pushing for action on climate change, gender equality, and LGBTQ rights, to dismantling racism, islamophobia, antisemitism and other forms of discrimination.

This energy and active participation in driving forward social justice has reached a new height with the overwhelming global response to the police killing of African American George Floyd in May 2020. The mass demonstrations led by Black Lives Matter and consequent debates about racism have highlighted both the need to expand knowledge about the histories of people of African descent and the urgency with which we must revise the teaching of colonial history in the Global North.

African Europeans is a response to these needs. It aims to provide multiple histories as a starting point to learn about the past and to dismantle racial oppression in the present. The book demonstrates that cross-cultural engagement is a powerful way forward to combat discrimination. Most of all, it is a celebration of long histories—African, European, and global—of collaborations, migrations, resilience and creativity that have remained untold for centuries.

1

EARLY ENCOUNTERS

FROM PIONEERS TO AFRICAN ROMANS

Modern-day Ethiopia presents us with various stories of exile or migration that date back centuries. However, scholars and students are more familiar with stories related to either empire and colonisation or Ethiopia's role in the world wars. Among the latter are stories of the Italo-Ethiopian wars. The exile of the emperor Haile Selassie is an example of a colonial story which became a European local story—relating in this case to the city of Bath in England in the second half of the twentieth century. Italian and Abyssinian forces entered into combat in October 1935, and the capital of Ethiopia, Addis Ababa, was invaded by Italy's fascist troops in 1936. The ruling emperor, Haile Selassie, was forced to leave his country the same year and stayed abroad until 1941. Selassie settled in Bath and made a home in the city for a few years. One could contend that, for a while, he became an adopted African European. His attachment to the city was such that he gave his home, Fairfield House, to Bath for use by the local community when he went back to Ethiopia. This positive example of Afro-European collaboration is well remembered in Britain, in particular by the British Rastafarian community in Bath and beyond.[1] This community, along with people living near the house, has been highly involved in preserving Haile Selassie's home, history and memory. However, the links between modern-day Ethiopia and Europe—Italy in particular— were established long before nineteenth- and twentieth-century colonial wars. This story started with the relationship between Meroe and Egypt, specifically between Ethiopian queens and Egypt's Roman governor, in 23 BCE.

Histories of the ancient Nubian kingdom of Kush and its capital, Meroe, clearly demonstrate that many of the encounters that took place centuries ago between Europe and Africa were far from peaceful. The Greek geographer Strabo of Amaseia (c. 62 BCE–24 CE), author of a seventeen-book *Geographika* which covered the history and topography of thousands of places, is one of few narrators whose work provides us with detailed accounts of the relationship between the Kushites and the Roman Empire. One of Strabo's most notable contributions in this respect concerns the Candaces or Kandakes (often known as Queens of Ethiopia), who fought against Roman invasion. In one of his volumes, he gives a striking account of how the Roman Gaius Petronius moved to attack the city of Napata, the royal seat of the Candace, only to find that she had already left for a more secure stronghold.[2] Accompanied by an army of thousands of men, the Candace launched an attack on the Roman garrison, but Petronius managed to prevent the invasion by entering and securing the fortress before the queen and her army ransacked the place. Local inscriptions have shown that this queen was in all probability Amanirenas (reigned c. 40–10 BCE). We learn through Strabo that the Kushites had threatened Roman holdings in Egypt; prior to this attack Amanirenas had, with the support of the Kushite prince Akinidad, defeated Roman troops in the city of Syene and on the islands of

Elephantine and Philae. In response, Petronius had invaded the strong city of Premnis and taken a fortress before he was confronted with Amanirenas's army.

What followed was an extraordinary series of negotiations, in which the Kushites sent ambassadors to engage with the Romans. Petronius demanded that the statue of Caesar that had been toppled be repaired, and eventually the Kushites capitulated. They finally signed a peace treaty in 21–20 BCE. These encounters demonstrate that the Roman Empire was well established in certain parts of the African continent, and one could contend that the inhabitants of these places were African Europeans. The episode with Amanirenas also shows that the balance of power was not always tilted towards the Roman Empire.

As far as gender roles are concerned, the stories of the Candaces challenge certain assumptions. The Candaces had always valiantly protected the Meroitic kingdoms as fiercely as kings. Although the term 'Candace' refers to the mother of the heir to the throne or to a royal wife, these women were warriors in their own right. Beside Strabo's accounts of Amanirenas, other stories are found in the writings of Greek historian Dio Cassius and in the Romance of Alexander.[3] Amanirenas was by no means the only Candace who fiercely protected the integrity of her kingdoms. The subsequent Candaces of Kush, Amanishakhete and Amanitore, followed in her footsteps.

These stories give us an insight into the way the relationship between Europe and Africa was built over time in areas where there was no strict delineation between the two continents. The term 'Europe' was used by merchants, soldiers and scholars to refer to their travels in various areas corresponding roughly to our modern understanding of the continent. It appeared in the sixth century BCE, and it included the regions around the Aegean Sea. The word 'Africa' has many possible etymologies, but one of the earliest uses dates back to 146 BCE, when the term appeared as 'Africa Proconsularis'. It referred to a Roman province in today's Tunisia, Algeria and Libya. The dispute about the etymology of the word matters because the term is thought to have come from a tribe that lived in the north of the continent, now Libya; if this is true, the hypothesis presented by various scholars, including Flavius Josephus, about the Latin or Greek basis of the name is ideologically dubious and Romano- or Grecocentric. Irrespective of such debates, the trade, war and political collaboration through which the populations of these continents came into contact with each other all defined their geographical borders. They shaped the journeys of the various historical figures in this volume.

When we examine the history of these places and their peoples, the question of otherness that is present throughout this study takes various forms. Otherness and othering played a role in delineating geographical spaces. The regions known as the Latin West, which included north-west Africa, Gallia and Italia, comprised several Muslim societies. Yet by the eleventh century, these societies had been grouped into entities that obscured their diversity of beliefs and social practices. Geraldine Heng notes that although names such as Agarenes, Ismaelites, Moors and Saracens were used to refer to Arabs, Christian Arabs were not defined in the same way. As time went on, the term 'Saracen' survived and came to be associated with negative traits.[4] Heng contends that those categorised as Saracens because of their religion did not respond in kind and homogenise all Christians, but instead recognised the diversity of regions and societies dominated by Christianity. 'Islamic historiography in Arabic and other languages, it seems, continued to specify territorial, national, and ethnoracial differences when they referred to Europeans as "Romans, Greeks, Franks, Slavs," and so on'.[5]

The next step towards racialisation was the attribution of specific characteristics to groups of people. This was achieved with the assertion that the birth of Islam was based on a lie and the prophet was 'a cunning, deceitful, ambitious, rapacious, ruthless, and licentious liar'.[6] As these traits characterised the prophet, all Muslims allegedly shared such negative attributes. Accounts of this nature circulated around the Mediterranean.[7] By the eleventh century, Muslims were presented either as horrifying animals, as in the French epic poem *La Chanson de Roland*, or as prone to indulging in shameful sexual exploits.[8]

Those who defined themselves first and foremost as Christian also perpetuated a narrative that informed racialisation. Crusaders, as Heng notes, carried a banner that symbolised their attachment to Christ. They perceived and defined themselves as the 'Christian race'. The step from racialisation through religion to othering based on skin tone also took place in literature. Heng provides an edifying example with a Middle English romance, *The King of Tars*. In the story, a fair princess is forced to convert to Islam and marry a Muslim king. The child born from the union turns out to be an inhumane monster, only saved and physically transformed through baptism. The father, who is defined as black, also becomes white after baptism and decides to convert his subjects.[9] Intermarriage was not an entirely fictitious practice. It was only in the second half of the eleventh century that marriages between European Christian noblewomen and Muslim kings became less common. However, Christian slave women were still kept in harems, so customarily that five Nasrid sultans of Granada had mothers who were enslaved Christians. Most of these women had been enslaved either during Islamic conquests or through a slave traffic which specifically sought white-skinned women.[10] Slave traders came from very different regions: the Vikings enslaved and sold Irish people, the English traded in human beings with the Franks, and the Venetians sold people from Central Europe. Some of these enslaved people ended up in the regions along the

Mediterranean, with a large number taken to Egypt.[11] The notion of African Europeans therefore takes on a different meaning when we consider the provenance and trajectories of all the people included in this group.

During the same period, Europeans also provided boys originating from Central Europe, Eurasia and the Caucasus to Dar al-Islam. Those boys were raised to be integrated into the military forces, which were composed predominantly of enslaved people. They were known as the Mamluks. In time, they became members of an elite group who could buy their own Mamluks and marry slave women who had originated from their own land or the daughters of other Mamluks, thus creating a 'military race'.[12] Heng demonstrates that premodern Egypt was dominated by Muslim Circassian Mamluks. Within a couple of centuries, they became the rulers of Egypt and enforced a strict delineation between themselves as a unique category of people from the Caucasus and other ethnic groups, forbidding marriages across these racial lines. The usefulness of Mamluks was undeniable. They were ruthless warriors and ethnically distinct, and their presence was encouraged in modern Egypt. Fifteenth-century travellers provide accounts of Mamluks from Hungary, Germany and Italy living in Cairo.[13] However, those Mamluks by their existence blurred the racial markers that tend to characterise Europeans and Africans. They were, in today's terms, white African Muslims of European descent.

Mamluks were not the only soldiers who broke barriers and influenced multiple worlds. The legend of Saint Maurice provides an interesting lens through which to further understand human geography. By the third century CE, Roman presence in the Thebes region had been strengthened by the incorporation of conquered populations into the Roman army. Their influence extended south, and the legacy of this era takes various forms. The figure of Saint Maurice is particularly revealing in this respect. One of the most famous images of Saint Maurice is a statue in Magdeburg Cathedral in Germany. The statue dates back to the thirteenth century, long after the birth of Saint Maurice in the third century CE.

Understanding how Saint Maurice became known as a saint sheds light on the formation of European hagiography. It also provides us with information about the place of saints in medieval art. Saint Maurice's story was transmitted from generation to generation. He became a legend over the centuries, and yet historians have very few details about his early life before joining the Roman troops. It is thought that Maurice was born near present-day Egypt and enrolled in the Theban legion posted there, by what is now the Sudanese border. He was allegedly sent to crush an insurrection in Gaul as a commander of Roman troops, and was asked to ensure that his troops pay their dues to the god Jupiter before battle, as was required of all Roman soldiers.[14] He initially agreed, but then changed his mind for reasons that may have been linked to religious freedom. The emperor Maximian sent troops to arrest Maurice and the most loyal of his soldiers. They were all executed in 287 CE. Maurice's origins have been the source of extensive scholarship. Most volumes tend to look at the legend's transformation over time, but a more modest number of studies examine its basis.

The starting point of the story is a letter from Eucherius, bishop of Lyon, to another bishop called Salvius, written around 450. Eucherius gave an account of Theban soldiers who had been killed in the Alps at the order of Maximian.[15] However, the accuracy of the account has been challenged. Denis van Berchem notes that there was a soldier named Maurice of Apamea whose martyrdom in Syria was erroneously conflated with the suppression of the uprising in Gaul under Maximian's reign. This story could have been confused with the story of Maurice of Thebes.[16] Other explanations have been provided in the work of military historians. The

Theban Legion referred to by Eucherius could have been misleading—he mentions *Thebaei*, which was the name of a specific Italian military unit in the fourth century.[17] We also learn from Eucherius that the original story came from Theodore, who was bishop of Octodurum in the late fourth century. Eucherius had taken Theodore's story and made it his own. Historians have suggested that the account of Maurice was a political story crafted by Theodore and aimed at encouraging people to rebel against usurpers.[18] As far as the relationship with Thebes is concerned, inscriptions recording work carried out by Theban soldiers under the command of one Mauricius circa 367–75 were found in Egypt near Syene. It would not have been unusual for the same Mauricius, or Maurice, to be sent up north near to today's Eastern Europe. The legend of Maurice spread up north itself, and reached the Rhine Valley. It became part of the region's history.

To understand how the story travelled, we need to look at how political and religious aspirations changed the history of this region. The erosion of the Roman Empire and the invasion of Roman-ruled provinces by the Goths, Lombards and Franks were followed by a relative stability with the accession to power of Charlemagne in 800 CE. After Charlemagne's death, his territories were divided into what was later known as France and Germany. In the south of the continent, King Frederick II— King of Sicily, self-proclaimed King of Jerusalem, and Holy Roman Emperor from 1220—was excommunicated three times by the pope. Yet he is also remembered as a cosmopolitan monarch who was said to have welcomed Jews, Turks, Arabs and Africans to his court. His tour of the Germanic region in 1234 is said to have caused a stir because of the noticeable number of African soldiers present in his army.[19] Frederick even appointed the African Johannes Maurus as Lord Chamberlain for the kingdom of Sicily.[20] Black musicians, servants and distinguished guests, alongside the legend of Saint Maurice, would have influenced and redefined the European gaze towards Africans at the time. African presence in European courts during the Crusades was modest in extent but consistent and long-lasting enough to be remembered and represented in various paintings. However, as Effrosyni Zacharopoulou has argued, this rather positive outlook on the influence of Maurice and other black people in European courts should not obscure another reality. The Pope and cardinals resented the fact that although individual scholars and esteemed guests accepted and recognised the power of the Christian church, Ethiopia resisted the influence of the pope; even Christian Nubia would eventually give way to the reign of a Muslim king supported by Mamluks in 1323.[21]

In the second half of the tenth century, representations of Maurice the African appeared up north under the reign of Emperor Otto I. The emperor, also known as Otto the Great, defeated the Huns at the Battle of Lechfeld in 955 and began a campaign of conversion that later took a significant turn with the foundation of the archdiocese of Magdeburg. By erecting a statue of Saint Maurice, Magdeburg Cathedral clearly stated that the place was a crossroads and a spiritual reference for the expansion and celebration of the Christian faith, as well as a powerful symbol of the status of the Roman church. Saint Maurice, now a patron of the Holy Roman Empire, was the mark of things to come. Beside religious and political considerations, Magdeburg was to be a central point for agriculture and trade. The figure of Maurice clothed in chain mail, an emblem of imperial insignia holding a reproduction of the Holy Lance, protected traditions embodied by European medieval knights. His African features did not pose any problems for contemporaries, as he was himself the expression of the common values across boundaries that were embodied by the strong Roman Empire. The popularity of the patron saint was so vast that the name Maurice became popular among the ruling elite, and first-born children were often named after him. Town centres and various other places also took on the name Maurice.[22]

In all depictions, Maurice is represented as an African and his features have been kept. Stefan Lochner's altarpiece *Dreikönigsaltar* (c. 1440, Cologne), Rogier Van Der Weyden's Bladelin Altarpiece (1452–55), and later on Albrecht Dürer's *Adoration of the Magi* (1504) bring the story of the three magi together with the figure of Saint Maurice. In each of these paintings one of the three magi (either Caspar or Balthasar) has become a Berber, a moor or a black African. The veneration of the magi and that of Maurice are merged in Lochner's painting, where an African is seen carrying a 'Maurice Flag'.[23] Balthasar appears as a black magus in several paintings, such as the work of Bartholomäus Bruyn the Elder and other masters, in the sixteenth century, while Saint Maurice appears again in Matthias Grünewald's depiction of *The Meeting of SS Erasmus and Maurice* (c. 1520–25). The veneration of both Maurice and the magi continued and led to numerous local representations of these figures in German territories. Later, Magdeburg once again pushed boundaries by creating a bust of Saint Maurice's imaginary sister, Fidis, under the leadership of Cardinal Albrecht in the second half of the sixteenth century.

These representations of origins, appearance and colour in medieval and early modern arts could be interpreted as an acceptance of otherness. Alongside such representations, the equation of blackness with evil seemed to be linked to ideas of morality rather than to black Africans. Yet this era saw a shift in perceptions. Scholars have argued that the notion of race that was defined in the nineteenth century was invented in the Middle Ages. David Theo Goldberg has contended that in the last part of the Middle Ages:

> race was emergent rather than fully formed, incipiently invoked to
> fashion nation formation in the early moments of national elabora-

tion as racial consciousness began to emerge out of—and later can be said to have taken over if not to have replaced—the mix of public religious constitution, the symbolics and architectonics of blood, the naturalizing dispositions—the metaphysics—of hierarchical chains of being, and the ontological orderings in terms of supposedly heritable rationalities.[24]

Other scholars have noted that a city such as Nuremberg, which saw a vibrant development in engineering, mathematics and navigation in the fifteenth and sixteenth centuries, was paradoxically governed by a relatively conservative religious interpretation of and approach to history. It was believed that the world was divided into several main parts that owed their existence to Noah's lineage. Many thought, for example, that Noah's son Ham, who saw his father's naked body and was consequently cursed, was the forefather of North Africans. However, no links were made between his colour and the idea of inferiority. Dürer's *Head of a Negro* (1508) and *The Negress Katherina* (1521) are artistic achievements because the artist managed to capture the nuances of expression of Africans, who had often been rendered different through the colouring of their features. Connections made between evil and blackness were striking, but evil characters were not necessarily depicted with African features in the sixteenth century.

Nonetheless, medieval Europe regulated the lives of those it perceived as 'other' and a danger to the majority group. The persecution of the Jewish community in the Middle Ages, for example, has been well documented. In England, a series of measures aimed at making the Jewish community more visible were passed. In 1215, the Church in England wanted Jews and Muslims to wear clothes that would differentiate them from Christians. In 1218, Jews were made to wear a badge. By 1222 they had to wear a revised version of that badge that had been crafted by the authorities in England, and by 1290 they were forced to leave England altogether. Alleged ritual murders of young Christian children were attributed to the Jewish community. References to those rituals were found in fiction, which was often conflated with reality and had dire consequences for Jews. In 1255, for example, ninety-one Jews were arrested and, under the order of King Henry III, one was executed following the accidental death of a young boy. The Jewish community were also othered through perception of their physical attributes, as represented in the King's Remembrancer Memoranda Rolls.[25] The rolls presented the Jews as a recognisable community, who could be identified through 'Jewish faces' that closely resembled caricatures.

Heng highlights that the question of race was fundamental to the formation of European identity. She notes that cultural creation in the medieval period was very much in line with this formation. For example, thirteenth-century *mappae mundi* such as the Hereford Map not only displayed places, but also contained objects, animals and people. Their representations of Europe are characterised by civic centres, cathedrals and examples of urban planning, while the rest of the world is noticeably lacking in these. Asia and Africa are populated by monsters, people with visible disabilities and creatures that are both animal and human, as well as 'troglodytes, cynocephali, sciapods' and other populations deemed abhorrent to Europeans.[26] However, Europeans were by no means defined as a homogeneous group that enjoyed the benefits of higher intellect. Ireland and its people were portrayed as a lower race that needed a firm hand to improve themselves. Heng notes that there were several configurations of race and racial hierarchy that existed in pre-modern and modern times. Medieval England had specific views about its neighbours. 'Caricatured as a primitive land—an undeveloped global south lying to the west of England—Ireland was accordingly positioned as a project in need of evolutionary improvement and instruction, in order to force the "savage Irish" ... to emerge one day from their barbaric cocoon into a state of enlightened civilization'.[27]

The colour black, as an entity that represented inferiority and the ugliness of human experiences on earth, was a component of Christian notions of good, evil and the redemptive opportunity for salvation through atonement for one's sins. Africans were black or of dark skin. They were the colour of evil, but they could repent, be saved and even become patron saints. The representation of Africans varied greatly between different settings in Europe. One of the facades of Notre-Dame Cathedral in the city of Rouen, France, clearly shows the execution of Saint John the Baptist being carried out by an African. The image dates to 1260. It forms a stark contrast with *The Beheading of Saint John the Baptist*, a 1608 painting by Caravaggio, which shows a white man reaching behind his back for a knife as he presses the saint's head to the floor.

Black saints appeared across Europe in the twelfth and thirteenth centuries, mainly in the form of sculptures. Erin Kathleen Rowe has studied the emergence and significance of black saints in the medieval and early modern Church, and in particular Black Madonnas such as Our Ladies of Montserrat, Guadalupe, Tindari and Le Puy.[28] How these saints came to exist has been the subject of long debates amongst scholars. While some argue that the Madonnas were initially white and the degradation that occurred over time changed their original colours, others note that as colour changes occurred, those saints came to be venerated as black Virgin Marys. Further scholars contend that the Madonnas were intentionally created black, while other versions of Mary were white with black hands, to symbolise the transformation from sinner to saint, the struggle of all believers, and the transformative power of the Catholic Church—or simply that spiritual beauty could accompany 'less aesthetically pleasing' black skin.[29] Rowe demonstrates that these female appearances had in fact been preceded by male black saints in late antiquity. Born in Abyssinia in the fourth century, Moses, also known as Moses the Black, the Ethiopian and so on, became an important figure in Western Castile. His former life as a thief and a sinner was used to show how a black man could become white and be saved after he had repented. Rowe looks at the careful editing of Moses's story and suggests that:

> the authors used the story to bolster a specific view of the aesthetics of blackness, and their decision to streamline Moses's life into a narrative of blackness, humility, and self-abnegation underscored the saint's lesser status—even lesser humanity. The themes echoed here—prejudice against black skin, the association of black sanctity and excessive humility, the interplay between interior and exterior— recurred in early modern hagiographies of black saints.[30]

A slow shift also occurred as many Europeans came into contact more often with Africans. Stories about the role played by the Ethiopian Prester John, a legendary king said to have ruled over an Eastern Christian nation, travelled and provided a hopeful platform for the expansion of Christendom. The representation of black saints took a new turn in the second half of the fifteenth century. Ideas about the blackness of sinners, as represented in the sculptures of black saints, or recognition of the role of black figures such as the magi in the foundations of Christianity were slowly replaced by a worldlier black presence. This was caused by the establishment of links between Ethiopian monks and Rome, Constance and Florence, and by the possibilities offered by potential alliances between the Catholic Church and the Orthodox Church, which were supported by Pope Eugene IV.[31] In the sixteenth century Southern Europe saw the emergence of a number of black saints, amongst them the Sicilian Franciscans Benedict of Palermo and Antonio da Noto.

Benedict of Palermo, also known as Benedetto da San Fratello or Benedictus de San Philadelphio, was born in Sicily to sub-Saharan parents. His mother was a free woman, while his father was an enslaved African. Both were devout Christians and raised their children to abide by Christian values and support the Church. Consequently, young Benedict became a hermit then joined a Franciscan brotherhood, before entering a convent near Palermo.[32] The story of Antonio da Noto differs greatly from that of Benedict. We learn from Antonio Daza's 1611 history of the Franciscans that Antonio, who was born in North Africa, was 'black as people from Guinea, Xalose and Manicongo but also a Moor, born and raised in the law of Muhammad.'[33] He was captured by Sicilian pirates and sold into slavery on Sicily, where he converted to Catholicism. Rowe has paid close attention to this source and notes that the question of conversion was discussed by Daza, who emphasised the salvatory aspect of Antonio's conversion to Christianity.[34] She argues that 'sacred blackness was constructed, both by the clergy and by Afro-Iberians. White clergy produced copious meditations on the role of black Catholics in the Church, with a rhetoric that tended to be grounded in the intersection of sanctity with color difference—that is, blackness.'[35] As a result, printed work destined for white audiences played a role in shaping racial categories.

It appears that medieval Europe was ambivalent about the place and role of black saints in society, both within and outside the church. Several examples, such as the stories of Saint Maurice and Sheba, shed light on these issues. The ambiguities mentioned previously appear again in relation to medieval European views on black women.[36] Thirteenth-century Europe became interested in the bodies of black women and their alleged abilities to produce higher quality milk and to give pleasure. Drawing on Aristotle's observations about the links between menstrual blood and heat, thirteenth-century medical scholars alleged that the milk of black women had more nutrients. Those claims produced debates in which some scholars stated that the best quality milk for any child was that of its mother, irrespective of her colour. The debates continued in European capitals. In 1300, in Paris, Cologne and other cities, it was argued that the body heat of dark and dusky women rendered their milk more digestible and therefore of better quality for the child. This discourse about mothers' milk took place at the same time as discussions about body heat and sexual attributes. Medical scholars argued over the desire and the sexual capacity of black and white women, a debate which had been ongoing for centuries and was derived from Greek and Arabic medical traditions. It was stated that black women had a greater desire to have intercourse because they came from hotter climates, while white women had more capacity for intercourse because of their alleged excessive menstrual blood. English theologian Thomas of Chobham was preoccupied with regulating the institution of marriage between a white man and a black woman in 1215, while Albert the Great's lecture of 1258 in Cologne was about pleasure and appetite. It was stated, for example, that the shape of a black woman's vulva provided greater pleasure to men.

These debates were not exempt from shame, confusion and morbid fascination. A firm set of widely accepted views appeared in the thirteenth century. For example, the medical profession in most European capitals believed that black people had certain characteristics which were related to reproduction, child-rearing and sexuality. Paradoxically, however, encounters between white men and black women had to be relegated to the private sphere and were not sanctified by the institution of marriage. There are a few examples of devout women who defied these perceptions and are recorded as having been devout Christians, such as Benedetta, Benedict of Palermo's niece. But overall black women continued to be negatively perceived, and the story of the Queen of Sheba is no exception.

Although there are doubts about the veracity of the story of the Queen of Sheba, her representation over time also provides an insight into changing views on the role of women and the weight of religion in communities. The Queen of Sheba appears mostly in Ethiopian paintings and arts, and in studies of the Bible and the Quran.[37] She also appears in both 1 Kings 10:1–13 and 2 Chronicles 9:1–12 of the Hebrew Bible, and in Surat 27:23–44 of the Quran.[38] In the Hebrew Bible, she is presented as a wealthy monarch who learnt about King Solomon's reputation and wealth and decided to test his wisdom. In the Quran, it is Solomon who received a report about the Queen of Sheba and threatened to invade her lands if she and her subjects did not stop worshipping their various gods. Both stories are about her conversion to a monotheist religion and submission to God's will. In the New Testament, her name is changed to Queen of the South (Luke 11:31 and Matthew 12:42). Further transformations of the story are to be found in the Aramaic version of the Book of Esther (c. 500–1000 CE), where Solomon sends a hoopoe bird to the Queen commanding her to travel to his palace. The encounter is given a new twist when, while crossing a glass floor she mistakes for a pool, Sheba pulls up her garment and shows her hairy legs. From that moment, Sheba was associated with demons because body hair was typically attributed to men or demons. In this case, it also indicates that foreign women who worshipped different gods were dangerous to family structures and the social order, as it was a woman's role to oversee the education of children and the wellbeing of the family.

The representations of the Queen of Sheba in European art also display interesting interpretations of otherness. According to many medieval readings of Song of Songs 1:5, it was the Queen of Sheba who declared to Solomon that 'I am black and beautiful'.[39] However, in a thirteenth-century sculpture of the Queen at the Saint Anne Portal of Notre-Dame Cathedral in Paris, King

Solomon and Saint Peter surround her and they are all the same colour, which one can assume is white. Later, in Lavinia Fontana's painting *The Visit of Queen Sheba to King Solomon* (c. 1600) she is again white. The fluidity of the colour of the Queen plays into the perception that otherness may not have mattered in instances where Africans, especially women, were at the top of the social ladder. In the following centuries, stories about the encounter between Sheba and Solomon mingled Jewish and Muslim traditions with folklore that depicted Sheba as a temptress or as half snake, half woman, seeking to seduce men and ruin lives. By an interesting twist, Muslim stories about the Queen being half snake and equating her with the Hebrew female demon Lilith were transformed and circulated in European literature. Nineteenth-century literature also used the figure of the Queen of Sheba, notably Flaubert's novel *La Tentation de Saint Antoine* (1874). The artist Odilon Redon produced an illustration of the Queen of Sheba (1896–1900), which presents us with a naked woman whose features suggest dual heritage and remind us of Charles Baudelaire's depiction of his muse, Jeanne Duval, as lascivious and exotic. Baudelaire's references to the Bible in his poetry focused on the idea of 'temptation'. The description of Duval in 'The Dancing Serpent' (in *The Flowers of Evil*, 1857) sends us back to the Queen of Sheba as an African European temptress.

From confrontations to collaborations, the relationship between Africans and Europeans has been tumultuous since the third century. The lost battles of the Kushite queens were followed by the incorporation of the Thebans into the Roman legions in the third century. The cathartic legend of Saint Maurice and the story of the Queen of Sheba have crystallized European aspirations of religious expansion and become symbols of power, as well as interesting tools with which to analyse the European gaze on Africans. The way the two figures were represented in art and literature provides an insight into social, cultural and scientific changes in Europe. They also challenge our understanding of gender constructs and the perception of black bodies in the European imagination since the Middle Ages. These stories are valuable additions to the history of black saints in Europe.

Rowe demonstrates that black saints' influence spread far beyond the confines of white Christian churches. In the second half of the fifteenth century, Portuguese traders were starting to fully engage with the slave trade. A century later, enslaved Africans in European capitals were encouraged to live Christian lives, but masters were faced with a conundrum. Baptism implied several responsibilities that fell upon the master, and those included the rights of the enslaved to be members of confraternities. This, in turn, meant they had the support of organisations that might work towards their liberation.[40] In addition to this, in the early decades of the seventeenth century the passing of Benedict of Palermo saw the development of a cult named after him which gathered a number of black Spaniards. The church saw these new developments as favourable, as they meant newly arrived enslaved people were more easily converted and assimilated. As Rowe notes, these black confraternities were highly organised, with constitutions and administrative organisation. They supported members in a variety of ways, from spiritual guidance to burials and dowries. They proudly displayed their roots and origins, as exemplified by the Nossa Senhora do Rosário dos Homens Pretos (Our Lady of the Rosary of Black People), who stated that 'we, black men, came from the regions of Ethiopia and its territories' and added that they had been worshipping in Lisbon since 1470.[41] These confraternities reached a global level as the slave trade developed in regions along the Atlantic Ocean.

The stories of Saint Maurice and the Queen of Sheba, and their subsequent reinterpretations, are grounded in the history of colonisation and conquest. Nevertheless, the brutal encounters they describe are not often linked to colonial slavery in medieval and modern Europe. One of the most studied periods of conquest remains the Roman Empire. Scholars have unearthed various stories. One figure stands out because he was both an African and a European; he was born in Africa and travelled to Europe. Emperor Septimius Severus's bust, located at the British Museum, interestingly shows the features of a man who appeared to be of European descent. However, Severus was born in 145 CE in Leptis Magna, a Carthaginian city that would be in today's Libya, known at the time as Tripolitania. He came from a wealthy family whose members had been involved in politics and possibly trade. His father did not hold a prominent office. Tripolitania was a maritime trading area, but was just a few hundreds of kilometres from trans-Saharan trading routes. Very little is known about Severus's early life in Leptis Magna. We are aware, however, that he moved from his birthplace to Rome, where he became friends with the ruling elite. This allowed him to rise to power. In 169, he became a Roman senator. It took him six years to be appointed as a tribune. He was later sent to various posts in locations involving Syria, and then became a governor at the Danube and in Gaul. Severus's ambition led him to return to Rome and seize power after the assassination of Emperor Pertinax by soldiers.

Historians Dio Cassius and Herodian have provided information about Severus's life.[42] Most details are embellished accounts of his character and his relationships with soldiers. Dio narrates his triumphant entrance to Rome after he punished the soldiers who had taken part in the killing of Pertinax, claiming that he took the time to change into civilian garments and marched on foot through the streets while his soldiers were still wearing their armour. The staged aspect of the entrance gives us an insight into the man's mind. He knew that, as an army leader, he might not convince a population that had seen their emperor killed by men of war. He needed to persuade civilians and politicians that he was a man of reason and intellect and a caring leader. Dio's account shows that he succeed in generating interest: 'The crowd chafed in its eagerness to see him and to hear him say something, as if he had been somehow changed by his good fortune; and some of them held one another aloft, that from a higher position they might catch sight of him.'[43] Either out of genuine admiration or in order to rally the deceased emperor's supporters, he erected a shrine for Pertinax and organised an elaborate public ceremony for his funeral, which was attended by senators, consuls, civil servants and their wives.

Herodian provides greater details about Severus's military victories, speeches, and familial relationships, his 'British Expedition' and the short reign of his two sons. The historian's accounts also give us insight into his ruling style. It appears that he was a clever politician who did not hesitate to make alliances with those who might threaten Rome's position. He also surrounded himself with people he trusted. For example, determined to keep close watch on his sons, whose dissolute lives of vice and unhealthy mutual competition were proving worrying, he gave them more power and provided them with wives. His son Caracalla was to marry the daughter of the praetorian prefect Plautianus.

Severus deliberately erased any association that could have been made between himself and Africa. Early in his career, he had distanced himself from his place of birth and managed to secure the support of powerful protectors in Rome. However, as emperor, he kept one man close to him. Herodian states that Plautianus was also born in Libya. The two were allegedly related. Detractors condemned the relationship, alleging that Severus and Plautianus were probably 'beloved' of one another when they were younger.[44] In any case, Plautianus was a poor Libyan who had been given great power and wealth by Severus, and did not hesitate to use violence to accomplish tasks the emperor had assigned him. Severus went further by bringing himself and Plautianus closer through their children. He could have forged any other political alliance by marrying his son into the families of opponents or of leaders in neighbouring territories. He deliberately chose Plautianus's daughter because he trusted Plautianus. He also believed marriage would help his son to mature, but was proven wrong; Caracalla utterly disliked his bride and threatened to kill her and her father once in power as emperor. Acutely aware of Severus's illness and his weakness towards his son, Plautianus feared for his life. He also knew that the emperor's unpopularity among the guards was not playing in his favour. He devised a plan to seize the empire and have his protector the emperor killed, along with his son. However, he made the mistake of putting his orders into writing. The plan failed and Plautianus was killed. Severus's sons continued to lead their lives of pleasure, and the emperor's only recourse was to punish those who kept them in a state of perpetual debauchery and competition against one another.

During his reign, Severus conducted several campaigns aimed at securing more territories extending south of Tripolitania, towards Mesopotamia in the east and towards Britannia in the north, securing Hadrian's Wall and launching a campaign of conquest against Caledonia, a province of Britannia in 208. Severus saw Rome as the heart of knowledge and civilisation as well as the seat of power. Once in power, he also understood that to strengthen Rome, he needed to further expand the Roman Empire. The Britannia campaign proved to be more taxing than the others. The emperor's illness prevented him from focusing on the campaign, and Caracalla, eager to seize power, tried to convince doctors to hasten his death. Eventually Emperor Septimius Severus died of illness in 211. Caracalla went on a killing spree to exterminate those who had been faithful to his father, such as the doctors who had refused to collude in his plots, and even those who had raised him and had been urging him to make peace with his brother Geta. Guided by their mother, the two sons would eventually be forced to rule together. As for Severus, the emperor's remains were burnt, perfumed and transported in an urn to the mausoleum of emperors.

Most African-born Romans did not foreground their origins. About a century before Severus, Marcus Cornelius Fronto's 'Africanity' was mentioned on several occasions but he rarely presented himself as African. Born around 100 in Cirta in Numidia, now Constantine, Fronto was from an African province that was under Roman rule. He is known as one of the most eloquent orators that Roman education ever produced. Fronto entered politics and was appointed consul in 142, but stayed in the post only two months as suffect consul. He was then offered the position of tutor to the adoptive sons of Emperor Antoninus Pius. His work that has survived is mainly his correspondence with his tutees Marcus Aurelius and Lucius Verus, who were later to become emperors, and other friends. None of the correspondence refers to his origins in a negative way. Various letters indicate that Fronto was respected and loved by his prestigious tutees. He was very fond of them too, as expressed in the physical contact, such as embraces and kisses, he had with them as tutees, and later as high-ranking civil servants and emperors. The picture that emerges is that of a man close to his family and held in high regard by the imperial household.

Fronto's rhetorical skills were credited to a Roman education which required a mastery of Latin. Jo-Marie Claassen notes that although he was not paid for his position, there are references to his possession of a Roman mansion.[45] In addition to this, an enviable proximity to the Emperor must have led to a few other rewards. Discussing the attitude of Romans towards Africans in elite circles, Claassen notes that Fronto's linguistic 'zeal' typifies the views of those who were born on the fringes of the empire.[46] They felt the need to overcompensate but excelled in an environment that encouraged assimilation. Using Edward Champlin's work, Claassen adds that elite families born in North Africa purposely adopted Latin and Greek as their *lingua franca*.[47]

Fronto applied for the position of proconsul in Africa but was given his second choice, which was a post in Asia. He eventually had to renounce the post because of ill health. As far as his links with Africa were concerned, Fronto wanted to go back to his birthplace. Several letters showed that he had maintained a close relationship with family and friends in Cirta. Other correspondence revealed that he was part of a wider network of African elites who lived and worked in prestigious circles across Europe. The grammarian Aulus Gellius, who had possible African origins, his Numidian-born friend Julius Celsius and the senator Arrius Antoninus, whose father was from Cirta, were among the friends who exchanged letters with Fronto and visited him on occasion. He was also the protector of several young people, and there is evidence that Fronto attempted to secure the protection of high-ranking notables in Cirta for his protégés. He was also interested in state matters which concerned Africa, as exemplified by a speech before the Senate in which he thanked Antoninus for his support of Carthage (now Tunis), potentially after a fire there.

Claassen notes that overall, 'Africans were at the time very rarely noted as "being different from Romans."'[48] Nevertheless, she also mentions an instance in which the background of an African man is foregrounded. A letter attributed to Marcus Aurelius mentions 'an African man, but with little of the African in him' in reference to Clodius Albinus, an 'African hero' who 'was appointed by Marcus to lead two cohorts and awarded a "double salary" and "quadruple stipend"'.[49] However, Claassen and others have questioned the veracity of these letters, noting that their source is 'dubious'.[50]

Fronto's views about himself as an African are revealed in a letter written, in Greek, to Aurelius's mother Domitia Lucilla, in which he refers to himself as 'a Libyan of the Libyan nomad'.[51] He never criticised Africa or Africans in his writings, and posited them as neither inferior nor superior to the Romans. He nevertheless always praised the Roman army's skills and victories. He saw himself as Roman who believed in the imperial project. This entailed using the army as a last resort but not shying away from battles. Fronto's Africanity therefore appears to be marginal to an otherwise extraordinary career and life.

Africanity, as defined by Jacques Maquet and many others, is a contemporary appellation that characterises African cultures by their unity and similarities.[52] This definition has been contested, but the term 'Africanity' also offers possibilities that include solidarity between those who were born in African provinces under Roman rule. It also encompasses a sense of community among those who had left their birthplace and made distinguished careers in elite capitals including Rome, Seville and others. Looking at the lives of figures such as Fronto and the philosopher and rhetorician Apuleius through this lens sheds further light on their trajectories as African intellectuals who lived in Europe.

Apuleius was born in Madauros in the Roman African province of Numidia. The son of a magistrate, he inherited a sizeable income that allowed him to study in Carthage, Athens and then Rome. The differences between Fronto and Apuleius are noticeable in the way they present their identities. Fronto mentions his foreignness by apologising for a lack of sophistication in his Greek:

> that famous Scythian, Anacharsis, didn't speak wholly Attic Greek, but he was praised for his meaning and his thoughts. Not that I would compare myself with Anacharsis for wisdom, good heavens, but for being a barbarian like him. After all, he was a Scythian of the nomad Scythians, I am a Libyan of the Libyan nomads.[53]

The idea was to show how profoundly Roman he was, but the term 'barbarian' also referred to his links with North Africa. In contrast, in his *Apologia*—a speech in self-defence against charges of magic—Apuleius proudly states his mastery of Greek to emphasise that he was an integral part of the Roman elite, who typically excelled in their knowledge of Greek. In a rhetorical joust, Apuleius also refers to his opponent's origins in Zarat, a poor African village.[54] Wytse Keulen suggests that because North African elites were competing for the favour of the Roman proconsul based in Numidia, some African scholars did not hesitate to disparage and discredit their North African opponents.[55] Incorporating his birthplace into his *Metamorphoses*, Apuleius demonstrated that there was pride in being born in North Africa. Praise of one's origins served several purposes. One of them was related to patronage. As Keulen states, men who had distinguished themselves in their birthplace were highly regarded. They could then earn the support of the elite in Rome. African Romans such as Fronto, Septimus and Apuleius paved the way for a strong tradition of African European intellectuals.

2

BLACK MEDITERRANEANS

SLAVERY AND THE RENAISSANCE

Alessandro de Medici, the first Medici duke of Florence, defies contemporary Europeans' perceptions of Renaissance Florence. Most studies, films and other representations of the fascinating Medici family focus on their political power and stories of rivalry and intrigue. Both academic research and popular culture foreground various aspects of sixteenth- and seventeenth-century Italy, and in particular the ascension to power of Giulio de Medici, later known as Pope Clement VII. The story of Alessandro, the pope's nephew, takes a relatively modest place in the turbulent history of the Medici family. Yet various studies have focused on the questions of reputation, sexuality and race it raises.

As John Brackett has demonstrated, it is undeniable that Alessandro troubled his contemporaries' preconceptions about Africans.[1] His mother is believed to have been a free African woman who lived in a village near Rome called Colle Vecchio. Her ethnic origin is still a debated issue; she was described as both *moro* (Moor) and *schiava* (slave) by Alessandro's contemporaries. Brackett contends that Alessandro was attacked not because of his mother's colour but because of her humble origins. She was a peasant.[2] Yet a number of writers have tried to demonstrate that she was not of African descent. According to Ugo Romagnoli, an Italian author writing in 1939, she was not a Moor but a white 'Eastern' peasant named Simonetta who was married to a coachman.[3] Both were in the service of Alfonsina Orsini, who was the wife of Piero de Medici. Romagnoli also stated that Alessandro was Pope Clement's son, and that he poisoned his mother to erase proof of his origins. However, Romagnoli was unable to convincingly explain the origins of Alessandro's features. No text confirming the origins of his mother exists to date.

Brackett uses portraits of Alessandro to show how his image and interpretations of his origins varied. All the representations were made after his death. A miniature from Agnolo Bronzino's workshop, painted after 1553, represents Alessandro with curly hair and African features. In a 1585 portrait from the workshop of Girolamo Macchietti, he is richly dressed and his features remain relatively similar to their presentation in the previous portrait. However, a 1534 portrait by Giorgio Vasari shows a Duke whose features are closer to those of a man of European descent, with an aquiline nose and thinner lips, although he still has curly hair and brown skin. Despite these disparities, Brackett argues that Alessandro's mother's ethnicity was not the object of attacks upon him. It was rather her place in society and his detractors' assertions that he was an illegitimate child, as well as 'a cruel tyrant, a monster and a murderer'.[4]

Alessandro de Medici lost his life on 6 January 1537, assassinated by his cousin Lorenzino de Medici. The circumstances that preceded the murder and the reasons for it were not immediately understood. Even after Lorenzino's written *Apologia* was made public years after the assassination, his motives were still a source of speculation. Nicholas Scott Baker, however, demonstrates that political assassinations were common occurrences in Renaissance Italy.[5] The reasons varied from personal vendetta to revenge to political rivalry. Lorenzino's *Apologia* presents him as a republican defender of liberty whose sole purpose was to rid Florence of an alleged tyrant. The 'revenge humanism' that was common at the time often masked the true pettiness and jealousy that had led to an act of violence against the offending party. The apology in this context was for the failure of Alessandro's assassination to pave the way for a brighter future for Florence. It was not about Lorenzino's remorse for killing a cousin, but for overestimating the repercussions of that act for the public good. However, we learn that his motives were anger, jealousy and revenge.

Lorenzino descended from the line of the Medici family that had on many occasions antagonised its ruling side. His father had left him with little, and he had to rely on the benevolence of wealthier relatives. In 1526 Giulio de Medici, then Pope Clement VII, had sought to help Lorenzino, but careless behaviour had lost him the favour of the pontiff. After 1534, he found a new supporter in his prominent cousin Alessandro de Medici. However, Baker contends that envy and jealousy were never far despite the closeness of the two young men. Lack of support for Lorenzino over a financial dispute with another cousin (Cosimo, later Alessandro's successor) may have led to resentment that turned into hatred against Alessandro. It is therefore evident, according to Baker, that the assassination had no political motives, despite the claims of the *Apologia*. It was carried out in secret and the culprit fled the scene without demanding any public discussion about his motives or a regime change. The assassination of Alessandro de Medici was not a tyrannicide, and no connections were made between his murder and his origins. Contrary to Brackett's arguments, in this instance illegitimacy does not seem to have played a role in resentments toward Alessandro. After all, the powerful Pope Clement VII had himself been an illegitimate child. The question of origins does appear in Lorenzino's account when he questions whether Alessandro can be called a Medici, but nothing more is said on this subject.

The discussion of motives that is at the forefront of studies regarding Alessandro's sexuality and morality is not necessarily accompanied by considerations of his dual heritage. The prince's political behaviour was often equated to his private activities. Alessandro's incessant quest for pleasure was not deemed acceptable according to sixteenth-century gender norms. As a man with responsibilities, he was expected to display restraint in the matter of sexuality. However, it is possible that the negative reputation of the young nobleman stems from the fact that he had been brought to power by Clement VII and by force. The Medici family had to leave Florence in 1527 but fought their way back through a siege that starved the city. Eventually, his cousin Clement appointed Alessandro as the first Duke of Florence. Despite attempts at reconciliation, resentment was simmering amongst those who had fought against the Medicis during the siege.

Although the narratives of those he financially supported contradict stories about the Duke's impatience and lack of generosity, historians have formed a rather negative view of Alessandro. Despite conflicting accounts about qualities the Duke might have had or lacked—he was accused of cruelty by Lorenzino in the *Apologia*—all reports converged as far as his sexual behaviour was concerned. The Duke was accused of relentlessly pursuing women from all backgrounds, not caring whether he ruined their reputation. This trait was frowned upon because it was an abuse of his privileges and evidenced a refusal to abide by social norms. The young duke's lustful attitude highlights a problem that many women faced at the time: it was difficult for them to refuse the attentions of men. Alessandro was the most powerful man in

Florence. As such, he was expected to protect Florentines both financially and morally. There are several instances when these expectations were not met. At the time, the question of rape was also being challenged in Florentine society. Baker provides a significant example which sheds light on the way those in power could face public anger on the issue. Nobleman Paolo Orgiano's behaviour towards women appalled the population of a small village, and despite his standing, wealth and proximity to power, he was unable to prevent them from testifying against him in court. Baker notes that nearly a hundred people testified, proving that honour mattered greatly to those who were at the bottom of the social ladder.[6]

In contradiction to these Florentines' attitudes towards women, however, it was also believed that women could have too strong a hold on their male companion and thus threaten the harmonious balance that kept society together. In these cases, men's identities were in danger. Social norms of the time reflected very restricted views on masculinity. In addition, as Baker notes, sixteenth-century men were expected to prefer the company of men.[7] A man who spent excessive time with women was deemed effeminate and lost the respect of his contemporaries. It was argued that the virtues that made a good ruler were weakened by promiscuity—this, in turn, made them tyrannical. Alessandro's cousin Lorenzino used the trope of a weak, uncontrolled and tyrannical man.

This notion of tyranny was further reinforced by the way Alessandro had come into power. The Medicis had been in control of Florence since 1434, and their power had been challenged several times. In 1526, the War of the League of Cognac started. Clement VII was determined to win the war against the Habsburg Charles V. In 1527, the Medici family was forced to leave Florence despite still having several strong allies there. The war gave detractors of the Medicis the opportunity to see power finally change hands. Florentines did not necessarily see the family as autocratic, but the fact that power had long been in the hands of the same family disappointed staunch republicans. However, the way in which the family regained control of Florence proved detractors right. They forced their way back into power using the army, and Clement then imposed Alessandro as the leader of the city.

As far as Alessandro's later reputation was concerned, these elements contributed to his profile as a born despot. In his *Apologia*, Lorenzino attempts to taint the reputation of the man who had been his companion in debauchery. It appears that Alessandro de Medici's negative reputation was not based on his leadership qualities but on his sexual behaviour. It was feared that his licentious attitude would result in a tyrannical behaviour, even though he had never displayed signs of it. The various interpretations of correspondence between Alessandro's contemporaries, from detractors to supporters, give a very controversial and mostly contradictory portrait of the young Duke. The accounts that are most likely to be impartial show that he was a capable leader, but his lustful behaviour also worried those who served him. Maintaining an impeccable public image was particularly important at a time when Florence was going through internal divisions and assassination attempts and coups were common occurrences. Most Florentines had welcomed the Medici family back, but their expectations in terms of governance were also higher.

Alessandro's family, including his successor Cosimo I, were determined to protect his reputation. Cosimo became guardian to Alessandro's sons and protected their social status. He allegedly later had Lorenzino assassinated in 1548. For Brackett, Italian society in the sixteenth century, despite occasional denigration of black Africans, did not find it appropriate to attack the nobleman Alessandro on his ethnicity in the public sphere.

There are no records of negative perceptions of Alessandro's dual heritage or ethnicity. However, speculation about his origins continued after his death.

Catherine Fletcher provides a fascinating analysis of the way race, prejudice and ideas about superiority were produced around the life and origins of Alessandro de Medici. Alessandro's half-sister Catherine, Queen of France from 1547 to 1559, was associated with figures such as Lorenzino, who had negative views about the Duke.[8] In 1564, a volume dedicated to Catherine mentioned Alessandro's 'Moorish' origins. In fact, his connection with Africa was seen here as a negative point.[9] By the end of the sixteenth century, Cosimo's historiographer, Scipione Ammirato, was describing Alessandro as having the features of a mixed-race man.[10]

The story of Alessandro has continued to attract writers. Alfred de Musset's 1834 play *Lorenzaccio* does not dwell on race, whereas other writers focus on the duke's ethnicity, physical attributes and differences. Colonel G. F. Young, for example, contributes to nineteenth- and twentieth-century discourses of race and intelligence by attributing traits such as incapability and viciousness to the duke because of his origins in his 1909 history *The Medici*. The way the story of Alessandro has been depicted provides an interesting insight into the history of race in Europe and in the United States. As noted by Fletcher, Arturo Alfonso Schomburg's article 'Alessandro, First Duke of Florence, the Negro Medici', published in 1931, showed how black activists used historical figures to encourage their community to learn about their history and take on the task of studying literature.[11] Remarkably forgotten, the work done by Schomburg and others failed to move the debate and bring about social equality and justice. In fact, more than four centuries after his death Alessandro's African origins still triggered negative comments, as exemplified by historian Georges-Henri Dumont's dubious remarks about the Bronzino workshop portrait of Alessandro that his fiancée 'must not have found him very attractive'.[12] The question of race remained a bone of contention, with uncertainty over whether to erase the duke's African ancestry or to posit it as significant in negatively shaping his character. As David T. Goldberg notes, 'Racism concerns the maintenance of homogeneities' contours, militarizing their borders, patrolling their places of possible transgression'.[13] Alessandro crossed those boundaries and did not conform to the norms of his times; neither, allegedly, did he fulfil the expectations of a ruler whose otherness should have invited him to tread carefully.

European views on black Africans in the fifteenth and sixteenth centuries were more nuanced than one would assume centuries later. The Church played a crucial role in shaping the status of Africans in Renaissance Italy.[14] The arrival of Africans in Europe was another opportunity to spread the gospel, and had clear implications for the conversion of the black population. As discussed in the previous chapter, one of the three wise men was increasingly depicted as black.[15] The slave trade was condemned by Pope Martin V in 1425. But a later pope, Nicholas V, did not share these views, allowing the Portuguese to acquire already enslaved Africans from non-Christian merchants. Calixtus III restated Portugal's right to trade in 1456, and Alexander VI expanded it to Spanish kings in 1493. By contrast, in 1462 we witness a different stance from Pope Pius II, who forbade enslavement of black people. Pope Paul III followed in his footsteps and added indigenous populations to the list of those whose enslavement was unlawful in 1537. Paradoxically, Paul allowed Romans to have slaves in 1548. The black population in question was a broad category that included Arabs, Berbers, Ethiopians and other people from the African continent. Slaving routes went as far as today's Chad, with internal slave routes in West Africa and the valley of the Nile. Enslaved populations were sent and sold to slave markets in Tripoli, whose capture by Spain in 1510 made the transfer to European capitals easier.

The religious beliefs of enslaved people were of great interest to the Church. At a time when the Church was fighting to convert poor populations, especially those in rural areas, measures to facilitate conversion were put in place, but the fear of losing already Christian populations led the Church in Spain to try to regulate the contact between enslaved people and white peasants. The Jesuits played a crucial role in implementing those measures, and generally in working with African populations in the fifteenth and sixteenth centuries. The Church tried to make alliances with African monarchs in Ethiopia and in Congo in particular. Henrique, the African son of the converted king of Congo Afonso I, was born in c. 1494. He was sent to Lisbon to be educated in theology and wanted to become a bishop. In 1518, Pope Leo X appointed him bishop of Utica in North Africa with the consent of cardinals.

Meanwhile in Europe, prejudice was rife and resistance to African integration, even after they had converted, proved to be a challenge for the Church as a whole. Ideas about race, racialism and racism had not been articulated as thoroughly as they were in the nineteenth century, but they were already present and shaping the lives of African Europeans. Slaves are often presented as a powerless group who had no agency in their daily lives. However, Debra Blumenthal's work paints a nuanced picture of these histories in fifteenth-century Valencia. She noted that sales of slaves entering the kingdom were regulated and taxes were paid to the crown. However, the resale of slaves obeyed different rules as these were private transactions, and slaves could play a crucial role in their own sale, especially during the interview that took place between the buyer, the seller and the enslaved.[16] An initial trial period was also allowed for the new buyer to see whether they were satisfied with their acquisition. Enslaved individuals could use this time to deter the buyer by faking illness or displaying off-putting traits.[17] Blumenthal also argues that expectations of slaves were sometimes 'gendered'. As she puts it, 'Contracts of sale for female slaves ... might include clauses assuring buyers that the slave menstruated or disavowing responsibility for a female slave's licentiousness. Some sellers stated that they did not wish to be held liable if the slave woman was found to be a whore'.[18]

The daily experiences of enslaved people in Valencian households varied greatly. The story of Ursola, a black slave owned by a mason called Francesc Martínez, is quite revealing.[19] Ursola could go to work for other people as a laundress and earn money. She was hoping to buy her freedom through such activities. She managed to get the forty lliures required, but her master declared that the manumission contract was null and void because Ursola had stopped coming back to his house to make him bread every day. That specific clause was indeed in Ursola and Francesc's agreement, and her manumission was invalidated. Anecdotal as this story may appear, it shows that the lives of slaves were still very dependent on their master's power. When pushed, slaves could damage their masters' reputations; alternatively they were able to solidify their master's place in society and spread lies against their enemies. However, they were still subjugated bodies whose lives obeyed certain rules that often operated along racial lines.

Goldberg has argued that the next centuries were characterised by the formulation and formalisation of racial boundaries and theories. Black and white slaves were treated differently in fifteenth-century Europe, even though life under slavery was still shaped by various forms of violence. As much as each country's unique experiences and history have shaped the question of race, there are commonalities that characterise the European approach to race, racialism and racism. Goldberg adds that this European approach emerged because of 'networks of racial conception and meaning, of racial value and power'.[20]

Drawing on the work of W. E. B. Du Bois and his own work on racialism, which posits that human beings inherit particular differential but non-hierarchical visible traits, Kwame Anthony Appiah notes that there is a thin line between racialism and racism. He argues that if we remove elements of hierarchisation which move from equal to unequal when it comes to evaluating these traits, racialism is a value-neutral term.[21] George Fredrickson, on the other hand, contends that racism is inherently about inequality between groups of people whose visible traits (and accompanying alleged sets of behaviours) are deemed inferior or superior.[22] Delving into the work of Fredrickson, Goldberg challenges the assumption that racism is necessarily about inferiority and inequality. Goldberg contends that in the case of 'racial historicists', nineteenth- and twentieth-century racial paternalism was characterised by the belief that Africans and Asians, deemed inferior, could improve their intellect and behaviour through education.[23] He concludes that racism goes beyond Fredrickson's initial definition. Racism implies 'more broadly that racial difference warrants exclusion of those so characterized from elevation into the realm of protection, privilege, property, or profit. Racism, in short, is about exclusion through depreciation, intrinsic or instrumental, timeless or time-bound'.[24]

Sergio Tognetti's analysis of the trade of Africans in fifteenth-century Florence provides a more detailed picture of the status of the enslaved.[25] They belonged to their masters and were allocated roles as domestic servants. In the fourteenth and fifteenth centuries in central and northern Italy, wealthy households were concerned with acquiring women for domestic tasks. 15- to 25-year-old workers were preferred, and the women came from the area that is now Eastern Europe, Russia and Central Asia.

With the fall of Constantinople in the second half of the fifteenth century, the country of origin of these workers changed, and they were predominantly imported from Africa. In southern Italy, Christians acquired enslaved people mainly through Arab merchants and slaveholders mostly bought men to work in the fields and farms.

In Florence, the powerful Cambini Bank, which operated between 1420 and 1482, dominated the trade. Although it was relatively short-lived, others followed its methods and adopted its supply chains. For example, in a statement of accounts by Giovanni Guidetti, one of Cambini's business agents, we learn that three young girls had been acquired. Not only did he have to pay for clothes for them because they arrived naked, he also paid different prices for each one. Isabell was black but seemed to have had lighter skin than the others, and because of this he paid 8,500 reals (a Spanish currency until 1864). Barbera and Marta, who had darker skin tones, cost him 7,500 and 6,500 reals respectively. The girls had been baptised but were still sold into slavery.[26] Other agents and businessmen followed in these footsteps. One of the wealthiest slave-owners Florence ever produced was Bartolomeo Marchionni. He worked for the Cambini Bank as an apprentice then as an agent, and moved to Lisbon in the early 1470s. Records from Lisbon show that between 1493 and 1495 Marchionni owned 1,648 enslaved people. Between 1489 and 1503 he sent 1,866 Africans to the kingdom of Valencia.[27] These records show the extent of the connections that existed between Spain and Italy. They also demonstrate that the slave trade was a lucrative business for several men who had developed a network of supply and demand in southern Europe. The question of colour and the value afforded to enslaved people was already established in Italian societies by this time. One can therefore assume that Alessandro's mother's origins were of importance after all, and may have played a role in contemporaries' perceptions of the duke at the time of his reign. One can also assume that as Duke of Florence Alessandro might have been unaware of those views because of his status, and because of his detractors' fear of being sent into exile.

Africans from the north, west and east of the continent had been using well-established trading networks for centuries before the arrival of Europeans. Internal slavery in African kingdoms, as in Europe during the same period, was one of the many forms of exchange that existed between merchants, explorers and navigators. Nonetheless, contemporary debates rightly point out that forms of subjugation varied across the continent at the time, and that grouping them all under 'slavery' would be historically inaccurate. The first records of European presence in sub-Saharan Africa date back to the fifteenth century. Between 1488 and 1498, stories of encounters between Africans and Europeans were based on the travels of navigators such as Bartolomeu Dias and Vasco da Gama. Portuguese monarchs were looking for gold to strengthen their political and trading hegemony in Europe. In order to achieve these goals, they attempted to find and conquer new territories. Using newfound maritime routes, West and East African as well as Arab, the Portuguese established partnerships with West African courts. In this respect, the history of transatlantic slavery that starts in the fifteenth century overlaps with the history of the Arabs and a period known as the Reconquista.

Muslim occupation of the Iberian Peninsula led to wars that lasted from 718 to 1492. The period of the Reconquista, characterised by Christian attempts to reclaim what they saw as their territories, resulted in complex narratives of collaboration, war and conversion. In order to fight efficiently against the last Muslim kingdom Granada, led by Emir Muhammad XII (or Boabdil), the kingdoms of Aragon and Castile were united in 1469 through the marriage of Isabella I and Ferdinand II. Granada was reclaimed in 1492. The period that followed saw a brutal Inquisition which was aimed at forcing Muslims to convert to Christianity. Inhabitants of Granada who had Jewish and Moorish ancestry were driven out or executed. By the time the scholar and poet Juan Latino was born, the relationship between North Africa, Spain and Portugal was based on mistrust and violence. Muslim influence in Europe has been widely studied, but often in terms of knowledge exchange and in relation to the crusades. Cedric J. Robinson has contended that:

> Islam, a faith that embraced a multiracial civilization incorporating peoples from Arabia, Africa, the Near East, the East, and southern Europe, would be known by its armies. And Africans were prominent in its armies from the very beginning. ... Africans had fought in the pre-Islamic Arabian wars, and within the first century of the Islamic era (the Christian seventh century), their presence had already been noted in the empires of Europe.[28]

Latino's life and work reveals a particularly complex kind of relationship between Africans and Europe. The scholarship about him is important to note here because it relates to his life as much as his writings, whose contribution to Renaissance poetry is now widely accepted. A close look at this corpus serves as an interesting backdrop, as analyses of his life, work and position in society shed light on conceptions of ethnicity and race.

Juan Latino or Johannes Latinus (c. 1518–c. 1594) was a slave in Granada who rose to prominence because of his mastery of Latin. He benefitted from his proximity to the third Duke of Sessa, Gonzalo Fernandez de Cordoba, his master's son. Juan de Sessa, as Latino was then known, followed the duke to the newly opened University of Granada. Studious and gifted, he was probably named Juan Latino because of his outstanding achievements as a Latinist. He received a Bachelor's degree in 1546 when he was about twenty-eight years old and still enslaved. In 1557, he received a Master of Arts degree. Later, Latino was manumitted and became a lecturer of grammar at the cathedral school.

Latino's origins, name and marriage remain topics of interest. In particular, the ambiguity between the term Ladino and the name Latino cannot be ignored. Ladino was the name given to enslaved people who were fluent in Castilian. The nickname could therefore have been a pun aimed at bringing together the mastery of Latin and Castilian by an enslaved man. Perceptions about Ladinos were based on stereotypes. They were deemed unreliable and somehow dangerous if left unchecked. In Cervantes's *Don Quixote*, there is a reference to an educated man described as 'el negro Juan Lati-'.[29] Some scholars assert that Cervantes was mocking Latino's knowledge of Latin in describing him thus, suggesting that his accomplishments in the language were 'a trifle enjoyed by amused owners'.[30] However, it has also been argued that Latino cleverly pre-empted others' perceptions by renaming himself, and that Cervantes in fact praised the scholar in the preface to *Don Quixote* through his poem 'Urganda the Unknown'.[31]

Irrespective of these analyses, Baltasar Fra-Molinero convincingly demonstrates how Latino used his origins to secure the support of Don Juan de Austria, Philip II's half-brother, by praising him while equating his own African descent with the Habsburg dynasty of Don Juan and Philip. In *Ad regem Catholicum et invictissimum Philippum elegia*, he wrote:

> This writer was not born of these parts of the world.
> His name is Latinus, and he came from the land of Ethiopia
> to sing the deeds of Juan de Austria with the admirable art of poetry.
> Unconquered Philip, on his bended knee this singer asks
> to be your brother's poet.
> If the wars of the Austriad make the poet famous,
> the poet's blackness will make Don Juan a phoenix.[32]

Fra-Molinero analyses how Latino links his blackness, signalled by Ethiopia, to his mastery of Latin and the successes of the Austrian Habsburg dynasty on the one hand, and on the other how he equates Don Juan with the stories and traditions of the Phoenicians through the symbol of the phoenix. His vision of Europe is thus also about the East and Ethiopia. In addition, he refers to Ovid's phoenix and the ability to rise from the ashes.[33]

Fra-Molinero also notes that Latino was very careful in establishing a clear difference between the Ethiopians and the Moriscos—Spanish Muslims who had been forced to convert to Christianity. In 1566, Philip II had prohibited his Morisco subjects from trading and owning black slaves.[34] Ethiopians could be Christian figures, just like Latino or Prester John. Former slaves, including Latino himself, had adopted Christianity and Granada's way of life. In addition, Ethiopians were amongst the first converted Christians, as related in the Bible. The reference to Ethiopia is therefore linked to the New Testament, the three magi and early Christendom.[35] Juan Latino had used racial and religious differences in the context of sixteenth-century Granada to signal to the elite and to readers that he had been assimilated into the society he lived in. In fact, he had gone further and adopted the values and language of poetry used by the elite. He acknowledged that he was not, however, the king and Don Juan's equal but was working towards their acceptance.

Latino's position could indeed have been deemed questionable. However, he had reached a status that very few black men were expected to in that context. He had carefully constructed a persona that gave him a certain amount of freedom and an income. Marrying a white woman could have been considered the ultimate marker of assimilation. As Aurélia Martín Casares and Marga G. Barranco have noted, intermarriages were not common occurrences by this time.[36] Nevertheless, the unusual union between Latino and a white woman was accepted, further demonstrating that he benefitted from the protection of the king and the king's brother. In fact, Latino also enjoyed the protection of Archbishop Pedro Guerrero, who had a comparatively soft approach to the Christianisation of the Moriscos. He believed in educating the Morisco elite in Spanish institutions and therefore promoting Latin. He was also in favour of using Arabic to convince Moriscos of the benefits of Christianity. He had been instrumental in the appointment of Latino at the cathedral school in Granada. Latino married Ana de Carleval, the duke's estate manager's daughter. It has even been suggested that Ana's inheritance allowed the couple to live very comfortably. Her father had hired Latino to teach her music and other subjects, and was forced by circumstance to accept the union. The couple had four children between 1549 and 1559. It has been alleged that although the church sanctified the marriage, Latino may not have been a free man when he married Ana.[37]

According to Martín Casares, wider fascination with Latino's work begun mainly in the twentieth century with Granada-born philosopher Antonio Marín Ocete, who dedicated his life's work to Latino's writing. Marín Ocete has been given little credit for his work. He patiently researched Latino's life, from his childhood, education and teachers to his connections and friendships. Martín Casares notes that Marín Ocete is probably the scholar who has provided the greatest insight into Latino's life. She also points out the importance of the way Marín Ocete viewed Latino's work, in particular his constant emphasis on the exceptional abilities of a black man as a question to be pondered. Marín Ocete's volumes referred to the scholar as the 'Black Juan Latino'. The frequent association of colour with ability by Western scholars seems to have played a role in Marín Ocete's quest to understand this 'black prodigy'.[38]

While Marín Ocete was working on Latino, Velaurez B. Spratlin and Carter G. Woodson, who founded the *Journal of Negro History* in 1916, also took an interest in the Afro-Spanish scholar. Spratlin's aim was to encourage African Americans to consider the contributions of people of African descent in

Europe. He investigated the life of Latino as well as other Afro-European figures. His mission to broaden the minds of his fellow African Americans was not solely based on the role of highly educated men and women in history. He also examined the presence of black figures in comedies in Renaissance Europe. Woodson, on the other hand, turned to the question of perceptions of race in sixteenth-century Spain and Portugal. In contrast with Marín Ocete, Spratlin and Woodson believed that Latino's abilities should not be attributed to exceptionalism. Latino's achievements in an environment that was not favourable to black people served as an important marker for the 'negro race'. They wanted to demonstrate that black people had the intellectual talents to achieve greatness when given the opportunity. In fact, Woodson achieved a similar rise to prominence. He obtained a PhD in 1912 and founded 'Negro History Week' in 1926. This became the international celebration known as Black History Month. In 1939, however, the scholar Otis Howard Green, who was racialised as white, published a review which saw originality in Spratlin's study 'Juan Latino: Slave and Humanist', but used the questions of education and achievement so dear to both scholars as ammunition.[39]

Further work followed in relation to Black Studies in the United States. It is notable that some of this work started to address the question of race more broadly, for example in relation to black people, Jews and Moors, while others examined enslavement. Since then, fifty or so studies have analysed the work of Juan Latino. What is remarkable is the constant shift between his work as a poet, as a humanist and as a narrator of stories of his time. Latino's work, which encompasses literature and what would now be considered social commentary tells us about Granada's views on the foreigner and the non-Christian, and about the fate of those who were perceived as a threat to the narrative the city was trying to create.

The creation of a narrative is precisely what Latino accomplished in *Austrias Carmen*, a powerful account of the Battle of Lepanto, which took place in 1571. The battle set the Republic of Venice and the Spanish Empire against the Ottoman Empire in the Gulf of Patras in Western Greece. It was a maritime engagement that the devout Christian Philip II of Spain needed to win if he were to send a strong message to the Muslims based in North Africa who supported the Ottoman Empire. It was also a confrontation between two determined men: Ali Pasha, Sultan Selim II's brother-in-law, on the one hand and Don Juan de Austria, Philip's half-brother and son of the Roman emperor Charles V, on the other. The battle was bloody; about 40,000 men were killed and 10,000 wounded. Latino published the chronicle in a volume of poetry celebrating Philip II, Pope Pius V and Philip's newly born son, the Infante don Fernando.[40] The poem was produced only eighteen months after the battle.

Elizabeth R. Wright demonstrates how economical the poem is. She states that it 'miniaturizes Virgil's twelve-book form', thus resulting in an efficient pedagogical tool that echoed the techniques of Latino's seminars. She also notes that the author's efficiency as an orator was successfully transferred to the poem, which is didactic and powerful.[41] Latino did not merely copy Virgil's style, but transposed the poet's interest in recounting battles to a Christian and Muslim world in turmoil. For example, he takes the reader on a journey to the Second Revolt of the Alpujarras (1568–71), which saw Moriscos rebel against Christian rule. Rules enforced in 1567 stipulated that 'Old Christians' should be housed in areas with a certain number of Moriscos, as they were suspected of still following outlawed practices. Constant surveillance, intrusion into their family lives and oppressive measures led to discontent and then rebellion. Don Juan de Austria managed to suppress the uprising. About 80,000 Moriscos were expelled from Granada and 10,000 were enslaved.

Latino linked the story of Alpujarras to the Battle of Lepanto in *Austrias Carmen*. Although praising Christian forces, he shifts the narrative from Christian to Ottoman viewpoints. The confrontation between the two empires through their leaders is thoroughly described. Ali Pasha is eventually captured and killed, and his head is put on a spike for his soldiers to see. Unexpectedly, his two sons also see their father's head on display. The reader cannot help but feel the pain of the children, who beg the Spaniards to kill them as well. The chronicle also takes the reader to Algiers, demonstrating the close links that existed between various parts of the Mediterranean. Wright concludes that although *Austrias Carmen* praised Christian efficiency and supported the king's decision to expel and enslave Moriscos, it would be a mistake to underestimate the complex dynamic that linked various protagonists and kept the door open for further unrest.[42] Latino's text emphasised the difficult and explosive nature of cohabitation between Christians and Muslims. If it celebrated the King and endorsed his decisions, it also highlighted that temporary peace came at a high cost. In 1573, Latino understood that Archbishop Guerrero's more tolerant views were not shared. The hardening of the royal attitude towards Moriscos and Don Juan's brutal suppression and subsequent vicious measures, supported by the king, had left Latino needing to clarify his position. In an environment where distrust and suspicion against perceived foreigners were reaching their apex, a public declaration of support for those in power seemed necessary. This may be one of the reasons that Latino wrote and published *Austrias Carmen*.

Latino is often defined as a Renaissance humanist. Henry Louis Gates Jr., Maria Wolff and Baltasar Fra-Molinero have all suggested that one cannot understand Latino's humanistic views without tackling the question of racial difference. Referencing an 1886 article by Antonio González Garbín, Gates and Wolff note that Latino was referred to as an 'erudite humanist' and a 'unique famous Ethiopian'.[43] However, this consideration of Latino's talents in relation to his race is mostly accepted in twentieth-century scholarship about the poet. Before the nineteenth century, the perception of Latino was that of an entertaining character whose noble attributes were related to his allegedly unusual intellect. In the nineteenth century, his life and work were deemed to shed light on the human condition.

Fra-Molinero tackles the notion of humanism by looking at Latino's complex environment, suggesting that he chose to define himself as a humanist in a context that was propitious to such stances. A 'Catholic universalism' that contradicted the social realities of Granada at the time served as an interesting focus for one who was both insider and Other; through it, he held up an embellished but nonetheless revealing mirror to his contemporaries.[44] Indeed, perhaps as a provocation that echoed his nickname, Latino named himself John the Ethiopian, signifying that he was both a Christian and a foreigner; a humanist and a black man. Fra-Molinero notes that these were contradictory categories in sixteenth-century Europe.[45] The colonial expansion towards the Americas that had begun a century before had already shaped European perception of an intellectual hierarchy. Arabs were not seen as uneducated but were still considered inferior because of their religion. Humanists were white Europeans. They were a superior category of men whose role was to educate, convert and rule. Latino's experience challenged established strictures and assumptions simply because of the colour of his skin and his status. He asked and obtained permission to write a poem about Don Juan de Austria before he wrote *Austrias Carmen*. Latino understood that although educated and mostly accepted by the elite, he still had to seek the sanction of the court because of his colour.[46] The poem was for elite consumption. *Austrias Carmen*, on the other hand, was aimed at an erudite audience that was familiar with the political, cultural and social tensions at play in the poem.

Andrew Lemons has suggested that alongside geopolitics and 'classical erudition', Juan Latino's work engaged in 'literary experimentation' with a series of unexpected alliterations.[47] It is also notable for the insertion of references to Roman poet Lucretius, in particular the introductory formula *omnia quae* ('all that').[48] Lemons notes that Latino promoted himself as a humanist and a neo-Latin poet whose intellectual and literary aspirations could also be traced back to the famed fifteenth-century poet and humanist Giovanni Pontano. Pontano had produced an analysis of Lucretius's poem *De Rerum Natura*. According to Lemons, interpretative texts such as Pontano's were salient in the way Latino experimented with words, sentence construction, rhythm, imagery and overall 'poetic technology'.[49] However, the other implication was that the dream of a superior world built by those who had enriched and supported Latin did not come to fruition. The new approach to philology did not offer a worthy place to the master of words, who had believed that literary superiority could remove all boundaries. Latino's peers, such as Cervantes and Lope de Vega, had relegated him to a caricature.[50] However, this reading of Latino's fate stands in stark contrast with the profuse commentary on his life and work that was produced over the following centuries. Contrary to Lemons's views, Latino has found his place as a Renaissance poet, a humanist and a chronicler of his time after all.

Yet the way Latino was represented clearly demonstrates that sixteenth- and seventeenth-century readers struggled to accept his journey. Seventeenth-century plays are particularly revealing in this respect. Black characters began to appear in Spanish plays at a time when the Iberian Peninsula was struggling with the close proximity of a relatively high number of people of African descent to the rest of the European population, and the challenges this posed for the ideal European discourse on monarchy and Christianity. Latino's story unfolded within the broader history of Spain, Portugal and sub-Saharan Africa. His African origins have been the source of numerous debates; it is still difficult to know whether he was born in Spain or was brought there with his mother. His mother's origins are also unknown. She may have been transported from West Africa to be sold as a domestic servant or a sexual object, as was often the case for African women brought to Spain in the first decades of the fifteenth century. However, Latino was often referred to as a 'full-blooded African', meaning that he was not of mixed heritage.[51] It has also been suggested that he may have been from North Africa. The recognised phenotype of North Africans often suggests that they have lighter skin than sub-Saharan Africans, but scholar Michael A. Gomez has given credence to Latino's potential North African origins.[52] The Berber Almoravid dynasty established in North Africa in the eleventh century stretched as far as Al-Andalus (Spain and Portugal). The Almoravid army employed Muslim West African soldiers. These men were eventually set free and were able to integrate into the Andalusian social fabric, where they frequently interacted with North Africans. After the Reconquista, the Moriscos and enslaved West Africans were assigned manual and unskilled labour. By the fifteenth century, these groups were cohabitating with one another.

A few records show that a stream of West African enslaved people was active in the first half of the fifteenth century. In 1444, 235 West Africans were sent to Lisbon. Determined to be closer to slave markets, Portuguese merchants were able to set up a permanent trading post in Mauritania in 1448.[53] Fifteenth-century Valencia saw an increase in the number of sub-Saharan Africans and Guanches, the indigenous population of the Canary Islands, arriving on ships rather than through North Africa. Italian and Portuguese traders had started to control those maritime routes. The Portuguese and the Italians had already started to roam the Mediterranean centuries before. By 1475 they had reached African coasts past the equator, and by 1488 they had reached the Cape of Good Hope. They travelled further east with navigators such as Vasco da Gama in 1497. By 1520, Portugal dominated the Indian Ocean.[54]

Annette Ivory notes that of the 429,362 inhabitants of Seville in the sixteenth century, about 14,670 were black people. She contends that competition for jobs was exacerbated by the availability of black labour. It was also at this time that black characters were ridiculed in plays. The portrait of the black buffoon was aimed at relieving social and economic anxiety.[55] In sixteenth-century Granada, until the Morisco rebellion of 1568–71, most enslaved people were of African descent. During the years of the rebellion, 90 per cent of enslaved people who were sold in Granada were Moriscos.[56] It was also in the sixteenth century that the term *negro*, or black, appears in legal documents instead of *esclavo*, or slave. Emily Weissbourd provides a striking example of such changes through documentation from 1559 to 1576 which refers to 'his majesty's blacks [negros]' instead of 'his majesty's slaves' in relation to people enslaved in silver mines near Seville.[57]

Changes in language use also revealed shifting positions within society. For example, in comic plays the character of the lady-in-waiting was often a woman of dual heritage, known as the *mulatta*. So-called mixed-race women who could speak fluent Castilian were considered acceptable companions for noblewomen. Nicholas R. Jones demonstrates the discrepancy between these women and black women, who were degraded through name-calling but also rendered anonymous in early modern Spanish literary texts.[58] Jones noted that 'black women from early modern Iberia have been aesthetically, culturally, and institutionally robbed of their agency and humanity.'[59]

'Black speech' (also known as Afro-Hispanic speech) was also an object of interest to playwrights from Diego Sánchez de Badajoz to Lope de Rueda. The pronunciation of certain vowels led to doubts around what the character meant. This ambiguity was aimed at creating a comical effect whilst reminding the audience that these characters were outsiders who could never speak the language fluently. White actors covered in black make-up played black characters. Jones looks at two black women, Eulalla and Guiomar, in Rueda's theatrical productions *Eufemia* and *Los engañados* and notes that the characterisation of female black bodies and the use of black speech contribute to a 'politics of opacity'.[60] Not only did these women contribute to Rueda's success as a playwright, but they also present us with examples of resistance and display a form of agency beyond Rueda's intentions. They existed outside the purpose of simply entertaining a white audience. Jones defines them as black divas, drawing on early African American feminist stances and theories. Quoting Sojourner Truth's famous speech 'Ain't I a Woman?', which both uses and transcends black speech in an address to contemporary black feminists, Jones posits black divas as voices of resistance who 'transcend masculinist and racist images employed by European dramatists, historiographers, theologians, and writers in their own self-representations.'[61]

In the seventeenth century, Portugal and Spain were not the only countries controlling the slave trade. The Dutch Republic, England and France were also involved in the so-called 'Africa trade'. The period was characterised by interesting changes in the way people of African descent were perceived. In Spain, the figure of the educated black man appeared in the plays of writers such as Lope de Vega and Diego Jiménez de Enciso. Enciso's play *La comedia famosa de Juan Latino* was written long after Latino's death. The play is about his life from his humble origins as an enslaved boy to his adulthood as an educated Latinist who was appointed to a prestigious school and married a white woman. As Ivory notes, the play is about blackness but more broadly about minorities in seventeenth-century Spain.[62] The main character lives alongside a community comprising Jews and Moors, who are the play's villains. For example, Latino must overcome the antagonism of the converted Jewish character Villanueva when he arrives at the University of Granada. The tensions between the two characters are based on racial differences. Villanueva does not accept that a formerly enslaved black man could be his equal in the institution. These tensions are further exacerbated by the honours bestowed upon Latino, whose legal status is still that of an enslaved person.

Ivory notes that the uses of the terms *negro* and *esclavo* for black and slave are important to analyse. Indeed, Villanueva uses them interchangeably to show that to be black is to be a slave, and vice versa. He goes a step further by trying to deny Latino's humanity in stating that '*esclavos no son hombres*' ('slaves are not men'), which equally means that black people are not humans.[63] At a time when 'negro' started to signify both black and enslaved in the rest of Europe, and when the dehumanisation of people of African descent served as a tool to justify enslavement and the alleged civilising mission of Europeans, it is interesting to note that these views were shared in the play by a community of people such as the Jews, even though they had also been placed at the margins of humanity.

The question of social mobility, assimilation and race also emerges through the marriage of Latino to Ana, a noble white woman. In the play, Latino must confront the question of his colour. Ana initially does not want to have a black teacher. Later, Latino has to convince her that his intellectual abilities far outweigh the negative associations of his colour. This is a clear indication that darker skin was devalued in Granadan society when the play was presented. Enciso plays with various perceptions of racial and religious difference. For example, in order to persuade Ana that he is a worthy teacher, Latino also positions himself as different from the Moriscos.

In the play, Don Fernando, a nobleman and a Moor, and Cañeri, a Black Muslim, have also tried to court Ana, but it is Latino who wins her heart. Don Fernando chooses to be a part of the Second Revolt of the Alpujarras and eventually embraces Islam. This decision leads him to death. He starts at the top of the Spanish aristocracy and ends up at the bottom. The character Cañeri meets with a predictably similar fate.[64] Having tried to tell Spaniards how to deal with their minority groups and refused to accept the place allocated to him as a black person and as a Muslim, he must also die. The tensions between Muslims, Moriscos and Jews had not subsided by the seventeenth century. The audience was in sympathy with their rulers' harsh decisions.

Ivory demonstrates that even Latino's character development in the play is flawed. He epitomises one who has assimilated fully accepted Spanish values, yet he remains legally enslaved throughout the play.[65] He elopes to marry Ana but is later accepted by her brother, who even decides to give him a sizeable sum of money. Yet no manumission is discussed at any point. The question of colour and enslavement was dealt with in different ways across Europe. Michael A. Gomez argues that Latino's journey does not provide a solid 'test case' in support of questions of 'enculturation' or 'hybridity'.[66] He had scant connections with his African ancestry growing up in the household where he worked as domestic servant. He was an enslaved child who knew nothing about his origins and could hardly bridge the gap between two cultures. Such would be the fate of Phyllis Wheatley, Olaudah Equiano and many others in the eighteenth century. There is, however, a case to be made about his position as an African European. The colour of his skin shaped his identity. Blackness was associated with Africa, and, whether or not he fully adhered to that epithet, he was seen as an African. He was the 'Black Juan Latino'.

In addition to this, Weissbourd notes that during the same period, Elizabethan England was dealing with the question of blackness with more nuanced black characters; however, black characters were more present overall in Spanish plays. Nevertheless, the common thread in both traditions of representation was negative stereotypes. In England, black was evil while in Spain it was characterised by stupidity and linked to enslavement. Taking Othello and Juan Latino as her examples of black theatrical characters, Weissbourd contends that black heroes in both countries were met with very different fates depending on genre. Othello's life ends tragically while Latino triumphs. Yet irrespective of the genre, black heroic characters in England were flawed whereas in Spain they were 'heroic or saintly', if also 'comical'.[67] Other differences highlight how Afro-Europeans were perceived in both societies. Othello carries the stigma attached to both black people and Muslims, whereas Juan Latino is allegedly redeemed through Christianity. Beyond the question of religious affiliation, one of the points that render these two characters heroic is their attachment to duty and to the notion of service. They are both rigorous and thorough in whatever they set out to do. They are both at the service of their king and city. Yet religion trumps those qualities and serves as a redeeming feature for Latino, whereas Othello, whose religion is indeterminate, has a disastrous fate.[68] Othello, contrary to Latino, was a fictional character, but as we shall see with Jacobus Capitein it was simply not enough to be an African European with status and education. One's religion determined one's fate.

In 1576, Archbishop Guerrero and Ana died. Don Juan de Austria and the Duke of Sessa passed away two years later. Juan Latino's health diminished. The exact date of his death is unknown, but he probably died blind around the age of ninety between 1597 and 1607.

3

THE TRANSATLANTIC SLAVE TRADE AND THE INVENTION OF RACE

Latino's life in many respects echoed that of Jacobus Capitein. Nonetheless, while Latino had interacted with one of the most powerful European monarchs and the elite in Granada, Capitein's fortunes were considerably more limited in various areas. Both men's trajectories highlighted the dependency of African Europeans upon the benevolence of the wealthy. The question of masculinity that often appears in the relationship between the white master and the black male remains absent in studies of these men's lives.

As with Latino, religion, opportunity and identity shaped Jacobus Capitein's journey. He was the product of a European education and benefitted from the privileges bestowed on those who were viewed as exceptional characters. He was also the medium through which part of the European elite attempted to implement its civilising aspirations. He was part of the 'middling' or 'buffer' class Gomez refers to as a marker, 'if not weapon', of modernity.[1] We know very little about Capitein's early years. When he was about seven years old, he was bought by a Dutch sea captain named Aarnout Steenhart. This new owner took the boy to Shama in the Gold Coast and gave him as a present to a merchant who was employed by the powerful West India Company (WIC), a Dutchman named Jacob van Gogh. Van Gogh left the Gold Coast in 1728 with Capitein.

What we know about the relationship between the two men has come from Capitein's writing. He praised Van Gogh's character and explained that the relationship was that of a father and son. Here, Capitein's views display the notion of paternalism analysed by Eugene D. Genovese and some aspects of the 'Sambo thesis' developed by Stanley Elkins.[2] Historically, paternalism was a way for slave owners to define their actions as care for allegedly unfortunate Africans, but also a means of survival through which enslaved people could navigate the troubled waters of oppression, as well as a resistance tool that allowed these groups to claim some agency over their lives. Capitein made no mention of the fact that he had been an enslaved child. Little was said about the global role of the Dutch in the history of enslavement. The WIC's role in expanding the colonisation of the Americas was also absent in his writings.

At first glance it seems that, as the product of a global market that traded in human beings, Capitein had no control over his body, let alone his soul. He was just one of the many Africans caught up in the race for commodities that made European kingdoms wealthy. Before he was born, the Dutch Republic had already challenged Portuguese and Spanish holdings in the Americas and on the West African coast. The Dutch provinces got involved in Atlantic enslavement as early as 1619, when twenty Africans were transported to the colony of Virginia. For the next thirty-five years the Dutch kept fighting to get hold of Portuguese plantations in northern Brazil during the ongoing Dutch–Portuguese wars. At the heart of these trading interests were the irreconcilable beliefs of the Catholics and the ultra-religious Dutch

Calvinists, as well as conflicts over crown successions. Europe was at war over religion and territory.[3] To finance these wars the Dutch also needed gold, and African sites were therefore extremely important for both parties. In 1637, the Dutch took the crucial Elmina Castle from the Portuguese and moved on to other West African territories in São Tomé and today's Angola.

By 1650, the Dutch Republic boasted a fleet of 16,000 merchant ships. They were also able to control many depots on the West African coast, and went on to settle in Cape Colony in South Africa. These victories did not assuage the appetite for land and goods. The Dutch continued their relentless pursuit of Portuguese-owned Brazilian holdings. However, a shift occurred when eventually, in 1690, they started to supply the Portuguese with various commodities including African captives. Prior to that, in the second half of the seventeenth century, Amsterdam had become a powerful trading centre. The rise in colonial trade had been bolstered by the regulation of trade through the WIC, which was set up in 1621. Trade had been at the heart of Dutch colonial expansion. The regulation and control of trading markets had not started with the WIC; the Dutch East India Company was established in 1602. A series of measures was put in place to replicate the so-called success of the East India Company in Dutch territories on both sides of the Atlantic. Governor-General Jan Pieterszoon Coen, a leading figure in the massacre of the Banda Islands who was in favour of the subjugation of local indigenous populations, declared the legality of the use of enslaved labour in the Americas. The Dutch had continuously sought to justify aggressive colonial conquest by seeking the advice of renowned jurists. Hugo Grotius, for example, made a case for Dutch war prizes. In 1625, an edict that allowed the WIC to become a slave-owning company was passed. Sugar, tobacco and cotton produced by enslaved men and women in the colonies was stocked in depots then treated in Amsterdam.

In the seventeenth century, Amsterdam became as important as Lisbon or Seville as a trading capital. In fact, the seventeenth century is known as the 'Dutch Golden Age'. The United Provinces had managed to become the European centre for overseas trade, excelling in manufactured goods, banking and navigation. The quest for commodities had also led to innovation in navigation with the fluyt, a lighter, faster and cheaper vessel that put Dutch merchants and sea captains at an advantage. Beside Amsterdam in Holland, other provinces such as Zeeland and Vlissingen ended up specialising in the slave trade. This was quite a stark contrast with these cities' previous stances. In 1596, for moral reasons, Zeeland had refused to have a slave market in its capital, Middelburg. By 1759, Zeeland saw the transatlantic slave trade as a crucial part of the province.

Capitein arrived at the epicentre of trade, religion and culture that was the Dutch Republic at a time when carefully crafted measures aimed at preventing too large a flow of enslaved people from the Americas and Africa were at odds with resistance to enslavement. The migration of black bodies had been tightly linked to centuries-old debates about the freedom and legal status of subjugated human beings. Strong support for enslavement went hand in hand with discussions about liberty and humanity. The Valladolid controversy in 1550 between Juan Ginés de Sepúlveda and Bartolomé de las Casas showcased two very different beliefs about the legal status of those who had been colonised by the Portuguese in the Americas. Las Casas had been against the enslavement of fellow human beings, especially the indigenous population of the Americas, on religious grounds. On the surface, it seemed that the Dutch Calvinists and traders had no such qualms. Capitein's presence on Dutch soil was neither legal nor illegal. The black presence in Europe had raised a number of questions about the moral and religious dimensions of enslavement, but by the seventeenth century the presence of people of African descent in the Dutch Republic had been normalised.

Reluctance to legally acknowledge black presence was accompanied by a reality that forced authorities to address the question in a few instances, as shown in the cases uncovered by Dienke Hondius. The records and burial grounds of Amsterdam's Portuguese Jewish community, as well as statements from Amsterdam notaries, show that there was a clear black presence in the city from the first half of the seventeenth century. Records from October 1625 demonstrate that the status of enslaved people brought to Amsterdam by a few Portuguese slave-owners remained unchanged while they were in the city. Yet in burial records after 1617, although information was provided about individuals' servant status and skin colour, the term 'slave' was absent.[4] It has been argued that the unease felt by the authorities was not linked to black presence, but rather to the involvement of the Dutch Republic in slavery. Ambiguity would become a feature of the Dutch position on the question of slavery.

Hondius notes the story of a woman called Juliana, which is symptomatic of the constant ambivalence between the law and unofficial positions.[5] In 1643, Portuguese trader Eliau Burgos bought Juliana in Recife. She was about eleven years old at the time. He tried to sell her years later but allegedly Juliana begged him not to and promised to serve him for the rest of her life. Interestingly, Burgos complied and even took Juliana to Amsterdam years later in 1656 when she was about twenty-three years old. Once in Amsterdam, she decided to leave him. She had been made aware that slavery did not exist in the city. She therefore could not be legally enslaved there. Burgos had decided to travel to Barbados and, seeing that the law was not on his side, he had a legal document drawn up which declared that because he had bought Juliana, he was entitled to some form of compensation. He offered her freedom once they arrived in Barbados if Juliana agreed to work for him there for three years first. It is unlikely that he would have kept his promise. Slavery was still legal in the Caribbean and Juliana would have had no way of forcing him to manumit her. Her fate remains unknown as no further correspondence has been found, but her story further highlights the difficulty Dutch owners and enslaved people faced at the time when it came to legislating on the question of freedom.

Dutch ambiguity was further evidenced by the debate about slavery and education to which Capitein contributed in some degree. Capitein arrived in Middelburg in 1728. He then travelled with Van Gogh to The Hague, where Van Gogh had a house. Two years after his arrival, Van Gogh sent him to German-born minister of the Reformed Church, Johann Philipp Manger. Manger's impression on the boy was important. In the 1730s the Republic was at its height in terms of trade and culture. The Dutch, Capitein amongst them, were proud of its achievements. Through Capitein's writings, one learns that The Hague and the whole of the country were a source of regional and national esteem. Manger's position as a vocal protector of immigrants and a tolerant Christian provided access to a more balanced and outward-looking perspective that greatly influenced the young Capitein.[6] Under Manger's tutelage, Capitein learnt French and was encouraged to consider university. In 1735, at nearly eighteen years old, he was baptised. He joined the University of Leiden two years later.

In 1742, Capitein rose to fame during his viva in Leiden before an audience of scholars who viewed him as a curiosity and a prodigy. His position was clearly enunciated in his thesis title: 'Politico-Theological Dissertation Concerning Slavery, as Not Contrary to Christian Freedom'. Despite the Bible's defence of freedom and its numerous passages both against and in favour of various forms of enslavement, Capitein focused on spiritual freedom rather than earthly concerns of emancipation for enslaved people. He argued that enslaved men and women should be baptised, but he contended that this should not mean emancipation.

According to him, Christian life was the ultimate goal for all human beings. He demonstrated that the Bible did not promote slavery, but rather that slavery was the result of human endeavour. The thesis used the malediction of Ham as the starting point for enslavement. It was perfectly in line with the ideas of Dutch Calvinist minister Godefridus Cornelisz Udemans. Udemans and his followers emphasised the necessity of leading a pious life above all else. Dutch piety was to trump personal quests, and supposedly selfish aspirations, including demands for freedom from enslavement, were thus deemed futile.

Capitein's lecture was met with enthusiasm. His sermons and dissertation were translated and printed several times. He even embarked on a tour in 1742.[7] Criticism of his position on enslavement has been virulent. However, one must remember that Capitein held a privileged position in the Van Gogh household, and the general reception he had amongst the elite—if we are to believe his lecture and writings, in which he profusely thanked his educators and former master—was incredibly positive. He had benefitted from an exceptional upbringing amongst the fortunate and had achieved a level of education often denied to those of African descent at the time. In addition, The Hague was not as multicultural as Amsterdam and it is quite possible that the Africans he encountered did not provide him with a clear understanding of what life in subjugation was like. He had been educated in Leiden where Grotius, and many other defenders of slavery, had studied. One could argue that he must have also been aware of the intellectual discussions that were taking place in favour of abolition. Nonetheless, purely intellectual debate could hardly provide him with the emotional experience that came from contact with those whose daily lives were regulated by their status in various households as enslaved men, women and children.

While Jacobus shared the views about enslavement that were widespread among Dutch Calvinists in The Hague at the time, it has been argued that his religious positioning was in fact relatively progressive. He followed the liberal and rationalist precepts of Johannes Cocceius, a professor of theology who had taught at the University of Leiden a century before. Cocceius's peer Gisbertus Voetius, theology professor at the University of Utrecht, opposed him and emphasised the importance of piety.[8] A true 'Cocceian', Capitein probably thought he understood the influence of the Bible in Christians' daily lives. Fate challenged some of those assumptions in 1742.

It is difficult to know what led to Capitein's decision to go to Africa, but it is very likely that the Reformed Church played a role in his African journey. Fellow Reformed Church minister Jan Willem Kals might have influenced him. Kals had been appointed minister in Surinam and was enthusiastic about the conversion of both the indigenous and the black population in 1731. He was determined to have colonists and colonised attend the same services and schools.[9] His approach was met with contention, and two years later the colonial administrators sent him back to Europe. Perhaps Capitein believed he could emulate Kals but in West Africa. However, it appears that he was not prepared for life there. He set sail for Elmina in 1742, full of ideas and determined to change and save souls. The reality turned out to be very different.

Capitein left for Africa as an employee of the WIC, which meant that he was to rely on his fellow Dutchmen in Elmina. However, we learn from the letters that he sent to The Hague, some of which were published, that he viewed this new journey as an opportunity to reconnect with his African countrymen. He was aware of the differences in their experiences and knew that his European education set him apart, but in time he developed ties with them and became attuned to their views on various matters. Nevertheless, he remained protective of Dutch interests in the Gold Coast, to the point that he viewed conquered commodities and territories as Dutch property. In his sermons, he even asked for God's support in prolonging the Dutch Republic's hold on the place. He declared in his first sermon that his aim was 'the gospel and promoting the interests of your Company'.[10] Capitein's refined and rather sheltered life also put him at odds with his fellow Dutchmen. Many colonists did not belong to the same socio-economic background. Alcoholism and disruptive behaviours were common on the Gold Coast. The racial divide between Capitein and those Europeans was probably blatant, but his letters do not provide information on the matter.

There were less than twenty members of the Reformed Church in Elmina, and overall very few people attended Capitein's church services. That was not the main problem as his aim had been to convert the local population, so it was important for him primarily to strengthen links with them. The economic ties that existed between the locals and Elmina Castle facilitated that part of his work. The authorities there paid them for skilled and unskilled work. What was left for Capitein was to ensure that the children of those workers had access to an education. He opened a primary school and was successful in enrolling twenty children. However, he was disappointed that more children, especially girls, were not sent to school. As Levecq notes, girls were groomed from a young age to anticipate becoming concubines for white settlers.[11] Any baptism would have hindered this practice, as various churches did not officially acknowledge those unions as acceptable Christian behaviour. Capitein refrained from expressing his views on the matter. In fact, he acknowledged that the economic advantages of these unions for the local populations were as important as the colonists' need for companionship. He became particularly involved in the education of dual-heritage children.

While looking into the interactions between white men and black women, Capitein was probably forced to acknowledge the complexity of human relationships. He became entangled in such difficulties when he found himself attracted to a black woman. He went to see her parents to ask for permission to marry her once she had been educated and baptised. However, he also needed to seek the permission of the Church back home. Unfortunately, permission was refused in 1745 on the grounds that the woman was a 'heathen'. One year later, we learn that Capitein married a young white Christian woman who had most likely been sent for him from Holland.

Disillusioned by the lack of church attendance, the dire state of church records and the Dutch settlers' general lack of commitment to his work of converting and educating the local population, Capitein asked the WIC to change the terms of his employment. One of the points that had troubled him was the lack of continuity when it came to the education of baptised children, including those of dual heritage. He asked for financial support so that he could sent up an institution where those children would be removed from their guardians' and parents' tutelage in order to prevent them from going back to 'heathen' households. He was planning to take full charge of their education, but he also insisted that they would then return to work on plantations as skilled Christian workers. It would take his church governing body two years to answer. When they did, pastors made it clear that they disapproved of errors in his translations of prayers and categorically disapproved of his intended marriage. He answered back explaining that the union would have been a celebration of two cultures: Europe and Africa united in matrimony. Several other points were of concern to him. For example, he worried about the fate of African men who could not find a good Christian woman because local parents did not want their girls to be baptised, hoping instead to attract a Dutch trader.

Capitein did not have time to pursue his dreams. He died in 1747. The causes of his death are unknown, but what is known is that he died in financial ruin. He owed money to several people in Europe. It seems that he had been living beyond his means, and yet we find out that he had asked the WIC to take 300 guilders from his salary to give to Van Gogh. As far as his position on slavery was concerned, Levecq notes that although the end of Capitein's first sermon at Elmina did not explicitly condemn the institution of slavery, he expressed a desire to provide young Africans with the few opportunities that were available in the restricted context of European dominance over enslaved people of African descent.[12] Towards the end of his life, he was well aware of the stance taken by the Republic towards the migration of Africans from the continent to Europe. He knew that, contrary to his experience, very few Africans had been taken to Holland and benefitted, as he felt he had, from Dutch culture and an academic education. Although he was criticised as having had a 'Sambo mentality', meaning he was an African who became subservient towards Europeans, Capitein's life needs to be understood in its context and analysed in light of Hondius's five patterns. He was perceived as exceptional and yet was still considered essentially a child, rendering him susceptible to the pattern of racial infantilisation. He fell from grace for deviating from what was expected of him because he thought he could become a force for change beyond set parameters. As Hondius notes with regards to paternalism, 'Failure to comply may lead to intervention, punishment, or correction'.[13]

The Dutch West India Company lost its monopoly in 1730. The slave trade was still important for the Republic, but harsher laws were adopted to diminish African circulation in European soil. While France, Britain and Portugal argued that slavery was not acceptable on European land, they found themselves in difficult positions when it came to addressing enslaved people at the service of wealthy owners. In 1739, slave-owners were asked by the Dutch authorities to acquire a travel document if they wanted to bring their enslaved servants from the Americas to the Republic. In 1742, free black people and people of dual heritage had to prove their liberty if they wanted to board a vessel. Marriage laws also changed. Marriages between white men and black women were facilitated while an administrative arsenal was put in place to discourage the marriage of black men with white women.[14] However, any enslaved person who arrived on Dutch soil was automatically free. The law changed in 1776, stating from this point that no enslaved person was to become free unless they had been manumitted by their master. The exception to this rule was if the master had stayed in the country for twelve months altogether but had failed to register their enslaved servants; then they would have to be set free.

The Dutch anti-slavery movement worried the authorities. The movement had built up in the 1760s and 1770s, but it was really in the 1780s, specifically after the French Revolution in 1789 and the publication of literature sympathetic to abolition, that it gathered momentum and attracted a vast number of sympathisers. In his treatise published in 1793, Pieter Paulus argued that slavery was abhorrent and violated the rights of men. However, he supported the idea that immediate emancipation would be a catastrophe. In the same year, law professor Hendrik Constantijn Cras also expressed his views in favour of ending the slave trade. However, he put forward the pervasive idea that enslaved people who were by law chattel slaves and were therefore at the mercy of their owner, and their owner's children and descendants, for the duration of their lives sometimes had better lives than free European labourers. This idea was in fact widely shared amongst European abolitionists, many of whom had never set foot in American and Caribbean plantations. They also considered the restriction of black bodies, the institution of enslavement and religious and philosophical justifications in the context of scientific discovery and interest in the anatomy of the Other.

In 1770, Dutch anatomist Petrus Camper set about convincing his peers that he had determined a set of ideal physical attributes in his *Facial Angles* lectures. Camper posited that facial measurements at the end of his established spectrum were unattractive. It has been argued that he and his followers did not equate facial measurements with intelligence.[15] Nonetheless, a few nineteenth-century anatomists and philosophers took it upon themselves to make those links. Camper's study of human anatomy had come at a time when European biologists were obsessed with classifying various species, including human beings. Colonisers were fascinated by plants and collected a wide variety of them; some exhibited them, while others were more inclined to study them. Prior to Camper, the work of Swedish botanist Carl Linnaeus became widely recognised, particularly with the 1735 publication of his *Systema Naturae*. He divided human beings into four different groups that were characterised by specific attitudes. In 1775, Johann Friedrich Blumenbach expanded this classification into five new groups, or races. Camper's use of taxonomy was in keeping with his contemporaries.

Decades later, French anatomist Georges Cuvier used Camper's work for the purpose of comparative anatomy. Cuvier's fascination with Sarah Baartman and the notion of missing links has been widely researched. Baartman, derisively nicknamed the Hottentot Venus, has often been presented as a powerless victim. Sadiah Qureshi offers a nuanced approach to these assumptions.[16] Qureshi's analysis highlights the violence and forms of subjugation that were at the heart of Baartman's experience. She also provides us with information about the way Baartman lived and the surprising agency she had over certain aspects of her life. But long before Baartman, the Dutch Republic's elite, through its scholars, was setting a strong precedent in the racialisation and regulation of colonised bodies.

In 1795, the Batavian Revolution provided the United Provinces with an opportunity to rethink its political destiny and its place in Europe and the world. Yet the question of colonial trade remained a thorn in the Provinces' side. Ideas of sovereignty and freedom were discussed comprehensively, but despite debates and reports on these subjects at the National Assembly of 1797, no mention was made of the protection of enslaved people in the colonies, let alone the abolition of the slave trade. The institution of slavery remained suspiciously absent from the parliamentary agenda. It was only in 1814, after Napoleon's defeat and the British victory, that the Dutch were forced to abolish the slave trade. However, slavery continued in Dutch colonies. Despite a relatively less profitable colonial trade with the Americas, the Dutch abolished slavery in the colonies in 1863, decades after the British and French. Slavery had been a matter of wealth and status in the European scene. There was pride in having colonies in the Americas, and through their legislation—or lack of it—on the question of slavery, European powers were demonstrating that they accepted the enslavement of millions of people as a fair price to pay for this pride.

Capitein, as a representative of Dutch interests in Elmina, was not fully conforming to what was expected from him. His interest in and sympathy for dual-heritage children living near Elmina Castle was negatively echoed in other settings in Europe. People of dual heritage blurred those racial lines that had been established by the anatomists. They were allegedly physically, physiologically and even emotionally closer to the white community. They could therefore inflict more damage on those racialised as white. As a result, it was felt that they had to be carefully monitored. Several kinds of bodies were monitored in this way. Ignoring the variety of their experiences and relationships with their heritage, people of African descent were essentialised as black. Yet the destinies of dual-heritage or so-called mixed-race children in eighteenth-century European empires varied greatly. People who were termed 'mulattos' in the eighteenth century were also called *gens de couleur* (people of colour) in France. Twentieth- and twenty-first-century France have named them *métis*, while the equivalent in English is often 'people of colour', 'mixed-race' people or 'people of dual heritage'.

Each term carries its own historical legacy, which matters when it comes to understanding various communities' relationships with these descriptors. The racialisation of the terms 'mixed race' or even 'biracial' is perceived in various ways by those belonging to relevant groups. The use of these terms stems from the decision to classify people according to the colour of their skin rather than their place of birth. The racialisation process that occurred during the colonial eras still weighs heavily on contemporary uses of language. It has been argued that, as race is a social construct, using these terms reinforces dated and dangerous views on visible biological differences. On the other hand, the word 'biracial' is deemed acceptable to some people simply because it acknowledges duality of experience in a world that still uses the categories of 'black' and 'white'.

'Mixed race' also has its supporters and its detractors. In an article written in 2015, the actress Meghan Markle, who has since become the Duchess of Sussex, self-identified as a biracial woman.[17] The piece provoked a number of responses. Some have embraced a 'mixed-race' identity while arguing that the imprecision of the term can leave people 'mixed up' as to where they stand in a society which forces them to choose who they are.[18] Others have contended that because of the long history of oppression that has led to classification based on people's skin colour, even people with one parent have traditionally been classified as black.[19] Per this argument, it is necessary to claim one's blackness once and for all. Equally contentious is the rejection of people of dual heritage by people from the black community. Karis Campion employs the useful term 'horizontal hostility' to analyse the reasons, historical underpinnings and tensions or jealousies that are at the root of 'mixed-race' rejection.[20] The mechanisms of these exclusions are different from those at play when rejection comes from the group racialised as white.

As Comedian Trevor Noah puts it, 'white is an "exclusive club"', while black is like an 'all-you-can-eat' buffet at which everyone is welcome.[21] The term 'dual heritage', used in recent years, acknowledges the multiple cultural backgrounds of the individual in question. It posits that culture shapes one's identity as strongly as perceived physical differences. However, in an attempt to claim their racialised identity nevertheless and to remove the stigma attached to it, many have decided to continue to use the terms 'biracial' and 'mixed race'. For many people, 'dual heritage' and 'biracial' seem to bear the same meaning. They encompass people whose identities are at the crossroads of racial and cultural boundaries. The use of the term 'dual heritage' in this volume is an attempt to acknowledge the complexity of the interpretations outlined here, while recognising the limitations of all the existing terms.

The complexity of individual trajectories, including the experiences of people of dual heritage, needs to be placed in its historical context. For example, there were specific cases that brought the question of the legal status of children of dual heritage to the attention of the French authorities. Africans were defined in various ways in the eighteenth century. Even those who had been born overseas and on plantations were deemed African because of the colour of their skin. The law regarding the migration of these groups varied greatly depending on whether they were enslaved or free. In reality, however, the question of colour remained at the forefront of legal debates. There were free black and dual-heritage people in France, but the assumption was that a black person was likely to be an enslaved person. The notion of the 'principle of freedom' or 'free soil' implied that once in France an enslaved person was automatically free. By law, they could petition the authorities to grant them official freedom. In the cases analysed by Sue Peabody, it appears that the legal basis for this freedom principle was established. Medieval law was used as a historical precedent, but this could have been challenged as the cases involved related to colonial slavery and involved very different contexts.[22] However, this point of detail was not widely known. Consequent misunderstandings led several black, enslaved men and women to challenge their masters before a court based on medieval law.

That was the case for Jean-Louis, for example, a 26-year-old enslaved black man who had been sent from Martinique to Rochefort and given as a servant to the wife of a naval officer.[23] When the wife died, the husband, Combes, kept Jean-Louis as his slave. He took Jean-Louis with him to Paris in 1775, and that is when Jean-Louis decided to petition the senior Admiralty court for his freedom. He even demanded 300 French livres from Combes because, as he argued, he had been working for him when he should have been a freeman. Three weeks later the authorities examined the case, but Jean-Louis had by then decided that 300 livres was not enough and raised the sum by 120 livres for each year following the date he set foot in France. Jean-Louis became entangled in a legal battle. The Admiralty court accepted his petition, and he was placed under the protection of the king. However, at Combes's instigation he was arrested by the police in Paris. Both the court and the police had the authority to give Jean-Louis back to or withhold him from his former master.

Over the following months, similar cases appeared. The authorities were forced to change the law. The *Code Noir*, or Black Code, of 1685 had established the parameters of the interactions between black and white people in the colonies. However, the law was primarily concerned with the administration of colonial matters. Enslaved people who came to France were both celebrated as exotic objects and stigmatised as untrustworthy. These contradictions were embodied at the time by France's main slave port, Nantes. Gérard Mellier, the mayor of Nantes, shared planters' views on black people but also believed in their right to marry in France. He went so far as to declare that children born from these unions should automatically become free French citizens. However, he recommended that masters who felt the need to bring their slaves to France limit the amount of time they spent there. These recommendations made their way into the Royal Edict of 1716.

In 1738, the law changed; the period enslaved people were allowed to spend in France was limited to three years, and marriages were forbidden. Also gone was the freedom principle. It appears that the number of enslaved individuals who had been left by their masters had increased at a time when authorities were worried that black people would demand treatment and even wages on a par with their white working-class counterparts. Colonial rebellions were rife in French and British plantations. White communities were worried that that spirit of rebellion would 'taint' France. Black people were not the only group who supposedly threatened France; dual-heritage children were not welcome either. Widespread distrust had, for example, led to the Edict of 1724 that took a harsher stance on mixed marriages. Given the tightening of laws, Jean-Louis's case was not easy to resolve. Historian Pierre H. Boulle contends that there was a sizeable number of cases in which the master was given royal prerogative to arrest the enslaved and send them back to their plantations.[24]

The number of legal cases involving black people led the authorities to suggest that a special unit should be set up. In 1777 the *Police des Noirs*, or 'police for black people', was created. Soon after, it became compulsory for black people to carry a *cartouche* (an identification card). Between 1777 and 1789, in Paris only, 765 people were registered.[25] The aim of the *Police des*

Noirs was to limit the number of black people in the country. It was not named a 'police for enslaved people', so the assumption by then was that all black bodies were also enslaved. Masters who had enslaved domestic servants in their service had to register them or risk paying a heavy fine. Enslaved people were to stay in detention centres for the duration of their master's stay. The costs would be the master's responsibility.

Outside Paris, many port cities resented the initiative, as it curbed the freedom of planters who had up to that point enjoyed the services of their enslaved servants. In Bordeaux, for example, authorities argued in 1778 that the prison was the only adequate space to serve as a detention centre, but enslaved servants incurred the risk of becoming ill or being corrupted by prison life.[26] Some people urged the authorities to find safe and clean spaces for their enslaved servants. The authorities' preoccupation was not with cleanliness. It was, they argued, with finding ways to avoid any collusion that would lead to an insurrection in those detention centres. Masters could have used white servants in France, but that necessitated paying them wages. The predicament was that planters visiting family and friends wanted their slaves with them, but the rest of the population and the French authorities did not want to see them on their streets. They also resented the fact that they had to contend with a wealthy group they would rather leave on the fringe of the empire. Consequently, all free black men and women from the colonies who arrived after the new laws had been passed were to be sent back to the colonies. A series of laws was also passed which aimed to discourage unions between black and white people. Marriages were forbidden but, as Boulle notes, Article 13 of the 1777 bill was redrafted. Instead of making such unions illegal, it stated that children born from them had to wait four generations before they could hold office. In the end, however, Article 13 was removed from the bill altogether.[27]

The question remained of how to fund the daily subsistence costs of those who were detained in centres across France. If the idea had been to keep the black population incarcerated while their masters were enjoying the perks of city life, it became obvious that sending the enslaved on the next ship back to the colonies was the best solution. But overall it was prejudice against black bodies that led to the series of laws and measures that forced all black people to register. The authorities had effectively managed to criminalise black people. However, enforcing these measures proved to be difficult. Some merchants refused to register their enslaved people. Some of the women who were supposed to stay in detention centres were also wet nurses. Some black and dual-heritage men and women chose not to register.

Other cases also highlight the difficulty the French authorities faced when the alleged master was the father of dual-heritage children. Such was the case for a plantation owner and merchant from Saint-Domingue called Aimé-Benjamin Fleuriau. Fleuriau had fathered eight dual-heritage children, five of whom he brought back with him to France, and owned an enslaved man named Hardy.[28] Once in La Rochelle, he tried to have them all registered. Fleuriau's trajectory had been one of rags to riches. He had come from a humble background. In 1729, at the age of twenty, he set sail for Saint-Domingue and, thanks to his family's connections, became an overseer on a plantation. After a few years, he was able to buy a plantation and acquire a sizeable number of slaves. He had eight children with a dual-heritage woman named Jeanne. She had been one of Fleuriau's slaves before he freed her. She then became the mother of his children. Despite the fact that all of their children had been baptised as free people of colour and Jeanne had been given a small allowance during their ten-year-long interaction, it was still the kind of relationship that existed in colonial settings and was thus dominated by financial and racial power dynamics. However, Fleuriau's behaviour was typical of white fathers with dual-heritage children in the colonies. He knew the value of connections and made sure that influential planters in neighbouring estates interacted socially with his children.[29]

Historian Jennifer L. Palmer has analysed the complexity of family units when dual-heritage children were involved, especially when they had left the colonies. As she notes, the nuclear family unit was complicated by the ability of fathers to choose their dual-heritage children as their heirs and even disinherit their white children.[30] Given that many of those colonists had been living side by side with free black men and women, some of whom were descended from white planters, the restrictions of life in port cities such as La Rochelle, Fleuriau's birthplace, proved to be challenging. France was, at the time of Fleuriau's arrival in 1755, tightening laws around race. In 1755, however, free people of colour such as Fleuriau's children still enjoyed the same legal benefits as their white counterparts. Fleuriau and other merchants in similar family units were not ready to let French authorities put dual-heritage children in the same category as enslaved people. Fleuriau eventually chose to register his servant Hardy but not his children. However, the children were not registered as his own and carried the family name of Mandron. He could not bring himself to abandon them, but refused to give them his name. As Palmer demonstrates, despite their family wealth, the elite in La Rochelle never accepted the children. If in Saint-Domingue their light skin and paternity protected them and even provided them with connections that could have helped them move up the social ladder, in La Rochelle they were viewed as having African blood running through their veins.[31] It was therefore unlikely that their fate would have been different if they had carried their father's prestigious name.

Fleuriau had white children upon arriving in La Rochelle, and they all integrated into the wealthiest circles of the city. In 1762, with a new ordinance that only took race into consideration, Fleuriau was forced to register his children. He registered them not as his children, however, but as free black people of colour he had ties with and whose working history was impeccable. He made a clear distinction between his *negre*, or 'negro servant', and his children, the *mulatre* (mulatto) Mandron family.[32] While the sons went back to Saint-Domingue, the two daughters stayed in La Rochelle in a comfortable house owned by their father and close to where he lived with his new family. Fleuriau left an inheritance to his children, including his dual-heritage daughters. It was only after the death of her father that Fleuriau's Afro-Caribbean daughter was able to put her sister's name beside their father's name on the death register.

Legally refusing to give his name to his dual-heritage children was not the path that Boulogne de Saint-Georges chose for his child Joseph. Joseph Boulogne was born in 1739 to a white, aristocratic French plantation owner and an enslaved Senegalese woman known as Anne or Nanon, on the French island of Guadeloupe. No record has been found of his exact place of birth and his father's precise name, given the number of Boulognes present in Guadeloupe and Martinique at the time. It is likely, however, given the findings of several researchers, that Joseph's father was Guillaume-Pierre Tavernier de Boulogne.[33] Guillaume took Nanon and Joseph to Bordeaux in 1748, then to Paris. At the time it was unusual for the father of a dual-heritage child to take the enslaved mother with them when they visited France or when they decided to leave the colony to return to their place of birth. There has been speculation about the nature of the relationship between the father and Nanon, and the reason she was taken to France. Given the colonial context, it is probable that she had little choice in the matter. One can only assume that given the choice to stay and risk life on the plantation or follow her child to France, she made the natural decision. No record has been found of other children fathered by Boulogne, or whether Nanon had other children.

Once in Paris, Guillaume decided to give Joseph the education of a nobleman. He probably realised that a lack of formal education and a life of relative obscurity, even as a nobleman, might be detrimental to Joseph's future. At the age of thirteen, Joseph was placed under the supervision of renowned master fencer Nicolas Texier de La Boëssière. The master was also in charge of his literary education. In his 1818 *Traité de l'art des armes*, La Boëssière's son Antoine celebrated Joseph's mastery of arms.[34] Another sought-after master, Chevalier Dugast, an equestrian who only accepted the sons of aristocrats, agreed to take on young Joseph's education in that area.

At the age of twenty, Joseph was considered one of the most handsome and accomplished young men in the kingdom. His abilities in swimming, dancing and even ice skating were admired. Some members of the elite French salons did not open their doors to all aristocrats, but they welcomed Joseph with open arms. His father's wealth could not be the only explanation for such popularity. Guillaume owned a plantation and had spent years in the colonies. Such a proximity to enslaved communities usually closed rather than opened doors in certain quarters. His money decidedly could not buy all privileges. Yet Joseph seemed to charm company of all varieties.

Guillaume did not limit his son's abilities to sports and literature. Musical education was also important in the education of wealthy young men and women at the time. For the aristocracy, it was paramount. Joseph's father decided that he had to have one of the best teachers in the kingdom. At the time, Jean-Marie Leclair, an old favourite of King Louis XV, was one of them. In 1761, Joseph was made a member of the *Gendarmes de la garde du roi* (Royal Guards), but he used his spare time to work on his musical and artistic education.[35] Composer François-Joseph

Gossec helped him to master the technicalities of composition. When Leclair died, Gossec offered his place to Joseph, who became the first violinist for the elite amateur concert group that had been created by Gossec.

Joseph's father had left him with the handsome sum of 8,000 livres, but he lived a lavish life in Paris. Despite the excesses of his lifestyle, in 1770 he decided to dedicate most of his time to practising, performing and writing music. In 1773, Joseph and Gossec became known as the first French musicians and composers to write string quartets.[36] Joseph's concertos became renowned, and drew people from European capitals. The Chevalier de Saint-Georges, as he was then known, continued to charm most people he met. There were, however, instances when he was met with a barrage of criticism. In 1775, he was the favourite for the position of assistant director at the Paris Opera. A few women from the Royal Academy of Music sent a petition to the queen, arguing that they did not want to be led by a 'mulatto'.

Undeterred by these setbacks, Joseph continued in his career ascension and earned further approval from most elite women in Paris. Joseph had played in a theatre that was dear to Madame de Montesson, a playwright with influence. She took Joseph under her wing and put him in charge of concerts at that theatre. Madame de Montesson, a marquise who had married the Duke of Orléans, was going to introduce Joseph to her husband. Shortly after that the two men became inseparable. The Duke, a freemason, introduced Joseph to freemasonry, and he became a member of the Lodge of the Nine Sisters. Joseph is believed to have been one of the first black freemasons in mainland France. In 1778, Mozart was in Paris. The Chevalier de Saint-Georges was the best composer and musician of the kingdom, but Mozart, despite his father's orders, refused to attend one of his concerts and meet him. Not all famous eighteenth-century musicians reacted that way, however. In 1787, Joseph asked composer

Josef Haydn for six pieces of music. Haydn provided them and Joseph directed them at an exclusive and highly praised concert. In 1785, the Duke of Orléans died. Joseph lost a dear friend and a powerful protector. This rapidly resulted in a severe loss of income for Joseph.

Joseph had been very fond of English history and culture. The passing of the Duke prompted a need for a change of scenery and a search for a new income. Despite his charm, the Chevalier de Saint-Georges had always earned an income by working very hard and devoting his time to a variety of activities. He made several trips to London, where his reputation had preceded him. In 1787 he fought an organised duel with another fencing master, the Chevalière d'Eon. The Chevalière, or Chevalier, had earned a reputation as a skilful spy and a fantastic fighter. By the time she crossed swords with Joseph she identified and lived as a woman. The Prince of Wales attended the duel. Joseph was inspired by his encounter with the Chevalière d'Eon. On his return to Paris, he wrote a two-act comedy entitled *La Fille garçon*, or *The Girl Boy*. The piece was extremely successful, and a positive review appeared in the *Journal de Paris* in 1787.[37]

The Revolution started in 1789. Joseph appears to have taken the new Duke of Orléans to safety. The duke, later known as Philippe Égalité, had got involved with the Jacobin Club and Georges Danton in particular. Joseph decided to return to France to help the revolutionaries. His mission was to find people of African descent who were ready to support and take up arms for the revolutionaries. He managed to find a few of them, including the son of a planter and an enslaved woman, Thomas Retoré Dumas, later to be father of the author of *The Three Musketeers*, Alexandre Dumas. By 1792, he had a small group called the 'Legion Saint-Georges' that became known later on as the 'American Hussars'. Despite his commitment to the revolutionary cause, in 1793 a high-ranking officer accused him of mismanaging the troops' funds and of using sums of money for his own expenses and benefits. The attack was noted but dismissed as preposterous. Joseph was still able to remain in charge of his troops, but months later attacks on his character started again. He was then dismissed with no recourse to challenge the decision. He continued trying to clear his name, bringing undisputable evidence before several committees. He was reinstated, but by then his troops had grown and been divided into two new groupings. Rivalry between Joseph and the new commander led to further disputes. Joseph was the one who was discharged.

Details about his journey after that have been vague. While Lionel de La Laurencie and Frederick H. Martens state that Joseph went to Saint Domingue, Claude Ribbe and Alain Guédé make no mention of that trip to the Caribbean. In fact, the revolutionaries imprisoned him for a year. Yet his reputation was not destroyed. After the revolution, he was once again asked to take the reins of the Royal Orchestra. He tried to continue to work despite an illness that had diminished him, but in June 1799 the outstanding musician and son of an enslaved black woman died. Three years later, in 1802, Napoleon settled the war with Britain and sent an army to re-establish slavery in the French colonies. Guadeloupe, where Joseph Boulogne was born, attempted to resist. An army of black and dual-heritage men and women, led by Joseph Ignace and dual-heritage colonel Louis Delgrès, fought against nearly 4,000 French soldiers. Two generals, Jacques-Nicolas Gobert and Antoine Richepanse, led the French army. The Guadeloupeans were eventually defeated in one of the bloodiest wars for emancipation that engaged people of African descent in the Americas. 6,000 of them perished in combat or were executed afterwards.

Once firmly established, Napoleon banned the Chevalier de Saint-Georges's music. His work was removed from all repertoires and he seems to have slowly disappeared from French national history. He was, however, never completely forgotten. Afro-Caribbean community groups in France, Guadeloupe and Martinique have worked tirelessly to have his music played and recognised by the French state. In 2001, a Parisian street named after General Antoine Richepanse, who was appointed governor of Guadeloupe in 1801 by Napoleon, was renamed; the new plaque reads:

Chevalier Saint-Georges Street
(former Richepanse Street)
1745–1799
Composer and Orchestra Conductor
Captain of the National Guard of Lille
Colonel of the American and Midi Legions

On 10 May 2014, during a commemoration of the abolition of slavery, then president of the Republic François Hollande talked publicly about Joseph Boulogne's enormous contribution to music, fencing and French history. The musicians of the Republican Guard Band paid a moving homage to the Chevalier de Saint-Georges by playing his music. The extraordinary life of an African-Caribbean-European was finally celebrated by the French state. But this seemingly positive ending should not obscure the virulent debate that has been taking place about the way France has remembered its past connections with the slave trade and slavery, as well as the impact that this past still has on French society. Crystal Fleming analyses the way in which salient questions of citizenship and identity are debated within Afro-Caribbean communities in France.[38] She demonstrates that racial discrimination continues to affect these communities, and yet a large number are fiercely loyal to the ideal of the French Republic and resolutely reject the alleged evils of communitarianism. Communitarianism is defined in France as sectarian divisions that threaten the principles of an indivisible nation. The racialist framework upon which these principles are based paradoxically clashes with a heavily racialised society where people of African descent are the least likely to benefit from social mobility. Fleming's detailed ethnographic and historical research clearly highlights the impact such paradoxes have on the questions of memorialisation and public commemoration.

4

NEITHER HERE NOR THERE

DUAL HERITAGES AND GENDER ROLES

Gender and race continued to trouble Europeans, and anything they saw as a threat to gender norms or racial hierarchy had to be neutralised.

Napoleon Bonaparte's aversion towards Joseph Boulogne, mentioned in the previous chapter, should be put into the much broader context of attitudes about African Europeans at the time in France. Napoleon was not the only one to have set views about black people in France and in the colonies. The increasing concern over gender and race hardened positions on and views about people of African descent. When they were out of sight, the question of race was really the colonists' problem. However, theories about the reasons for differences in skin tone had already started to intrigue European naturalists and other scholars, as we have previously noted. Colonial slavery brought about renewed interest in and new hypotheses about those racial differences. Race and gender dynamics also played out very differently in different places, with views on the Other varying from France to Senegal or Ghana.

The origins of Africans' skin colour troubled seventeenth- and eighteenth-century naturalists and philosophers. In 1665, Italian doctor Marcello Malpighi contended that there was a colouring system below Africans' skin. In 1684, doctor François Bernier suggested that the sun might be responsible for darkening the skin of North Africans, indigenous Americans and South Asians, but that the skin colour of sub-Saharan Africans was hereditary.[1] By the first half of the eighteenth century, others held the same views but wanted them to be scientifically tested. Among such people were Dutch botanist Frederik Ruysch and French naturalist Georges-Louis Leclerc, Comte de Buffon. The latter suggested that to verify these hypotheses, one could take an African up to Denmark, isolate him from the rest of the population and see whether he lost his colour.[2] Meanwhile, American surgeon and anthropologist Josiah Nott was suggesting that the further north one travelled, the fairer people's skin got and the cleverer populations became. Ironically, if one followed that logic, indigenous populations of the Arctic region were the cleverest communities on earth and not, as Nott suggested, white Europeans.

Although the idea of a colour change, or the possibility that black people might not be black under certain circumstances, was incongruous, the theory was not novel to seventeenth- and eighteenth-century scholars. Such ideas have been circulating for centuries. The Greek novel *Aethiopica*, written by Hellenised Syrian Heliodorus of Emesa around 3 BCE, was found in the fifteenth century and translated into several languages. The story is about Chariclea, the daughter of King Hydaspes and Queen Persinna of Ethiopia, who was allegedly born white because while in the throes of passion her mother looked at a painting of Andromeda. Ashamed, Persinna hid Chariclea and then sent her away. She ended up in Egypt and later Greece, where she met Theagenes. The story ends with Chariclea being reunited with her parents. Karel van Mander III's series of paintings about the meeting in court, with Chariclea trying to prove her affiliation to her parents, brings to the surface notions of transmission, gender and representation. In Mander's paintings black characters are richly clothed and beautifully positioned. It was expected that African courts were as sophisticated and colourful as those in Europe. Mander's work was deemed outstanding by the eighteenth-century educated elite.

Although a work of fiction, Heliodorus's novel contributed to the idea that wealthy Africans were, at some time in the past, Europeans' equals. Heliodorus's own origins troubled the strong delineation that existed between Greece and those who were simply called 'non-Greeks'. It was believed that intercultural dialogue could transcend race in many cases. Black people could have white children.[3] Andromeda herself, an Ethiopian princess, could have been black, as has been suggested in numerous literatures.[4] The colour of Chariclea's skin could therefore have been a fluke. In her work on *Aethiopica*, Marla Harris addresses these questions by quoting Elaine Ginsberg: 'when "race" is no longer visible, it is no longer intelligible: if "white" can be "black", what is white?'[5]

French merchants and Enlightenment thinkers struggled with the notion of equality when it was applied to Africans and people of African descent. In 1716, the mayor of Nantes Gérard Mellier, discussed in the previous chapter, contended that Africans were prone to 'theft, larceny, lechery, laziness and treason' and that they were 'only fit to live in servitude, and to be used in the labors and in the cultivation of land on the continent of our American colonies'.[6] A few philosophers were of a similar opinion. Although he had displayed ambiguous views about Islam and the Quran in his 1736 play *Fanaticism, or Mahomet the Prophet*, French philosopher Voltaire changed his mind twenty years later and enthusiastically supported trading connections with the East in his *Essai sur les moeurs et l'esprit des nations* in

1756. No such change of heart was to be found with regards to enslaved people, or Africans generally. Despite his criticism of the treatment of the enslaved through the figure of the 'Negro of Surinam' in his 1759 satire *Candide*, Voltaire had trading interests in the colonies.[7] Those with vested interests in the slave trade tended to try to justify enslavement. The Marquis de Chastellux, one of Voltaire's admirers, wrote in his *Voyages dans l'Amérique septentrionale* that the negroes' 'natural insensibility' played a part in mitigating the pain they might feel while working on the plantations.[8]

Napoleon's views on black people were based on the evolving situation in the colonies. In 1799, he promised to the 'brave black men of Saint-Domingue' that the abolition that had been granted in 1794 would be maintained. People such as Admiral Lacrosse who were ready to launch expeditions against the rebellious colonised in Saint-Domingue were amongst Napoleon's inner circle. Using Yves Benot and Claude Wanquet's work, Erick Noël has demonstrated that Napoleon's opinions about black people were complex. For instance, he wondered how freedom could be granted to Africans, yet also viewed them as people who had no respect for property rights. He was also ready to grant more powers to Toussaint L'Ouverture, a leader of the Haitian Revolution, so that Haiti could take part in the fight against Britain.[9] Pragmatism seems to have prevailed when it came to colonial matters, but not entirely.

Napoleon had married Joséphine de Beauharnais in 1796. She was born Marie Josèphe Rose Tascher de La Pagerie in 1763, the daughter of a wealthy plantation owner whose family had been trading in enslaved people and sugar for centuries. She was the eldest child of noblewoman Rose Claire des Vergers de Sannois and aristocrat Joseph-Gaspard Tascher de La Pagerie. Joséphine spent her childhood in Martinique. She married Alexandre de Beauharnais, who was later killed by the revolutionaries. She then married Napoleon but was unable to have children with him, even though she already had children from her first marriage. Napoleon eventually divorced her in 1809. Prior to that, particularly between 1799 and 1801, she had been influential in the decisions he made regarding French colonies of the Americas. She had fiercely defended her family tradition regarding the slave trade, and the potential loss of colonies was perceived as a real threat to white planters' social and economic interests. The first French abolition of 1794 had been a blow to them. Napoleon's views on people of African descent have been attributed to her influence.

We rightly associate the history of African Europeans with journeys across the oceans and attempts to adapt to new environments in Europe. The stories of black figures have dominated European arts for centuries. However, the representation of black people in the arts changed significantly between the seventeenth and the end of the nineteenth century. The exoticisation of black bodies still played a part in their representation, but a power relationship was also on display in many paintings. From the household of a wealthy nobleman or merchant in London to the salon of a trader in Nantes, Seville or Lisbon, black figures were a sign of wealth. The black page in William Hogarth's *Marriage à la Mode* (c. 1743) was typical of art across the rest of Europe; such representations were as common as paintings of renowned black models. In all cases, the European gaze was as much an anthropological attempt to normalise societal changes as it was a journey fantasised by the artist and the audience. From the frescos of African figures dating back to the second millennium BCE found in Crete to nineteenth-century paintings of female black models, one could say that if beauty is in the eye of the beholder, so is fantasy.

Artists' relationships with black subjects took on a different turn when African arts and artefacts shaped European artists' perceptions. Art is universal, or so we have often been told. The appropriation of art forms disputed today, such as Picasso's artistic reinterpretations of African and European arts, was also, allegedly, both a matter of artistic expression and a way to document cultural transformations. The question of the gaze and how it shaped European mentalities has, however, been at the forefront of an increasing number of studies of the black figure in European arts. These volumes reflect changing attitudes, but also record limited or skewed views about people of African descent. Representations of black people's perceived social identities have strongly marked the history of the white gaze, as Naïl Ver-Ndoye and Grégoire Fauconnier clearly demonstrate. As they put it, not only is the 'history of Europe sewn of black thread', but it presents us with an interesting further aspect. They contend that the overwhelming number of paintings with black subjects posited the continent of Europe as an 'imaginary black museum'.[10]

Robin Mitchell's extensive research has brought to light the complexity of the question of the gaze, in particular the European gaze towards women of African descent in Europe. The gaze changes across time, from one geography to the other and from one social circle to the other. Mitchell looks at the lives of three women: Ourika, Sarah Baartman and Jeanne Duval. Ourika was likely born in Senegal, where she was purchased and offered as a gift to a French aristocrat. From Mitchell's research, we learnt that her master was fond of her and that she was taught to read and write. At the age of fourteen she was manumitted, put under a guardianship and provided with an annuity. Ourika died at the age of eighteen, single and buried in a town on the outskirts of Paris. Although little is known about her short life, numerous paintings and memoirs and a novel celebrate her. However, as Mitchell notes, these artistic productions only highlight how 'she clearly played multiple roles in elite identity, serving as plaything, status symbol, rescuer, benefactor, confidant, and muse, often simultaneously.'[11] The positive views they exhibit existed alongside racist considerations. She was the colour of sin and had redeemed herself through an exemplary life.

Sarah Baartman, on the other hand, served a different purpose. She came to be known to the French at a time when the losses of Napoleon were viewed as the failures of a whole country. Her alleged deformity served as a ploy to entertain while restoring control to bruised French masculinity and providing a sense of superiority to white French women at a time when fascination for black women's supposedly sexual attributes verged on obsession. Mitchell notes that 'Sarah Baartmann's representations facilitated a new collective narrative intended to secure white superiority in a historical moment of flux, change, and uncertainty.'[12]

Jeanne Duval, the third woman whose life was transformed by the European gaze, played a different role in French society. She was the poet Baudelaire's muse and lover. Criticisms of Baudelaire's dissolute lifestyle often attribute it to Jeanne. To survive in a bourgeois society that distrusted black bodies, she became a model and a sex worker. Unapologetic, she defied social norms through her profession. Mitchell notes that Baudelaire would not have been the poet he was without Jeanne, as she influenced him deeply. In addition, Mitchell argues that Baudelaire's lifestyle challenged the expectations of his circle; because of his tumultuous relationship with Jeanne, he failed to represent, in his contemporaries' view, the essence of whiteness and Frenchness. Jeanne in a way tainted him and blurred gender and identity norms: 'Because Baudelaire's defenders could not find a way to incorporate Duval and other black women into the definition of Frenchness, they demonized her and expunged her from the record as much as possible.'[13] Mitchell's work insightfully shows how these women were used to patch up failing narratives of empire, and to reinvigorate French ideas of identity and masculinity.

Shifting this analysis of the white European gaze to a view of European geographies as vibrant spaces comprising a multiplicity of identities allows us to further explore the questions of gaze, power and 'mixity' or 'hybridity' in different settings. Understanding and theorizing hybridity as it was defined by Homi K. Bhabha, Stuart Hall and Paul Gilroy in his notion of 'double consciousness', and before them other post-colonial scholars such as Frantz Fanon, Aimé and Suzanne Césaire and Paulette and Jane Nardal, expands our understanding of space, memory and identity.[14] Hybridity and trauma in colonial contexts were generally seen as inseparable. The survival techniques chosen by those who were born in those settings and tried to circumvent forms of oppression have been largely studied. What has been considered less is the way colonial subjects in West Africa tried to create spaces where they could have forms of agency. Looking at the stories of a few European Africans who lived on West African coasts makes room for a broader interpretation of the way identity was shaped and performed in colonial spaces.

Histories of 'European-African' women have been the object of notable scholarship, mainly from researchers based in the African continent. A plethora of Master's and doctoral dissertations have looked at the history of the Signares in Senegal. These innovative studies are concerned with understanding how the Signares contributed to ideas of gender, colonial trade and even religious identity in the sub-region. The term Signare originates from the Portuguese word *senhora*, which means 'lady'. Stories about the Signares are closely related to two islands off the coast of Senegal: Gorée and Saint Louis. They are also linked to questions of ownership of land and female bodies. The history of the ownership of Gorée Island has common features with other narratives of European settlement on African coasts.

The literature of conquest often uses the term *terra nullius* as a justification for European appropriation of local lands. In the case of Gorée, local fishermen might have inhabited the island in the fifteenth century before the arrival of Europeans. Despite Dutch trader Pieter de Marees's statement that the island was not inhabited, it was bought by Holland in 1617. It is unclear from whom the Dutch bought it. In 1444, Portuguese soldiers had arrived on the island and claimed it as their own. They had named it Palma. The Dutch seized Palma in 1588. Over the seventeenth and eighteenth centuries, the island changed hands between the Dutch, French and English multiple times. In 1677 the French took Gorée from the Dutch, but it was only in 1763 that property ownership there was legalised through deeds. The population of the island increased noticeably from 257 inhabitants in 1749 to 1,840 in 1785. The black and dual heritage population went from 197 in 1749 to 1,566 in 1785.[15]

Economic opportunities provided by proximity to Europeans brought a few Africans closer to the coast and to Gorée. Most European traders spent a few years on the island and left once they had managed to make a fortune in the Atlantic trade. Those traders and sailors did not take their European spouses with them. While in Africa, they sought the company of local women. They often settled with these women for a few years and even had children with them. European trading companies understood that one of many ways to retain the Europeans was to facilitate settlement. They built a few houses for their officers. As time went by, the Signares, who were in fact the children born from relationships between Europeans and Africans, managed to effectively claim those houses for the duration of their European companions' stays. By 1723, Marie-Hélène Knight-Baylac notes, at least four Signares women had a house to themselves.[16] These had been the property of European settlers. Most houses in which Signares and black African women lived, however, were huts or had a hut-like construction. Stories of legal disputes were not unusual. Hélène Aussenac, for example, used written documents when a dispute occurred to demonstrate that her mother, Signare Caty Louet, had bought a piece of land from a French officer years before. It appears that not only had Caty been one of the wealthiest Signares in Gorée, but she had managed to claim a house that allegedly belonged to an officer. Legally speaking, however, there was some ambiguity regarding the ownership of these houses. In fact, some of them had not actually been the property of the officers. As for Caty, in addition to the officer's house, she had also managed to claim the plot on which the house had been built.

Prior to 1763, French authorities had allowed a number of African women to settle on these plots, but had not provided written documents. As time went by colonial administrators moved back to Europe, and the British occupied the island in 1758, two years after the beginning of the Seven Years' War. During this period the question of ownership became thorny. In 1763, it appeared that the women had legitimate claims over the plots. Caty Louet's land ownership highlights the power that some of the Signares held on the island. Of the seven women who were landowners, six were Signare women. Louet was the wealthiest of the women. With wealth also came ownership of African captives. Records show that in 1775, Louet had seven of her enslaved servants baptised. Baptism meant that they had been deemed worthy through their behaviour to be integrated into the household.[17] The wills of some of the Signares could also provide information about the lifestyle of these women. For example, in 1769 Signare Jeanne Laria's will stated that her daughter was the sole heiress of her property. Her wealth consisted of six captives, various garments and silverware worth 839 livres, as well as beds, furniture, huts and a house in Senegal.[18] Jeanne also had a son, and yet she did not leave anything to him. One can speculate about the relationship between mother and son. However, the reason might have been that her son, named Ghusban, had married the daughter of one of the most powerful families in Gorée. His wife, Marianne Porquet, was one of the descendants of an employee of the notorious French East India Company.

Not all Signares in Gorée were as powerful as Caty or Jeanne, but Signare women married either Europeans or wealthy dual-heritage men. Being a Signare in Gorée meant that one's family and their networks in Gorée, Saint Louis, Nantes or Bordeaux secured one's financial place in society. Historians have documented the lives of those women well, but very little has been written and is known about the Signares' black mothers. They often disappeared from official registers, even though most of them had been free black women. There was and still is a stigma attached to slave descent in Senegalese culture. This might be one of the reasons we know so little about most of the enslaved women who gave birth to Signare women and dual-heritage men on Gorée Island. Despite the lack of details about their relationships with European men and how they approached questions such as child-rearing and networking with Signare women, black African women continued to shape the history of Gorée and the population continued to grow, reaching nearly 3,000 people in 1800—a population density of 42,857 per square mile.[19]

The economic contributions of African women to the hinterland of Gorée in the eighteenth century have been documented. Enslaved women were tasked with food production while waiting to be transported across the Atlantic. African women performed all tasks necessary within and outside of households, from sewing, ironing and cooking to dressing attendants. In fact, they were indispensable in Signares' homes. External signs of wealth included having African women perform tasks that were deemed unsuitable to one's social standing. Rich garments and elaborate headdresses were social markers signalling that the Signares were free from domestic chores such as carrying water or pieces of furniture on their heads. The Signares relied heavily on enslaved women. The slave population, and consequently domestic slavery, grew with urbanisation and the increasing social requirements of this group of women. Enslaved men were also important in these port cities, as they were rented out to merchants for various jobs. However, as Bronwen Everill notes, although slave labour was valuable overall, the number of enslaved women was higher than that of men.[20] Nearly half of all households had more than six enslaved men and women. While male slaves who were rented out as sailors could earn wages to be divided between themselves and their masters, enslaved women could use their skills by selling food or as seamstresses and weavers. This income was similarly divided between themselves and their mistresses. Enslaved women therefore contributed to the local economy as labourers, consumers of goods and insurance assets for loans.

The island of Saint Louis, located about 300 kilometres north of Dakar, followed a similar path and developments. An analysis of individual stories alongside the history of colonial connections give a fuller picture of the links between the population of Saint Louis, its hinterlands, its social and cultural norms and the place of its Signares from the seventeenth to the nineteenth century. The population of Saint Louis was divided into three main groups: the enslaved population, the free black population and the white European population. The dual-heritage population lived alongside the free men and women of Saint Louis. The diversity of Saint Louis's inhabitants is reflected in their varied regional origins. The free black population counted groups as different culturally as Wolofs, Peuls, Toucouleurs and Moors. Yet all these groups found common ground living and working on the thriving island of Saint Louis in the eighteenth century. The role of black women in the development of the island was significant. They were indispensable providers of a variety of services. As in Gorée, they were cooks, cleaners, seamstresses, and so on.

They carried out domestic work for both the free and the enslaved populations. Men were equally valuable. Again recalling Gorée, enslaved men were used as sailors and soldiers. Their skills were rented out. Even enslaved, they were able to acquire goods from the hinterlands and sell them on the coasts. The community of dual-heritage offspring also played a crucial part in the development of the islands. They either worked for the French or the British crown, or they were independent traders. The separation between work and domestic life within all of these groups was ambiguous.

Traders, colonial administrators and employees usually arrived in Saint Louis alone. Some had left their family at home. Others were not married and were determined to make a fortune. They were mostly able-bodied men, and were prone to alcoholism and sometimes gambling. They settled with local women. Most of their unions were monogamous, but some men lived with several African women. There was a shift from the seventeenth to the eighteenth century in the way these unions were understood. What appears to have been a form of cohabitation with African women, often perceived as concubines, became a legal form of arrangement known as *mariage à la mode du pays* ('marriage in the custom of the country').[21] A European man who wished to marry a free young African or dual-heritage woman had to gather people of influence around him to go and ask for the consent of his fiancée's parents. A long process that was often known as the ceremony of bride-wealth followed. The parents generally consulted the rest of the family, friends and respected members of the community. Each group made their demands for consent. As the power of the Signares grew, about 10 per cent of what the groom was expected to pay also went to the community of Signares in the island. Discussions were then held about the bride and groom's families' contribution to the wedding. The ceremony was both a private and a highly public matter. A procession through the streets of Saint Louis or Gorée was expected. It was common to see several people from various communities joining the walk.

The *mariage à la mode du pays* was legally recognised. When the European husband died or left the country and it was confirmed that he would never come back, the woman could remarry. These women had the support of their communities if they then wanted to start anew and have children within a second or third union. The children born from the marriages had their father's name and could enjoy the benefits of his wealth. However, these unions were not recognised by European laws, meaning that the father's European assets could not go to his African children. In 1830, the law changed, stating that European African children in Senegal could no longer inherit their father's property. However, a French Royal Ordinance of the same year stated that children born before 1830 were still allowed to inherit their father's property in Saint Louis.

These unions were based on mutual advantage and economic advancement. A few deeds suggest that in the early days some of the women had shares or interests in slave commerce or traded in rubber. Early unions between Europeans in Saint Louis and local women seem to demonstrate that the latter were usually enslaved women who had been manumitted by their masters. Aissata Kane Lo notes that the manumitted women mostly belonged to the Bambara ethnic group, while free women were often Peuls and Sarakolles. She adds that these were among the most conservative groups in Senegal at the time, and yet some of the Peul women remarried. A renowned Signare named Comba Poul had married a Frenchman named Blondin, but later remarried an Irish-English governor named O'Hara.[22] More revealing, however, was the fact that although the French East India Companies forbade their employees to trade as individuals, some men used their concubines as proxy owners.[23] When some of these employees left the Royal Company to work as independent traders, the women in question had been able to accumulate enough wealth to carry on investing in various trades. However, most Signares focused on ownership of enslaved people. These enslaved people were mostly rented to Europeans for various tasks. The second highest earning activity for Signares in the nineteenth century was trade in rubber.

The identity of these female Saint Louisians has been the object of several studies. They share traits with the Signares of Gorée. Saint Louis was the bigger island, and it was an important colonial capital for Europeans. The way identities were formed there was strongly informed by local imperatives. Overall, the Signares became a distinct social, economic and cultural category of people in Senegal. The most visible element of these women's difference beside their skin colour was their attire. At the beginning of the eighteenth century, their garments were relatively similar to those of the Senegalese aristocracy. They were made from elaborate woven cloth, and it was common to see the women with sophisticated African braids. In the second half of the century, their attire changed and tended to conform in many ways to European styles. For example, they would walk around with a set of servants, who carried a parasol, jewellery and musical instruments. This complex dress code included European undergarments and dresses, with about six layers of African cloth on top. European materials arrived with traders or family members. In some instances, wealthy Signares placed orders to and in Nantes, Bordeaux or Paris. As for African cloths, the Signares had strong relationships with the best local or regional weavers. The colourful headscarf and Madras cloth that appeared in the eighteenth century in Saint Louisian circles became indispensable accessories to the Signares. The Madras cloth was a stark reminder of European global connections and the way commodities shape social and cultural practices within empires. Saint Louisian

Signares had various costumes for different occasions. Attire worn at home remained elaborate, as it was still important to maintain status before enslaved servants and visitors. Their sophisticated jewellery was generally made of gold. Jewellers along the main river collaborated with gold owners from the kingdom of Galam to produce intricate pieces of jewellery.[24] The wealthiest Signares were covered in gold from their necks to their ankles.

Religion was not an impediment to unions between French or British Christians and Senegalese women. It did, however, play an important role in Saint Louis. Before the arrival of Europeans, Islam had been the dominant religion since the eleventh century. The religious history of the island in the second half of the eighteenth century developed in line with the presence of various French royal trading companies in Senegal. There were a few Catholic parishes with a modest number of priests. This number did not change dramatically when the island came under British rule in 1758. The British, who were more interested in trade, saw no advantage in bringing Church of England clerics to the island. Even after they left in 1779, the number of churches did not grow. However, the French authorities were keen to control the role of ecclesiasts on the island. The Signares, on the other hand, were pragmatists, but religion played a role in their daily lives. Some followed the expected tenets of religion in the public sphere but continued to pray to various gods. Others adopted Catholicism and even left their property to the Church. Due to Saint Louis's location, most of its inhabitants were of Muslim faith. In this context, the religion of the Signares was characterised by syncretism.

In the latter part of the eighteenth century and throughout the nineteenth century, religion played a bigger part in Saint Louisian households and in the education of Signare children. In 1819, a congregation of six Catholic nuns led by Mother Javouhey left France for Saint Louis. They wanted to convert the population and teach the gospel. They knew that they had the support of the Church, and by this time Senegal had been in the hands of the French for several centuries despite two British occupations. Educating girls and boys in Saint Louis was not enough to support the long-term project of upholding Christian values. Mother Javouhey therefore decided that the education of a few chosen children should be undertaken in France. In April 1824 she sent a letter to the Marquis of Clermont-Tonnerre, requesting his help in establishing a seminary for young boys and girls in the Oise region in France. She needed him to open his house at Bailleul-sur-Thérain to the children and their supervisors. She was also asking for the costs to be covered by the king's finances. She had the support of a few powerful people, such as the important Abbot Claudel in Beauvais.

The following year ten children from Saint Louis (seven boys and three girls aged between eight and thirteen) were sent to Bailleul-sur-Thérain. Two years later, seven more children travelled to France. Some of them were sons of Signare women, while others had black parents. In 1828, the enslaved child servant of the governor of Saint Louis was sent to the same place.[25] A child named David Boilat was among those who left Saint Louis in 1825. He later became an influential Catholic priest and the first person to write a book on Wolof grammar. After 1828, the living conditions where the children had been placed were harsh, and one of them died. This prompted Mother Javouhey to transfer the rest of the children to a warmer institution in the Aude region, in the south of France. Nevertheless, living conditions were still difficult and proved taxing for the young African learners. Eventually, worried parents who had heard about their children's experiences had a letter sent to the colonial secretary asking him to send some of the children back to Senegal. However, some of these children died before they could return home. Others died on the way back.

David Boilat was among those who survived. Boilat was born in 1814 to a Signare mother and a French father. When he came back from France, he was allocated a post as an auxiliary in the Catholic Church. He was eventually ordained in 1840. Boilat shared his views widely on what he saw as the benefits of a European education. He was keen to share ideas with parents about religious and academic education. His project of school reform was met with resistance because he was also vocal about what he saw as the immorality of the *mariage à la mode du pays*. Boilat also attacked Islam and contended that Saint Louis, and Senegal as a whole, were going through dangerous times. People had turned away from Christianity and greed prevailed, claimed the priest. He wanted to establish a free school to fight against these perceived faults and to promote social mobility. He took charge of a secondary school, but disputes with other schools and with his school staff led to the demise of the project. In 1852 he left Saint Louis for a post in the diocese of Meaux, in France. He died in France in 1901. The extraordinary journey of one of Senegal's most renowned Catholic priests and educators ended in a country that had become increasingly hostile to people of African descent who settled in European cities.

Boilat had established his reputation as a scholar who was able to communicate and write in several African and European languages. He played a crucial role in the education of young minds in Saint Louis, as an African European who had left the country for Europe for several years, but also as an intermediary whose mother had secured a network of connections that granted Boilat's generation better prospects of social ascension. Most Signares had married within their own groups of dual-heritage people or with Europeans. They had been forced several times to find new ways of surviving in a society that either celebrated or despised them.

In this context, Boilat demonstrated that education and closer relationships with Europe did not have to be gained through what he saw as immoral means, based on the sexual gratification of Europeans. He had failed to grasp the complexity of the survival techniques that Signare women had been obliged to develop. From 1809 to 1817, the British had occupied Saint Louis. They had made the slave trade illegal in 1815. The Signare community relied on enslaved labour. All slave owners in Saint Louis were entitled to compensation for the loss of their property, but they complained about the administrative barriers that delayed an already insufficient, in their view, amount of compensation money. Signare women had to turn to other trading ventures in a world where their roles had previously been clearly defined. As Saint Louis moved away from the trade in African captives, so did most European countries. A lower number of Europeans were travelling to the island, with many choosing to focus on plantations in the Americas.

Another group of European and American colonisers were, however, attracted to the trade around rubber and Senegal's hinterlands. Kane Lo demonstrates that beside the abolition of the slave trade, the implementation of several laws that diminished the power of women in French colonies showed that the balance of power had shifted. Up to that point, the Signares had been able to trade and associate with Europeans on an equal footing. After the 1830s, they failed to understand that Senegalese society, as well as the European approach to trading, was changing. They were not indispensable anymore. Some of them had contracted debts that they were struggling to pay. Others were still very wealthy but instead of investing in businesses that belonged to local black populations, they still focused on European trading networks. In a few instances, some of them continued to marry newly arrived young European men who had little means but were determined to make a fortune. Indeed, it became a trend for some of these penniless French men to get to Saint Louis so that they could try to marry a wealthy Signare. In the latter part of the eighteenth century and the nineteenth century, the Signares of Saint Louis went through another career change. Kane Lo analyses how they relinquished their links with trade to become healers in Senegalese society, thus ending centuries-old relationships with Europeans but succeeding in reinventing themselves in the area of health and wellbeing that had existed in Senegalese society for centuries.

Religion and the baptism of women in particular had not had strong bearings on trading links between the Signares of Saint Louis and Gorée, and the religious education of young girls destined to become partners to European traders was resented and discouraged by the local black population in the Dutch settlement of Elmina. Nevertheless, christening became a way for African European women of dual heritage to secure a brighter future on the Gold Coast in the eighteenth century. The Danish presence in West Africa needs to be understood within the context of ruthless competition between European kingdoms. The Danes' interest in West Africa was ignited by their desire to find means of funding the military and covering expenses incurred by the Danish crown.[26] Danish economic development and industrialisation remained relatively modest compared to its neighbours. Denmark's dependency on them was evidenced in various areas. For example, in the Dano–Swedish War of 1658–60, they received help from the Dutch, who were nevertheless trying to get rid of the Danes in Guinea at the same time.[27] The Danish presence in Guinea began with their first voyage there in 1649. Soon after, in 1650, Hendrik Carlof arrived there and through various, often questionable, means, managed to obtain several outposts. Carlof worked for the Swedish Africa Company but changed sides with the Dano–Swedish War of 1657. By that time, he had managed to institute Fort Carlsborg and several other outposts, including one in Osu that we will examine later, and claimed them for Denmark.

A couple of years later the Swedes regained Fort Carlsborg and the Dutch took the other holdings. However, the Danes continued to fight for outposts. They were successful in Legu, Osu, Labadi, Teshi, Old Ningo, Trubreku, Ada and Keta. Danish interest in and exploitation of what was known as the Gold Coast rested on their wish to be close to the source of gold and the Akans' *savoir faire* regarding its production. As the rest of Europe's interest in plantation economy grew, a significant shift took place in Danish interests, with the transatlantic slave trade surpassing gold as the most lucrative enterprise for the Danish crown and its traders.[28] Christopher R. DeCorse notes that Denmark was also the first country to abolish the slave trade. Economic reasons were at the heart of this decision, although it was not without humanist considerations. For example, the harsh treatment of enslaved people in plantations in the Americas had led a few traders to consider a less costly system of plantation on African coasts that would employ free black workers. However, the project proved to be unsuccessful as it failed to gather wider support from officials.[29]

The Danish made the fort of Christiansborg in Osu their headquarters in 1685, and this castle remained the heart of the Danish presence and the most important trading post in the Gold Coast until 1850, when they sold it to the English. The population of Osu was made up of several ethnic groups, including the Ga.

The story of Ga woman Lene Kühberg bears similarities to the lives of the Signares in Senegal. Lene was born to a Ga mother and a Danish father, and lived in the Gold Coast. She married the interim governor, a slave trader named Frantz Kühberg. Pernille Ipsen's portrayal of Lene gives us a glimpse into the experiences of Ga women in the 1760s.[30] Due to Lene's entrepreneurial skills, she accumulated enough wealth to lend money to employees of the fort when her husband passed away. She remarried, thus continuing the local practice of *cassare* marriage. The term comes from the Portuguese *cassare* or *calissare* ('to marry'), and referred to marriages between Danish men and African women. The legal implications of *cassare* marriages seem to be different from those of *mariage à la mode* in Senegal. Indeed, Danish men often saw the women in question as concubines rather than wives in the European legal sense. Nonetheless, Lene was able to keep her house when Frantz died. Ipsen tells us that Ga women were able to baptise their children and to provide them with an education by sending them to the fort's church school.[31] The Danish approach to these unions was not always positive. In 1717, for example, the Danish West India Company emphasised its disapproval of unions between African women and Danish men.[32] But employees of the Company, including the Governor, continued to ignore the warnings. Eventually the Company ceased to intervene. Pragmatically, it even took measures to encourage Company employees and traders to get children born from those unions to church for a religious and academic education.

By the time Lene married her Danish husband, Ga people had been intermediaries who acquired various goods to sell to Europeans for a century. They went to the hinterlands to get the goods that were needed by fort employees and independent traders. The most significant difference between Senegal and the Danish settlement of Osu was that even though Lene and other Ga people risked being enslaved, they were powerful providers who became necessary for commercial exchanges. Danish traders and authorities who had settled in the town of Osu had no legal power to control the local population. Ga women chose to enter *cassare* unions for economic gain and the Danes did not have the legal power to subjugate them.

However, the racial markers that separated dual-heritage Ga women and enslaved Africans came to be associated with social hierarchy in the eighteenth century, although there were also free black women who continued to marry Danish men. As time went by, dual-heritage Ga women chose to marry Europeans rather than free Africans. One of the reasons for this was that Ga communities were dominated by patriarchal rules. Once they were married, the husband had the power of life and death over his wife or wives. Bride-wealth paid to the bride's family during the marriage transaction denied these women the support of their own family. The degree of freedom that they enjoyed when they married a Danish man, as well as the financial benefits, was certainly appealing to many young Ga women. Equally revealing is the fact that eighteenth-century Danish women were not free from their husbands' control either, but Danish men in Osu could not enforce Danish norms in an environment where local cultural and social literacy was facilitated by their African wives. These men paid a higher bride-wealth than African men but were in some measure dependent on their wives in many areas.

Marrying a Danish man presented Ga women with other advantages. For instance, they had access to European goods such as fabric and household materials. Their children could benefit from a pension that was provided by the Danish government for dual-heritage children. Most Danish men gave their wives a monthly allowance, whereas Ga men did not. Ipsen notes that Ga wives relied on their husbands for food, although they did often trade independently and thus had some access to commerce to provide for themselves.[33] Irene Odotei analyses how external factors and influences shaped the Gas' economic, social, political, religious and cultural practices. Encounters with Europeans saw a shift in Ga commercial practices, with the Ga community moving from free trade to forms of protectionism. This resulted in conflict with other neighbouring traders, including the Akwamu, who ruled Ga society and expanded their boundaries to Accra between 1680 to 1730.[34] In addition, Ga communities were patrilineal, and their prolonged interaction with the Akans resulted in changes in marital practices.[35] Akan societies were matrilineal, and in unions between Gas and Akans the question of inheritance often became a bone of contention. Odotei notes that overall, with the help of the court, a compromise was usually found. In this context, it is likely that some Ga women married to Ga men found ways to circumvent stringent patrilineal practices.[36] Nineteenth-century Ga society, with its imperatives changing due to European influence, may have presented a different picture, however, with the question of gender roles more nuanced and women's agency more complex.

Ipsen presents a society based on intercultural marriages, in which exchange seemed to take place on an equal footing as far as trading interests were concerned. Dual-heritage men were employed at the Danish fort and so were enslaved Africans. Yet this apparently equal relationship should not obscure the fact that the West African coast was dominated by a constant power struggle between traders and local populations that could lead to the captivity of those who had previously been commercial partners. Europeans incurred the risks of being imprisoned by the sizeable local population or losing their lives through illness. They were highly reliant on locals for subsistence, and specifically for food.

Danish men who interacted with Ga communities abided by their cultural practices. For example, they accepted that they could not live under the same roof as their wives and children, as in Ga communities husbands and wives did not live in the same house. Mothers were tasked with looking after their children. Europeans had a chance to get involved in their dual-heritage sons' lives by providing them with a trade when they reached puberty—usually they joined the army to become trained soldiers. European governors nonetheless paid them less than white soldiers of equal skill.[37] The situation was very different from that of dual-heritage communities in Saint Louis and Gorée. However, *cassare* unions benefitted the economies of coastal towns for everyone concerned, and for Europeans in particular. Governor Frantz Boye, for example, had participated in colonial trade in the Americas before using his connections to get a position in the Gold Coast. He had married an English woman a year before he arrived at Christiansborg, where he entered into a union with a local Ga woman named Koko. He was forced to leave in 1717 when the Danish government found that he had been conducting private trade. Boye was nonetheless able to return as an employee of the British Royal African Company years later. Koko's connections with the Danes meant that her father was granted regular payments from Christiansborg as a contractor.[38]

Danish settlers shaped Osu society in many ways. By preferring to trade with dual-heritage people or giving preference to that group for certain tasks that could equally be performed by the majority non-baptised community of Osu, they set a hierarchy that lasted for centuries. Religion played its part in their relationships. Some Danes refused to enter into a union with Ga women who had attended school in the fort and had therefore been baptised, because it meant that according to local expectations they were obliged to make the relationship official in church. A church wedding implied a degree of restriction, including monogamy and the duty to support a companion financially if the Danish man lived in Osu. Ga families understood the implications of such unions. Many therefore refused to send their daughters to school. Not all Ga women were able to marry into wealthy families. For these communities, even temporary access to a European partner was a gain.

Further global expansion of the slave trade led to changes in the relationship between Ga communities and Danish traders. Christiansborg used a workforce with more enslaved people. The increasing number of dual-heritage children meant a greater number of African European soldiers were recruited. However, while Europeans expanded their trading links in the Americas, Ga communities did not see corresponding financial gains. The sums they were paid were not sufficient to acquire substantial wealth; instead, they were consumed by continuing day-to-day trading exchanges. Fears of being kidnapped then sold or held to ransom in an environment where intermediaries were also competing to survive rendered Ga societies even more dependent on Europeans and other ethnic groups that wanted access to European wealth via the sale of African captives. In the second half of the eighteenth century, Ga men and women constituted a small group of people who had to adapt to new trading alliances to survive.

Their European descent provided some protection for dual-heritage Ga families. As difficult as their lives appear to have been, dual-heritage Ga women managed to carve themselves a place in society in the eighteenth and nineteenth centuries, as a few individual stories have shown. Lene's daughter Anna Barbara carried on the tradition of marrying Danish men of a certain rank, wedding a wealthy trader called Johan Emanuel Richter. In 1785, she gave birth to a son called Henrich who became 'the wealthiest man on the coast'.[39] Such experiences were perceived as positive social ascensions, but the context of racial hierarchy should not be understated. Most male dual-heritage children spent their time in Africa. While Europeans were able to travel as often as they wished, their children were confined to the coast. The story of dual-heritage man Christian Petersen Witt is a remarkable example of this dynamic. He asked one governor after another for permission to travel for years, but was denied what he saw as the opportunity to make a fortune. Witt had probably observed generations of Danes coming to the Gold Coast, succeeding in making a fortune and moving on or going back to Denmark with a higher status. He probably believed that as a dual-heritage man whose place in Ga society was deemed enviable, he was entitled to ask for further advancement. Reality must have hit him hard when he realised that he would never be considered a white man's equal. He repeatedly appealed to the governors nonetheless, convinced of a positive outcome. Finally, in 1730, the governor granted Witt the right to travel to Copenhagen. No evidence has been found that his life in Denmark was better.[40]

The story of Severine Brock and Edward Carstensen gives us a clearer understanding of shifting social norms based on the European gaze towards African women and the fate of those of dual heritage.[41] Edward Carstensen came from a long line of colonial high officials who had made a fortune in Africa. His father was consul general in Algiers, as was his maternal grandfather. He spent his childhood there before being sent to Copenhagen to study law. He was not sufficiently successful in his studies to remain in Europe, and instead chose to further enhance the family fortune by following in his ancestors' footsteps in Africa. He chose West Africa—a significant choice given its historical ties with the Danes.

Beside career advancement, Edward wanted to strengthen his connections with the local people and acquire a deeper understanding of trading links. He soon met Severine Brock, a 14-year-old dual-heritage Ga teenager; he married her in 1842 when she was sixteen and he was in his late twenties. It was not unusual for upper-class Danish men to woo the girl and her family for a lengthy period. They married at a time when intermarriage was highly discouraged, if not illegal. His reasons for marrying her were not directly linked to the trade in African captives. In 1792, King Christian VII had signed a decree that was supposed to stop Denmark from trading in enslaved Africans. Yet it took a decade for the decree to be implemented, with Denmark officially abolishing the slave trade in 1803.

Plantation owners continued to exploit enslaved communities until 1848, the date Denmark abolished slavery altogether.

Instead, Edward's marriage to Severine was to do with the opportunities that continued to exist in the nineteenth century. The colonisation of African hinterlands and access to goods such as rubber were at the heart of the European race for commodities. Edward may have sought companionship rather than economic advantages, but it is significant that he chose to marry a Ga woman of dual heritage whose family had trading connections. As tradition required, he had not asked her but her family. The transaction had been successfully conducted on both sides. However, we have a glimpse into Edward's perspective as far as racialisation was concerned. The changing landscape of racial views in nineteenth-century Europe was echoed on African coasts. Ipsen's analysis of an 1843 meeting between the prince of Joinville and Edward, by then governor, provides further details about the relationship between gender and race.[42] Through the prince's diary, we learnt that Severine was not present at this lunch with Edward. Instead of doing the honours, as most elite women in Europe would have when welcoming an eminent nobleman, Severine was absent and the prince and the governor were catered to by barely clothed black women. A painting by the prince captured the occasion. Referring to these black women, Ipsen notes that 'they look almost the same, and they should not be considered realistic renderings of African women, but rather an ethnopornographic fantasy'.[43] One might wonder why Edward felt the need to expose his host to naked African women. The reason may be that as a host he was expected to provide some form of entertainment and it may have been common for these servant girls to be paraded naked before European visitors.

These expectations also bring to the surface the question of 'familiarity' explored by David Theo Goldberg. These Europeans, meeting in a foreign land, shared common characteristics. Goldberg refers to the racialist's idea of familiarity, which posits that 'Abstract familial connection—loosely sharing some traits or characteristics or bordered dispositions—becomes the basis in turn for an abstracted familiarity.'[44] Although often applied to black and brown bodies, this idea of racial familiarity is based on the assumption that 'I can claim to know you intuitively on the basis of presupposing peculiarly to be like you.'[45]

Severine's absence could be interpreted in two different ways. She may have been excluded from the lunch because Edward did not want her in a place that was deemed unsuitable for the wife of a governor. Alternatively, it may be that he was trying to protect her from the prince's lurid gaze. However, he could instead have chosen a more private setting without the service of naked African women. The prince's painting brings to the surface the question of ownership of black women's bodies in colonial contexts, recalling in many ways plantation life in the Caribbean and North America. These women were shown to a guest by a host who was familiar with European social norms and had first-hand experience of how black women were perceived under the European gaze. The stories of these encounters are numerous, and they continued with the arrival of the English on the Gold Coast in the second half of the nineteenth century. They left tangible marks in the form of a Europeanised landscape characterised by several forts. They also left social and psychological scars, which are still visible and remembered in contemporary Ghana.

Despite tourists' visits to the house of Danish trader Wulff Joseph Wulff in Ghana, most Europeans do not know the history of Denmark's connections with the Gold Coast. It took the work of activists and historians to initiate a debate about European colonisation of and settlements in Africa, including Denmark's role in the enslavement of Africans centuries before.

Demands for apologies and answers to the question of Denmark's contribution to reparations started in the 1990s. In 2012, a researcher argued that if Denmark apologised for its role in the slave trade, it would jeopardise its ties with the United States.[46]

The debate about Denmark's involvement in the slave trade and slavery was more virulent in the United States Virgin Islands. These islands located in the Caribbean were Danish possessions (and were known as the Danish West Indies of the Kingdom of Denmark–Norway between 1754 and 1814). The kingdom sold them to the United States in 1917. As Astrid Nonbo Andersen notes, the islands had been concerned with the question of memory and reparations long before the demands of the Caribbean Community for reparations in 2014.[47] In 2004, the African Caribbean Reparations and Resettlement Alliance (ACRRA) was established and began to campaign for reparations. A year later, the NGO decided, as Nonbo Andersen contends, to focus on 'truth telling, reconciliation, and proper memorialization'.[48]

That entailed telling the story of the indigenous Taino and Kalinago people, who had been eradicated before the Danes' arrival, as well as highlighting the history of slavery and the harsh system of fixed-term contract that kept the islands' population in poverty after the abolition of slavery in Danish Caribbean territories in 1848. The period following abolition was characterised by several incidents of violence and revolts, such as the revolt on the island of Saint Croix in 1878.[49] Economic changes and a series of increasingly prominent roles in the Caribbean region continued to shape the history of the United States Virgin Islands.

In 2017, for the centenary of the islands' transfer from the Danish to the United States, a new controversy was ignited over the question of guilt and reparations, which has been at the heart of ACRRA's work and has influenced multiple public debates organised by NGOs and officials.[50] To mark the centenary, Danish prime minister Lars Løkke Rasmussen gave a speech in Christiansted, Saint Croix. His words focused on Denmark's own reflections on its role in colonialism. As Mathias Danbolt and Michael K. Wilson argue:

> it marked a willingness to discuss the depths of Denmark's relationship with *itself*, more than its relationship with its former colony. The Prime Minister's idealized description of sharing the same view of colonialism with Virgin Islanders, then, glosses over, if not dismisses, the highly contentious politics of memory at play in the Centennial.[51]

Echoing debates about the disparity between the Virgin Islands and Denmark in spaces and memories, an artist from the Virgin Islands, La Vaughn Belle, and a Danish artist, Jeannette Ehlers, unveiled a seven-metre-high statue in Copenhagen of Mary Leticia Thomas, one of the group of women that led the 1878 Fireburn revolt in St. Croix.[52] The statue, created for the centenary, troubled the city's urban landscape and gender positioning, as well as popular assumptions about women's role in resistance movements against oppression. It was aptly named 'I am Queen Mary', a striking reminder of the historical role of the crown and a challenge to received ideas about royalty and queenship.

In December 2018, the Danish government apologised for the country's involvement in enslavement and the transportation of African captives across the Atlantic. Denmark's participation resulted in the transfer of 111,040 captives aboard Danish and Baltic vessels.[53] In a historically significant visit, which marked the first time a Danish monarch had set foot in Africa, Queen Margrethe II arrived in Ghana determined to bring past and present into dialogue. After the apologies, the Danish foreign minister Anders Samuelsen highlighted that Denmark had been supporting Ghana through the Danish International Development Agency and hoped for stronger business ties with Ghana. The geopolitical situation in Africa, and Chinese involvement in West Africa in particular, have been worrying European countries for some time. Denmark saw an opportunity to present an apology alongside an offer to strengthen bilateral trading links. The debate about the legacies of the past and more specifically the question of reparations was left aside, as were the migratory policies of Denmark as a member of the European Union. Denmark's stance on the black presence in Nordic countries will be further examined later in this volume.

5

FLEETING MEMORIES

COLONIAL AMNESIA AND FORGOTTEN FIGURES

The questions of memorialisation and reparations have been a concern in former colonial empires and post-slavery societies. Another layer needs to be added to the double jeopardy of memory by which former colonisers have erased parts of history (by focusing on abolition) and legacies of colonial slavery while refusing to consider the question of compensation.[1] This new layer concerns the process of completely un-remembering one's involvement and then claiming one's superiority for not having been involved in human trafficking. It regards countries that seemingly have little to do with colonial slavery. While Portugal, Spain, the Netherlands, Britain, France, Denmark and Sweden have been recognised as the main European colonial powers from the sixteenth century onwards, the territories of Brandenburg-Prussia are often left out of the equation. The reason is that their participation in colonial conquest was modest and eventually deemed unsuccessful.

Brandenburg-Prussia truly emerged in 1648 when it came out of the Thirty Years' War and managed to acquire a few territories, including the Duchy of Magdeburg in 1680. Eager to get involved in a trade that had made the fortunes of many, Brandenburg decided to create a company that could manage colonial transactions and investments. The Electorate Brandenburg African Company was created in 1682. It went through several name changes before ending up as the Royal Prussian African Company. Two years later, it established a trading post on the Gold Coast and a fort on the island of Arguin.[2] Adam Jones estimates that it started to decline in 1698, despite concluding an agreement with Denmark to occupy part of the island of Saint Thomas in the Caribbean. Surprisingly enough, most employees of the company were Dutch and its trading relationships were mainly with Dutch traders. Brandenburg tried to seize several territories in the Caribbean and then, when this failed, to negotiate their acquisition, but neither the English nor the French were interested in the offers.

These setbacks cannot, however, fully explain its demise. We need to look at the history of Brandenburg at the time to understand what happened. Frederick III, the Elector of Brandenburg, became King of Prussia (as Frederick I) in 1701. The same year, the War of the Spanish Succession also started. Brandenburg, now mostly equated with Prussia, had little appetite for dedicating its resources to colonial conquest when territorial expansion and questions of succession were at stake at home. The involvement of Brandenburg in the slave trade and the number of vessels and African captives it transported are difficult to evaluate because of its Dutch connections and the possibility that some of the Dutch officers based on the African coasts also traded in their personal capacity. However, valuable pieces of information are provided by the company's correspondence, including details about internal disputes related to its management. Other interesting information concerns an 'anti-French alliance made between the English, Dutch, and Brandenburgers on the Gold Coast in 1703'.[3]

Some of the information about Brandenburg's colonial history emerged in the nineteenth century when German officials decided to bring a second colonisation project to life, and invoked stories of previous attempts at colonial conquest.[4] The first attempt took place in 1755 when Frederick II, then King of Prussia, decided to revive the East India Company.[5] Documents were produced at the time about Brandenburg's colonial history, but these were circulated only among a select group at court. The resuscitation of the colonial company failed years later in 1766. Again, historical documents written at the time of this failure were intended only for military officials. In 1885 this information was uncovered, purposely coinciding with the German Reich's procurement of its first colonies in Africa and New Guinea. It was published to support Chancellor Otto von Bismarck's new endeavours. Military staff worked swiftly with the archives to promote the politician and link his story to a glorious national narrative of colonial endeavour.[6] Further volumes were subsequently published by the General Staff.

Daniel Purdy contends that the aim was to create a story which used a wealth of primary sources while focusing on nationalist aspirations and providing a background that would encourage readers to support the colonial project as part of Germany's historical tradition. Frederick William, the 'Great Elector' who had overseen the establishment of the Electorate Brandenburg African Company, and his great-grandson Frederick II, King of Prussia, were praised as pioneers who fought against other imperial powers while struggling to find German investors. Richard Schück, the author of a second volume about Brandenburg's early attempts at empire published in 1889, claimed that he had rediscovered crucial archives. Purdy argues that this purported retrieval of archives that were never lost resembles to an extent the Freudian unconscious. However, there are significant differences: 'Far from repressing knowledge of Prussia's colonial past, the state's management of the archive is eager to retrieve, promulgate, and to re-enact this history.'[7] Ideology, historical research and scholarship went hand in hand. Historians such as Schück constructed a past that never existed so the new regime could present itself as the heir to a long and successful colonial power. In the nineteenth century, gathering enthusiasm for past initiatives, the German Reich embarked on the project of colonial conquest with gusto.

German colonisation of African territories, from Togoland to Kamerun to Namibia, has been widely studied. The question of migration at the heart of this volume brings to the surface the vastly diverse interactions that took place between the colonisers and the local populations. When the Germans set sight on the territory near the equator that had been known to the Portuguese since 1472 as *Rio dos Camarões* (River of Shrimp), the race to gain access to territories which had been a source of African captives and other commodities became a pressing matter. As with other European colonists, German settlement started with a relatively modest trading post in the form of a warehouse. In 1868, the Woermann merchant firm settled on the *Rio dos Camarões*—the Wouri River in today's Cameroon. Previous employees of Woermann formed another company, Jantzen and Thormählen, in 1874. The companies were determined to start several new ventures; initially reluctant, Chancellor Bismarck supported them. Commissioner Gustav Nachtigal was to supervise the colonial move. He concluded a treaty with Douala kings Bell and Akwa, thus allowing Bismarck to claim Kamerun as one of the first German colonies.[8] Legally, Kamerun was to become a protectorate of the Reich. The treaty stipulated that the kings were responsible for providing the colonisers with labour. Although the Douala territories represented a relatively small portion of what is now Cameroon, that treaty was used by Germany to impose a

German rule that extended to Lake Chad in the far north, and eventually to unlawfully seize Douala lands.

German traders wanted to impose forced labour, so they used conscriptions and labour taxes to make the population work on plantations and build roads and railways. Education through vocational training and religion was a key instrument for achieving those goals.[9] However, it proved to be a challenge for the colonial administration. Prior to the arrival of the Germans, the languages used in the region had been local languages and English. These were taught in the schools established by British Baptists and American Presbyterians. As the German administration grew in strength, it forced the London Baptist missionaries to give up their missions to the Swiss German Basel Mission in 1885. American Presbyterians had to use German as the main language in their schools. In 1887, Theodor Christaller, a German officer in charge of education, was sent to Kamerun. He soon set up the first German government school. Shortly after that, four more schools were established in the centre, west and north of Kamerun. German Catholic Pallottines and German Baptists set up mission schools in the years following 1890. From 1897, German was the only language allowed in schools, and by 1910 subsidies provided to schools and churches and legislation had paid off. German had replaced English as the dominant language in institutional settings. It would be naïve, however, to assume that local languages completely disappeared. They were simply not spoken in the presence of colonial officers.

Trade remained the strongest vector for German colonisation. In 1885, the Woermann and Jantzen and Thormählen companies bought some land in the western part of the territory, near Mount Cameroon. The idea was to start an intensive cultivation of cocoa, rubber and palm trees. Land purchase gave way to ruthless land appropriation and by 1914 these plantations were deemed successful by German traders and the colonial administration.[10] Yet brutal force was not sufficient to sustain a colonial regime. Education and language played a role in subjugation and, one might argue, acceptance of colonial rule by local populations. Colonisation worked both ways.

The influence of the colonised has been generally dismissed, with the rise of a colonised elite rightly attributed to colonial officers' calculated endeavours to strengthen their hold by creating a category of people who would act as intermediaries. Rarely do studies investigate the impact of this elite on the colonisers in both Africa and Europe. Quantitative evidence for such an impact is difficult to obtain. However, studies of writings in Cameroon have provided us with information about some degree of mutual influence between colonised and coloniser as far as literary production is concerned. Centuries-old stories about the territories later known as Kamerun under German rule were based, until the nineteenth century, on the oral transmission of histories. In the nineteenth century, European and American missionaries started to learn local languages and put these stories into writing. It was also at this time that indigenous populations from the south of the region started to write in English, while the north used a version of written Arabic. Setting stories down in writing became paramount for Sultan Njoya. He developed the Bamun script between 1896 and 1910. An innovative pictographic language, it attested to the sense of emergency felt by those who believed that German colonisation might erase their histories. Narratives which were important for local communities thus needed to be turned into a written form.

The prevention of erasure was not the only reason the elite learnt to read and write European languages (or, in Ndjoya's case, developed a new one). Written forms of local language were also used to show allegiance to the colonisers or express gratitude for the Gospel. Reverend Joshua Dibundu, who had vigorously voiced his disapproval of the removal of English Baptist missionaries by the Germans, published a volume of praises to God in the Douala language in 1896. Mutual influence was also visible when the Seminar for Oriental Languages was founded in 1887 in Berlin. It signalled early interest in a German centre for the study of Africa; two decades later, in 1908, the Colonial Institute was launched in Hamburg.[11] The vibrant African diaspora started to produce laudable pieces of literature. Cameroonian Njo Dibone published a compilation of Cameroonian tales in German with Elli Meinhof in 1889 (*Märchen aus Kamerun*). Dibone had previously worked with Elli's husband Carl Meinhof, a scholar of African linguistics. In fact, he had taught local languages at the institute and contributed to Carl's research. Dibone was by no means the only Cameroonian to contribute to African Studies in Germany. Josef Ekollo's work provides us with an interesting insight into German society and the way it viewed Africans. In 1908, he published an autobiography about his experiences of Germany (*Wie ein Schwarzer das Land der Weissen ansieht*, or *A Black Man's View of the Land of the White Man*).[12]

Further examples can help us measure the impact German education had on the colonised. Intercontinental exchanges were visible in the case of a minority of Cameroonians who served German officers and then left for Germany with them. Similarly to French and British colonial administrations, Germany worked towards the idea of a useful Cameroonian elite. In fact, a large portion of those who were sent to Germany in the last decades of the nineteenth century were the children of upper-class Cameroonians. The well-known king Ndumba Lobé Bell had his children educated in Europe. When he died, a short article entitled 'The Last of the Cameroons' Kings' was published in *The Times* on 5 March 1898.[13] The king's death signalled a new era. Although his son Manga Ndumbe Bell succeeded him, the Germans made it clear that they held the reins of trade between the Cameroonians and other European nations. The new king had less power than his father. The news of King Bell's death was thus of great interest to the British; the paper noted: 'The German government allow British traders the same privileges as their own countrymen. Manga Bell who will be now looked upon as a big chief was educated in Bristol, and christened in 1868 at St. Mary, Redcliffe, Church there.' It was noteworthy that Cameroon's rulers had been demoted to the status of chiefs.

Robbie Aitken has examined the stories of a number of children who were sent to Germany as apprentices and students in the 1880s and 1890s.[14] Equalla Deido was one of them. He had been born into a prestigious family; his father, Epee Ekwalla Deido, was one of the leaders who had signed the treaty that led to the settlement of Germans in Kamerun. There have been various speculations about why those leaders accepted German rule. Many thought they could manage and even direct German administrators while keeping the English at bay and safeguarding their communities' interests. Aitken notes that one of the points on which they insisted was that Germans set up a school in the land that had been given to them. The population was already literate, and it was believed that German influence would provide a healthy balance of power between over-eager Europeans. A school was set up and a teacher, Friedrich Flad, took charge of it.[15]

Deido, his brother Ebobse, Rudolf Duala Manga Bell (Manga Ndumbe Bell's son), and other elite children were sent to Germany in the late 1800s. Ideas of experimentation and assessment of the abilities of the colonised, which would supposedly be enhanced under European supervision, were also at the heart of these migration projects. The children were taught academic subjects, such as German, other languages and mathematics. It appeared that they did well, and thrived academically. However, the tight control over their behaviours and movements proved to be taxing at times. They usually lived with the family of the

German headmaster, who was expected to send regular reports to Berlin about his African pupils. Aitken's detailed research shows that, despite the lack of information about these learners, there are a few documents which give us a glimpse into their lives in Germany.[16] Examples of verbal abuses are not numerous, but those recorded show that the children were not necessarily welcomed by most people. In one case, a school report praised the self-control of a student who had been verbally abused but did not condemn the abuse itself.

Most of the children were baptised in Germany. However, a number of them died of tuberculosis and pneumonia. Those who survived were looking forward to enviable positions within the colonial administrations. Unfortunately for them, those expectations were not met. Once they were back home, German officers' attitudes towards them were blatantly hostile. They were accused of aspiring above their station. While they had been away, the balance of power had tipped into the hands of Germany. Less educated German officers could not accept working alongside them, favouring workers educated in Cameroon over those who had left for Europe. Disappointed, some of them attempted to go back to Germany, but failed because by 1910 the German central government had enforced the heavy travel restrictions demanded by colonial officers.

In Cameroon, confrontation between the Douala, formerly allies of Germany, and the German colonial administration took another turn. In 1914, German officers executed Rudolf Duala Manga Bell, by this point King Manga Bell. The confrontation has been interpreted as a fight between coloniser and colonised over land expropriation. The Doualas found it unacceptable that racist German colonial rules stipulated that the lands of the indigenous population were to be confiscated for German settlers and traders (and their descendants), while these populations were pushed further into the hinterlands. Manga Bell rallied other

Douala leaders and they appealed to central government in Berlin and to other European nations. Trying to find a legal solution, Manga Bell had experts look into the initial treaty. His appeals to the Reichstag, the German parliament, remained unanswered. The case became a legal battle. Manga Bell's team argued that the Germans were violating the terms of the treaty, while the colonial administration stated that they were managing the lands as the treaty stipulated.

Eventually Manga Bell was dismissed as a German civil servant and replaced by his own brother. He had managed to rally other Cameroonian leaders and kings, and the Bamun ruler Sultan Njoya informed the Basel missionaries that his contingency plan was to unite all leaders against German rule. In 1914, Manga Bell was arrested for high treason. It was alleged that he was planning to overthrow the German colonial administration with foreign support. The war between Germany and the Allies had just started. Despite all German missionaries, including those from the Basel Mission, supporting Manga Bell's release, Governor Karl Ebermaier gave the order to execute him and his assistant Adolf Ngoso Din, nearly two months before the Allies took Douala.

After 1910, travel permissions were denied to nearly all Cameroonians except for those few deemed highly useful to the colonial administration. Cameroonian Charles Atangana was amongst such people. For two years from 1911, he was employed by the Colonial Institute in Hamburg as a lecturer in language and culture. In 1919, he published an Ewondo-language volume of fables and indigenous stories from his community. He then translated the volume into German. When the First World War broke out, a number of Cameroonians were trapped in Germany. Dualla Misipo was another one who had been allowed to go and stay there. He had been sent to study medicine in 1913, but ended up working on literature. He wrote a novel about love, cultural differences and discrimination, which was a fictionalised version of his life with his German Jewish wife and their son. In 1931, forced to flee, they eventually left for France.[17]

The interwar period saw several changes related to the status of Africans in Europe. Cameroonians in Europe played, like many Africans, a crucial role in the debate about colonisation, autonomy and the rights of the colonised. In this debate, the issue of representations of the colonised came into question in a rather alarming way. In 1921, *The Times* published an article about Prince Alexander Duala Manga Bell titled 'Prince's Dishonoured Cheque'. The article stated that the prince had been brought to Berlin by the Kaiser in order to receive an education. It went on to note that after the war Manga Bell went to Paris, where he led a 'gay life' and had a cheque drawn without the money to honour it, before leaving for Cameroon. The article carried on: 'in his Absence he was condemned yesterday to three months' imprisonment and fined 1,500 francs (£30) and ordered to restore 5,000 (£100) to the defrauded bankers.'[18] Manga Bell was simply presented as a dishonourable thief. However, a closer inquiry into context provides a more nuanced perspective on the relationship between Manga Bell and Europe.

In 1902, King Manga Ndumbe Bell had gone to Berlin with his son and grandson, Rudolf Duala Manga Bell and 4-year-old Alexander Duala Manga Bell, to try to use his influence in order to curb what he viewed as oppressive land appropriation measures taken by Governor Jesko von Puttkamer. When his father and grandfather returned to Cameroon, Alexander was left to be educated in Germany. In 1918, after Germany's defeat, France and Britain seized its territories of Togoland and Kamerun. France wanted a permanent hold on the majority of these lands, whilst Britain was wary of that decision and argued that the duration of French sovereignty should be limited.[19] France also had to deal with the demands of the Doualas, which did not die with the execution of their leader Manga Bell in 1914. France resented what they saw as demands for a form of Cameroonian semi-autonomy led by the Doualas. A letter from all Douala leaders to the French had made explicit the fact that, while they were grateful to have been liberated by the Allies, they also expected a discussion about their future relationship.

In 1919, Alexander had turned twenty-one and was expected to represent the family. He had been educated in Germany and did not speak French. He had even been part of the German army. This close relationship with Germany worried the French. It was decided, with the support of an elder from the Bell family, that Alexander would spend a year in France. Advance money was provided for him to go to Paris, and it was agreed that he would subsequently go back to Douala and lead his people. However, he was put under very close surveillance and supervision while in France. This took the form of 'well-wishers' who befriended Alexander, his close advisor Elong Ngando and his German wife; he had married Andrea Jimenez Berroa, the daughter of a German woman and an Afro-Cuban musician. These new friends were working for the Ministry of the Interior. None of them managed to prove that Alexander was particularly pro-Germany, but they all worried that he had ambitions to study medicine rather than return to Cameroon and lead.

Alexander went to great lengths to try to convince the French of his loyalty to France. He even went so far as to get rid of his German passport and ask for a French one. He nearly succeeded in convincing the French authorities, but opposition came from the French governor based in Cameroon, Jules Carde. Carde was born in Algeria and worked for the governor of Martinique before being sent to Ivory Coast as secretary general. His distrust of colonial subjects was known, but authorities in Paris respected his experience. Alexander asked for a passport for his wife so that she could go to see her mother in Hamburg for the last month of her pregnancy. The request was denied. In 1920, Jimenez

Berroa once again made a request for a passport, this time to go to Berlin; it was also denied. As Richard Joseph explains, the couple had run into financial difficulties and the French authorities viewed them as particularly vulnerable to any German offer.[20] It was only when Alexander went to Cameroon that his wife was allowed to travel to Berlin. Alexander was himself denied the right to see his own family in Germany, despite the support of respected black French member of parliament Blaise Diagne. French authorities' ambivalence regarding Alexander's status was further evidenced by their refusal to recognise his status as a prince. Although he always signed his name with this title, the French administration referred to him as Monsieur, meaning Mr, Manga Bell. In fact, they denied him the right to call himself 'Prince' on the basis that he had been prince of a territory that was under German rule. As it was by this time under French rule, the title was null.

In addition to this, a change of heart led the French to reconsider Alexander's return to Douala. They worried about the influence he might have over his fellow Doualas, and decided that it was probably preferable for him to remain in France after all. Yet after several lengthy discussions, it was decided that Alexander could go back to Cameroon without worrying the colonial administration. He had run into debts during the three years he had spent in France. An inflated sense of himself as a prince who had been 'courted' by the French and was taking his rightful place had led him to believe that his status needed to be more ostentatiously displayed. The previously mentioned 1921 article in *The Times* provided factual information but also discredited his character. He was by no means the only young aristocrat to have a lavish lifestyle beyond his means, but because of his background, and in a context of distrust towards those who were viewed as extra-European subjects, he was expected to show some decorum, a degree of gratefulness and, most importantly, a stronger sense of purpose regarding his lineage and the fate of the Doualas he claimed to care about. What has been ignored in various analyses is that he had grown up in Europe. He was Europeanised and probably saw himself as part of the European elite as well as a prince, giving him a strong sense of entitlement.

Alexander led a life of leisure in many ways. He married Andrea when he was nineteen years old. She was seventeen. Their first child, a son, was born in 1920 and their daughter was born a year later. Alexander travelled to Cameroon in 1919 and returned the same year. He went back there again in 1922, but by then the couple had grown apart. Andrea had been allowed to move to Germany and Alexander never saw her. He allegedly refused to provide for her unless she relinquished custody of their children, so she had to work to provide for them. It was only after the Second World War that Alexander reunited with his daughter. His relationship with his son, José Emmanuel Manga Bell, remained contentious. Alexander shot his son while he was on a visit to Cameroon in 1947.[21] The circumstances of the death remained unclear. Alexander and Emmanuel were African Europeans who were caught between both identities at a time when colonial rule was shifting from German to British and French powers.

The Manga Bells were not the only Africans and African Europeans to struggle with the question of sovereignty and political engagement. Many political activists tried to rally other African Europeans who had established themselves in London, Paris, Berlin and other capitals at the beginning of the twentieth century.[22] The framework of Black Internationalism created a way for African European activists to exchange ideas, organise and find practical routes of action. It was based on the idea of shared ancestry and lived experiences as colonised subjects. It brought together people born in Africa, the United States, the Caribbean and Europe, and took various forms including Pan-

Africanism, a movement that was born in the eighteenth century and was particularly strengthened in the 1900s. During the interwar period it gave way to a variety of movements across the world. The common thread of these movements was an anti-colonial stance that led some activists to support certain political parties. The French Communist Party counted several African-born members, such as Tiemoko Garan Kouyaté, a Sudanese intellectual and teacher who founded the influential monthly paper *Union of Negro Workers* (*Union des travailleurs nègres*, or UTN). Kouyaté had studied in Ivory Coast and in France. He was expelled from the Communist Party but had been successful in convincing a number of black students in France to join it and engage in the anti-colonial fight. He also reached out to other African American and Caribbean Pan-Africanists.

The era of these collaborations has mistakenly been inter-preted as a peaceful historical moment for anti-colonial move-ments and those involved in them. However, constant police surveillance and arrests shaped the lives of African Europeans. The fear of close proximity between them and the white French population was not simply related to political views. Along with anxiety that anti-colonial sentiments would gain momentum amongst white French people, official concerns also stemmed from allegedly too close relationships between black men and white French women. African women seldom travelled to Europe at the time, and African students, who were mostly male, found themselves able to integrate more comprehensively into French society and understand French customs through friendships and unions. As Michael Goebel demonstrates, the Special Police went so far as to influence or intimidate the family of the bride to prevent marriages in these cases.[23] The correlation between intervention in the private sphere and political oppression in the form of surveillance was also ambiguous. The Special Police recruited some anti-colonial activists to work for the French government as informants. This recruitment was sometimes costly, as it spanned long periods. As Goebel notes, rather than weakening some of those groups with the intelligence they had obtained, the Special Police allowed them to continue and, in that respect, contributed to the anti-colonial movement. The reasons for such choices are open to speculation, but Goebel argues that anti-colonialism legitimised the existence of those special forces and allowed them to employ a number of French citizens.

The French Special Police by no means uniquely targeted sub-Saharan Africans. Former soldiers who had fought in the First World War and stayed in France, African migrant workers, and Malagasy, Indochinese and North African men all suffered the same fate. Two special police units were set up specifically to observe these groups of people. The *Service des affaires indigènes nord-africaines* (SAINA), or North African Indigenous Affairs Service, for example, focused on North Africans because of the legal status of Algeria, Morocco and Tunisia. North Africans were numerous in France, and the special service was set up to manage certain aspects of their status and their lives there. Its rationale was distrust and fear of the colonial 'Other'. By contrast, a pro-natalist stance in the 1920s led the French government to encourage migration from European men and women.

As the census of 1926 showed, of the 72,173 Africans who lived in France, only 2 per cent were women.[24] In 1930, of the approximately 75,000 North Africans who lived in Paris, 5,000 were in a relationship with and 700 were married to a French woman. The colonial population represented roughly 100,000 people in 1930.[25] These unions posed new problems for the French administration, who had a hard time accepting Muslim first names for children born from them. The Vietnamese community had similar problems with regards to Asian European children born in Paris in the interwar period.

Most Africans in Europe at the time were in low-skilled jobs. Some of them had fought for France, Britain or Germany during the First World War. They had experienced hardship on the battlefield, discrimination from local populations and unfair treatment from army officers and fellow soldiers. There were some attempts to rebel, such as the 1918 Taranto Mutiny which involved West Indian soldiers stationed in Italy, or the 1917 rebellion of French African soldiers, or *troupes noires*, of the 61st Malafosse Battalion in France. Despite these experiences, some had stayed in the country and survived by working in port cities and in factories.

Outside of this world, but in close proximity to the workers, was the world of entertainment populated by African American artists, intellectuals and activists. It was a world that saw 19-year-old Josephine Baker perform the opening act at the Théâtre des Champs-Élysées in 1925 before rapidly taking other European capitals by storm. The 1900 World Exhibition had brought a number of African Americans to Paris, and 1920s France later welcomed several Harlem Renaissance artists and thinkers. Paris was an intellectual hub which attracted activists and educators from the other side of the Atlantic, such as African American educator and activist Anna Julia Cooper, who was granted a PhD in 1924 at the Sorbonne. Caribbean intellectuals, and women in particular, also helped shape the anti-colonial movement and Pan-Africanist calls for action. One could argue that Caribbean intellectuals found a more determined community with the African diaspora in France, and yet the movement also gave Caribbean men and women a clearer sense of identity. They were from the African diaspora but they were fighting for their Caribbean identity and their rights as French subjects. In 1848, with the abolition of slavery, they had become French citizens, and in the 1920s they had a different status from most sub-Saharan Africans.

There were some exceptions, however, including Senegal. Blaise Diagne was elected in 1914, thus becoming the first black

Senegalese man to sit in the French parliament. He fought for and won the right for African-born Senegalese to enjoy the same rights as Creole and French people who had settled in Senegal. When the war broke out, he also managed to convince the government and the army that Senegalese men would fight for France. He thus secured French citizenship for colonised men and women. Born in Gorée in 1872, Diagne travelled to and served in several French colonies, from Congo to Guiana, and became a valuable asset to the colonial administration. He married a white French woman and had the strong support of his fellow Senegalese. Diagne was an astute politician who was respected by the French political elite. He initially showed some support for Pan-Africanism, but this stance wavered when the question of Black Internationalism was brought up. Diagne remained convinced that assimilation was the way forward.[26]

While African American women were travelling to France and sometimes making that country their home, overall the role of black women in the emergence of strong anti-colonial movements during this crucial period was for decades underestimated. Paulette Nardal and her sisters Jane and Andrée may not be viewed as African Europeans, and they certainly affirmed their Afro-Caribbean identity, but their activism was echoed by African Europeans such as Diagne. Paulette Nardal's writings also bring together questions of class and gender. The sisters were born in Martinique in an upper-middle-class family, and received an education in Martinique and France. Paulette and Jane were amongst the founders of the influential journal *La Dépêche africaine*. From its inception in 1928, the journal was aimed at a broader audience than the other black papers. It sought to attract the support of black and white audiences from all social backgrounds, while still focusing on black matters. As Jennifer A. Boittin notes, the journal's wide circulation clearly demonstrates its popularity despite its niche market. In 1929, the

Special Police were provided with the information that between 12,000 and 15,000 copies had been printed. This was in stark contrast with the fewer printed copies of black papers such as *La Race nègre* or *Le Cri des nègres*.[27] Although *La Dépêche africaine* counted thirty-six men and only five women as contributors, the Nardal sisters' articles brought white feminists, such as journalist Marguerite Martin, to the cause. Black women such as the Nardal sisters and white female contributors wrote about a variety of topics, from politics and literature to domestic issues. As Boittin contends, Paulette and Jane Nardal had managed to carve a space for women to engage in a dialogue that crossed racial, class and gender barriers.

It had also been argued that the Negritude movement born in the 1930s owed the Nardal sisters a great debt. Besides writing in *La Dépêche africaine*, they also participated in debates in various salons, which a number of men and women, from journalists to lawyers to entertainers, attended. In fact, discussions in those salons led to the publication of a new journal in 1931, *La Revue du monde noir*, aimed at bringing people from the African diaspora together and providing information about black culture and history.[28] In this publication, the Nardal sisters and others questioned a number of assumptions regarding the role of black men and women with regards to entertainment. The problem of othering through exoticism, which restricted and predetermined ethnic relationships, was key to the debates. Jane Nardal in particular worried about the way black women's bodies were fetishised, and the impact that could have on their wellbeing. The notion of race consciousness explored by the sisters and others led to the formation in 1935 of an influential paper, *L'Étudiant noir*, which published the writings of the fathers of the Negritude movement: Aimé Césaire, Léon-Gontran Damas and Léopold Sédar Senghor. Nardal even noted that 'Césaire and Senghor took up the ideas that we had sown. They expressed them with much more panache and brio. We were just women. We had shown the path to the men'.[29]

Paulette Nardal's activism led her back home to Martinique, where she fought for the rights of women to take a stronger role in education and politics. From 1945 to 1951, she wrote a series of essays, published in the journal *La Femme dans la cité*. It has been noted that Nardal's views were in contrast with those of Simone de Beauvoir. Nardal believed that women had predispositions which made them fit for certain tasks, as did men, while de Beauvoir made the case for an existentialist over an essentialist view.[30] The question of identity that was at the heart of Paulette Nardal's activism after the Second World War remains an important point, and was later explored by other Afro-Caribbean women such as Suzanne Césaire and Mayotte Capécia.

The process of exoticising black bodies, discussed by the Nardal sisters, provided a number of African Europeans and African Americans with a means of survival in societies that tended to confine them to menial jobs. While black women were seen as sexual objects, black men were equated with brute force. The life of Senegalese-born boxer Battling Siki seemed to conform to those parameters. Yet the complexity of his trajectory brings to the surface the obstacles met by those who were born in their ancestors' homeland but spent their formative years as teenagers in Europe. A trip to twenty-first-century Saint Louis, where Siki, or Louis M'barick Fall, was born, reveals nothing about his early life in the fishing community of Guet Ndar. Guet Ndar has maintained its reputation as a defiant and vibrant community of fishermen, where loyalty to one's neighbours is celebrated as much as a visible distrust for outsiders. When wandering the streets of Saint Louis, a flâneur will ineluctably come across a pretty facade with warm, inviting colours. A hotel bearing the name of Siki located feet away from the River Senegal on one side and the Atlantic on the other offer a glamourised glimpse into the tumultuous life of the boxer. The Spanish-owned establishment has chosen to pay homage to Siki by displaying images of him prominently in some of the rooms, or even customising lampshades and other bedroom accessories.

The hotel is the only visible reminder of Siki's life as a Saint Louisian. Little about the boxer is remembered by the city of Saint Louis as a whole, beside a double-page spread displayed at Saint Louis's *Centre de recherches et de documentation du Sénégal*, a library which also hosts a museum about the island's history. In fact, few public places commemorate his life and achievements. Siki's story and tragic death seem to have fallen into oblivion in Senegal. One reason may be that he reached fame outside the country, and never came back to celebrate his victories with his fellow Senegalese. The reasons he stayed abroad throughout his lifetime are open to debate.

The circumstances of Siki's departure to Marseille at the age of nine or ten are unclear. It is assumed that he had a European benefactor who paid for his passage, but he was abandoned soon after he arrived in Europe and was left to fend for himself. As a teenager, he became attracted to boxing, which he practised in the little time he had for leisure. He seems to have spent his time between various jobs, including doorman, messenger and cleaner, and at a boxing club. He moved from Marseille to Toulon, Nice and other cities in the south of France. Boxing was a dream, but turned into a reality when he was offered his first big break as a professional boxer in 1913. Between 1913 and 1914 he continued to train and fight, and he put on the required amount of weight to challenge middle- and heavyweight boxers. Like many African Europeans in Europe, he enrolled in the army when the war broke out. He was barely seventeen and yet he fought alongside the *tirailleurs sénégalais* (Senegalese riflemen) and other black regiments. After the war, he was decorated with the *Médaille de Verdun*, the *Croix de guerre* and the prestigious

Médaille militaire. Those achievements alone should have been enough to have had him recognised as a hero in both France and Senegal. He was wounded in 1916 but showed what the army considered to be outstanding bravery.

After the war, once Siki had recovered, he continued boxing, but his erratic if not self-destructive behaviour became more pronounced. Post-traumatic stress disorder had not yet been recognised as a medical condition suffered by war veterans, and the view of African soldiers by both French and German military leaders as human war machines made it even more difficult to acknowledge that they could suffer from mental illness as a result of their involvement in the war. Instead, Siki's drunkenness and quarrelsome attitude were attributed to arrogance, or to his social and racial background. As a black man, and a boxer in particular, he fit prejudiced interwar views about both categories of people. From 1920 to 1922, Siki continued to fight in France, but also fought in Holland, Germany and Spain.[31] Winning and losing in equal measure in early days, the boxer continued to build up his career and reputation. He had married a Dutch woman, Lijntje van Appelteer, and in 1921 they had a son called Louis Jr. Race must have been an issue for the family, but unions between African men and white European women were not illegal in France at the time. Racial prejudice in public spaces and newspapers was not illegal either. As Benson notes, the boxing journal *La Boxe et les boxeurs* had no qualms implying to their readers in 1922 that even if Siki had continuously won several matches that year and the year before, he could never erase the stigma of his colour.[32] In addition, the audacity of a black man aspiring to become the equal of a white man through marriage was perceived as an affront.

Yet, in 1922, Siki finally managed to fight against the European and world champion, Georges Carpentier. Judges overturned the referee's questionable decision to declare Siki defeated. He became the world heavyweight champion in September 1922. The boy from Guet Ndar had made his dream come true. Siki continued touring and started to fight in the United States. However, his boxing match with Irish champion Mike McTigue signalled the beginning of the end of a successful career. The match between the two boxers, and its results, were heavily disputed, but victory was granted to the Irish boxer and Siki lost his world championship title. An attempt at reviving his career in the United States proved to be unsuccessful. Spiralling further into alcoholism and bar fights, he also ran into debts. In December 1928, he was found dead in New York. He had been shot, but the murder inquiry did not turn up any culprits. There has been speculation about Siki's connections to the underworld of crime and his relationship with boxing promoters. The world of boxing was as much about material gain as it was about the sport itself. Promoters could decide to fix matches, and boxers had little power to change accepted practices. Siki's second wife, Lillian Werner, stated that he was killed because of a twenty-dollar loan. A few months prior to being shot dead, he had been stabbed.[33]

The story of Battling Siki may not be at the heart of the history of Saint Louis, but his influence outside Senegal led the country to reclaim his remains from the United States in 1992. During his lifetime and after, his 'Africanity' was given as a justification for his attitudes and his choice of a career. Battling Siki was a black man who had fought for France in the boxing ring and on the battlefield. However, France did not claim him, and allowed his story to be discarded from the national narrative of First World War heroes. In the last two decades, however, several documentaries, films and articles have been written about Siki. Renewed interest in his life has shown that his extraordinary journey intrigues many, and could be noted as a celebration of a boxing champion. Throughout his life he longed for a relationship with his peers. He seems to have felt at home in the ring rather than in his domestic life as a father and a husband (he was allegedly still married to his Dutch wife when he wed American-born Lillian Werner). However, his death barely interested the public. Forgotten in many ways, his story has also apparently been of little concern for decades after he died. It was only when the world champion boxer Muhammad Ali referred to Siki as an important figure that the boxing world started to pay close attention to him again. His name became a respected reference in boxing clubs.[34] Black boxers paid further homage to Siki when his body was returned to Senegal. Finally, and perhaps at peace, he was moved to an ancestral land that he had not chosen as his final home while still alive.

Siki's story is both an interwar and a post-war story of migration and survival. His trajectory reflects the resilience of many African Europeans who, in contrast to him, did not reach fame but managed through entertainment to find ways of living in societies that often despised them.

Theodor Michael's life takes us on another journey across Europe during the interwar and post-war periods. Several articles have been written about Michael, but the most in-depth information we have comes from his own autobiography. It is another story of resilience, as well as an extraordinary volume which leads its reader to interrogate the value of an autobiography as both a literary production and a means to reach a specific kind of audience. Stories written by people of African descent about their own lived experiences were relatively scarce prior to the eighteenth century, when several abolitionists in Britain in particular tried to denounce the cruelty of slavery and give more prominence to the cause by creating spaces for those who had managed to escape. The voices of enslaved people appeared in the form of testimonies. In Britain, the autobiographies of Ukawsaw Gronniosaw, Olaudah Equiano and Mary Prince, amongst many others, brought to light the power of black voices in the fight for emancipation.[35] However, black intellectuals in the eighteenth century were not writing solely about the question of slavery, as seen in the social commentaries of Ignatius Sancho.

The nineteenth century was deemed the century of abolitions, but it also produced a number of African European and African American writers who were involved in the fight for emancipation and engaged in debate about the relocation of Africans back to Africa, and other forms of Pan-Africanism. Twentieth-century Europe brought new waves of intellectuals of African descent, who wrote about various topics beyond their own trajectories. Those powerful black voices belonged mostly to people from highly educated backgrounds. In this context, Michael's autobiography is very particular in both its content and its intended audience. Its narrative is framed as one of success, describing a man who rose above his class and race. It also presents us with a thorough investigation into and documentation of Michael's ancestry. Michael was an eyewitness to and a victim of Germany's interwar and post-war race, family and labour laws, and his experience was marred by pain, rejection, extreme poverty, ingenuity and survival. He navigated the very specific experiences of people of dual heritage; for example, he was German by birth but denied German citizenship.

African Europeans born in Europe had a different perspective to African Europeans born in Africa and bred in Europe. Young Theodor lost his mother when he was just a year old. The story of the relationship between his mother and father is little known, and was never really discussed around him. We know, however, through his remarkable autobiography, that his mother Martha Wagner was a single mother who left a previous son with her sisters to marry a Cameroonian man named Theophilus Wonja Michael. The couple had four children altogether, and after Martha's premature death Theophilus remarried, but this second marriage did not last. Theodor mentions cultural differences—for instance, the absent father expected his new wife to raise children that were not hers without his input, or opened the door to fellow Africans even when the family was already struggling to adequately feed the children in the household. Theodor also felt unloved by his siblings, especially his oldest sister Juliana who, at the age of thirteen, had to manage the care and education of her younger siblings. She also had to juggle house chores while still going to school. The children witnessed their father's financial struggles and his increasing reliance on alcohol as a coping mechanism. Theophilus struggled to take care of his young family financially. However, from time to time he appeared in silent movies and convinced the directors to hire his children as well.

After the First World War led to the loss of territories, the subjects of Germany's protectorates saw a change in their status. Work was scarce and Germany was suffering from high unemployment. It became increasingly difficult for Theophilus to find work. He enrolled the family in what was called a *Volkerschau*, or human menagerie. These were part of a circus act that employed Africans, and Theophilus and his young family were expected to dress and behave like 'savages', making noises and pretending that they were unable to understand German. This meant that the children were not in school. Eventually the Bureau and Guardianship Court removed them from Theophilus's care and placed them in an orphanage, then in the care of foster parents. Trapped in the foster system, the children ended up with foster parents who made them work in the *Volkerschau*. Although compulsory, school became intermittent from that point onwards.

In the years 1932–33, growing support for Hitler amongst the population allowed Hitler to access power. In 1935, at the age of ten, young Theodor learnt while on the road that his father had died. Even though they had been separated for a while, the news seems to have devastated the Michael children. Mistreated, barely fed and behind in terms of school education, they had settled with their foster family in Karlshorst, a suburb of Berlin, where they had to carry on with various duties. The same year, the Reich Citizenship Law established that Jews were German nationals instead of German citizens, and children of subjects of former protectorates were declared stateless. Juliana, Theodor's oldest sister, succeeded in joining their brother James in Paris, but Theodor was prevented from travelling and had to stay in Germany, exploited by the foster family as an unpaid servant.

This was the time that Theodor started struggling with his identity as a dual-heritage child. A poignant passage from his autobiography demonstrates that along with racial isolation, loneliness and poverty were playing a part in young Theodor's sense of belonging and self-worth:

> When people talked about 'we' or 'us', they didn't mean me. And when I looked in the mirror, I saw it really was true ... I swung back and forth between rejection, doubt, self-hatred and pride in being different from the others ... I had no place at all in the world! Neither in German society, nor in Cameroon ... I had no house, no home, I was a nobody in the family and the country where I lived.[36]

The question of race was exacerbated by the 1935 Nuremberg Laws, which were articulated around the notion of alleged identity and citizenship based on 'German blood'. Paradoxically, Theodor did have German blood, but as a child of a former protectorate subject he was erased from discussions about citizenship, as Germany by then had no colonies or protectorates to speak of. Determined to make a living, however, he left school to try to find work at the age of fourteen. The foster family agreed but demanded that any earnings be given to them. He was persistent despite several rejections, and finally found a job as a bellboy at a prestigious hotel. However, his good fortune would not last long. All hotel staff had to be members of the official union set up by Hitler's administration, the *Deutsche Arbeitsfront* (German Labour Front), or DAF. Theodor applied for membership but was rejected, which meant that he was dismissed without further notice. The motive for the rejection was clearly explained in writing: 'Theodor Michael cannot be accepted as a member of the DAF because his negroid blood makes him too alien to our kind'.[37]

Extraordinarily, it was not the reference to his African ancestry that hurt the young man but an inability to understand what 'our kind' truly meant. His anger was based on the vagueness of what German identity was supposed to encompass, and probably on the definitiveness of the letter. Anyone seeking permanent and official employment at the time had to have a DAF membership card. In 1940, at the age of fifteen, Theodor's future had already been determined by these arbitrary categories. He continued to work in low-paid but regular jobs, ranging from hotel staff to playing small parts as an African in films. Some of those roles took him abroad. The circulation of black bodies became contentious during the war period. Black soldiers captured by the Germans were forced to play in German movies, while black or dual-heritage German actors classified as stateless in passports issued by Germany were allowed to travel across Europe, but could be deported back to Germany once their visas had expired. They were stateless and yet somehow German. Theodor had to come back to the only home he had ever known. He knew that he had nowhere else to go. Running away was not an option, as he would be caught and would also lose the roof over his head that had so far been provided by his foster parents. In fact, the opportunity to work abroad had been provided by his foster father, who in return had of course kept his salary.

Once back home, Germany required all workers, including 'aliens' such as Theodor, to work in factories for the Reich's war effort. This could have been the opportunity for the young man to find solace in the company of his father's 'countrymen', but he was of dual heritage and was suspected by foreign workers of being a German informant. The racial line was clear on both sides. Other Europeans forced to work for the Reich formed a group, while Africans interacted with one another when they could. Theodor did not speak any African or European languages other than German. As a man of dual heritage, his loyalties were constantly questioned. Colonial legacies had played a key role in the formation of stereotypes which are relevant here. From plantation overseers to colonial administrators, white fathers across the Atlantic had used their dual-heritage children in various roles as intermediaries.

However, Theodor's strong attachment to his father from a very young age until Theophilus's death at the age of fifty-five, despite their physical distance, had been undeniable. He never rejected his African ancestry. His foster father was of Moroccan ancestry, while his foster mother was German. They both mistreated him. Young Theodor did not value ancestry, but the warmth and kindness of people he had encountered in his life. The ugliness of war and the treatment of Jews, from the discriminatory laws to the exterminations in camps, did not escape Theodor's observation. He did not meet people from the Jewish community, but recalls encounters with those who had participated in the exterminations and the impact it had had on them. Some boasted about their roles, while others were suffering from what appears to have been post-traumatic stress disorder. Theodor did not dwell upon those experiences, however. His loathing of violence and quest for survival did not leave much room for extended inquest into the Nazi mindset. He was a starved young man who was trying to survive while praying for better times to come, in spite of the sheer violence around him— air raids, forced sterilisation of those called non-Aryans, constant stop and search practices, and other humiliating schemes.

Theodor also encountered the kindness of ordinary Germans caught up between the war and fear of the Nazis' demands for obedience. Some of these people, such as the traumatised former Nazi executioner, provided food and shelter to him.

Better times came eventually, and when the war ended Theodor was twenty years old and stronger both physically and mentally. Germany had to be rebuilt, and many German cities were managed by the Red Army or occupied by Americans. Theodor resourcefully managed to gain admission to a military camp, but was refused the status of a displaced person. He was legally a stateless foreigner but still German-born, and therefore could not be taken to the United States or any other country. After the war, the racial divide was still in place. Theodor's experience showed him that white Americans had more sympathy for white Germans, even if some of them had fought alongside the Nazis, than they had for him, or for Africans and African Americans. However, the love of a nurse from Upper Silesia, today Poland and the Czech Republic, gave Theodor hope, and the birth of a son in 1947 brought a new sense of purpose both to him and to his wife Friedel. It also signalled the beginning of a literary education and an outward-looking perspective on issues of race equality and philosophy.

Reading and learning English proved to be useful for employment. Theodor found work, after a series of setbacks, as an interpreter for the US army in Germany, three years after the end of the war. Family life also seemed to take a positive turn when he was reunited with his siblings. His brother James had been forced to join the Foreign Legion, while his sister Juliana was working for a famous circus in Paris. However, his career proved difficult. He lost his post as an interpreter while his wife was expecting their third child, and his status as a 'stateless German' provided the excuse most employers needed to dismiss him for jobs. He resumed his search for employment as an actor in films and plays. That was the start of a relatively regular flow of work in the theatre, cinema, radio and television industries, but income was low and Theodor's recurring tuberculosis forced him to seek help. He spent three years in a sanatorium, returning to a poor and broken family of four children whom he had not been able to support financially and emotionally. That role had been left to his wife, which seems to have created resentment between the couple.

Theodor turned to reading and studying, managing to get a diploma and then a scholarship to go to Paris in 1960. When he finished his studies in France, he was able to secure a post at a publishing house in Cologne, where his family eventually joined him. His interest in African politics and culture was fulfilled through deeper research into the continent's history and relation-ship with Europe; Theodor delved into diplomatic relations and European ties with African embassies. He started cultivating relationships with people working in this area and keeping abreast of events and publications related to Africa, and eventu-ally he got a job at *Afrika-Bulletin*, a German magazine covering African current events. However, as with most Africans who had grown up in Europe and had never set foot in their father's land, Theodor's expectations of his reception from and connection with a family and homeland he had never seen turned out to be a disappointment when he finally visited Cameroon. He wrote:

Word had got round in Victoria that a prodigal son had returned to his poor homeland from rich Germany. Accordingly, people had expectations of me, which of course I couldn't possibly fulfill. People I had never heard of would turn up and ask me for all kinds of help, even medical aid. My financial resources, which were tight anyway, were soon completely exhausted ... In the end I had just enough money left for the bus to the airport in Douala. Friedel picked me up at Cologne-Bonn airport, otherwise I would never have gotten home.[38]

Life back in Germany improved, however. A job offer at the German Federal Intelligence Service, a recognition of his services to the nation and, later, further acting opportunities demonstrated that Theodor had been right to keep hoping while working for better tomorrows. Racism never disappeared from the equation, but he also reflected more deeply about the ways in which black people experience racism. He was a resolute anti-racist who never understood this unfounded hatred towards fellow humans. He also refused to be burdened by the prejudice of others. In a compulsory three-year job review he challenged a report that stated: 'he has overcome initial problems with colleagues'. As he put it, 'I had no problems with my colleagues; it was the other way round'.[39] Racism was the racist's burden to bear, not his. Towards the end of his life, Theodor found a community of Afro-Germans who were actively involved in fighting for their rights and against all forms of discrimination in Germany. His father's countrymen might not have been a constant and supportive family, but new generations of Afro-Germans were creating new family networks that extended beyond the immediate bloodline. In October 2019, halfway through Black History Month in Britain, Theodor Wonja Michael passed away at the age of ninety-four. The fight for social justice and political and cultural representation continues in Germany. As Tiffany Florvil demonstrates, ongoing struggles to maintain Black History Month there highlight the appetite for new narratives which foreground the histories of people of African descent. The resilience of Afro-Germans, in collaboration with various other communities, puts the issue of forgotten histories into perspective.[40]

6

CLAIMING A PAST, NAVIGATING THE PRESENT

Theodor Michael's commitment to engaging with Afro-German communities in the last part of the twentieth century echoes the trajectory of several African Europeans. Beyond documenting aspects of the black presence in Europe, one of the most prolific aspects of black activism in twenty-first-century Europe has been a greater emphasis on the collective production of knowledge and on self-documenting African European experiences in various areas across the European continent. In Italy, Afro-Italians, alongside other children and descendants of immigrants, have been able to challenge common discriminatory practices that plague Italian society. The question of citizenship, for example, was brought to the forefront of political and societal debates when those communities mobilised and questioned the validity of the principle of citizenship based on 'right of blood', which states that children of immigrants born in Italy can only apply for citizenship when they reach their eighteenth birthday. This process is a race against time, as they then only have one year to gather the documentation needed to submit their application. Associations such as Rete G2 and many others have worked collaboratively to place pressure on institutions, and shifted the debate in parliament from 'right of blood' to birth right.[1] The question was debated in the Italian lower house in 2015.

These groups have also been tackling questions that have a poignant impact on various aspects of Afro-Italian identities. Academic Annalisa Frisina and Afro-Italian academic Camilla Hawthorne have analysed how young Afro-Italian women trouble Western beauty norms in their own daily 'aesthetic practices', as part of an organised and collective form of resistance against discrimination in a society that has denied them citizenship. Using the work of Philomena Essed, Frisina and Hawthorne tackle the issue of 'gendered racism' and analyse what Anita Harris calls 'everyday multiculturalism'. The women in the study use their bodies as sites of resistance by refusing to conform to Western hairstyle norms and adopting '"fashionable" Islamic veil[s]'.[2] Interviewed by Frisina and Hawthorne in 2014, they candidly discussed the currency of light skin colour for women in Italian society, as well as in Africa, in the twenty-first century. The question of race central to the debate manifests itself in various ways. We are indeed conditioned to accept certain norms of beauty that work in conjunction with skin colour and follow a certain hierarchy. As argued by Frisina and Hawthorne, certain characteristics such as hair, weight, body shape and forms of movement, as well as clothing, are read according to the 'grids' we have been provided by society, which 'work to reproduce racialised relations of power'.[3] Using social media to connect, share their experiences and support one another, the groups of women interviewed have developed tools to claim their Italian roots.

Two different groups were interviewed. Women of North African descent born in Italy used their Facebook group *Hijab Elegante* to resist islamophobia, isolation and fear, and to set their own beauty standard while wearing the hijab. The second group was *Nappytalia*, a Facebook page mostly aimed at discussing Afro-Italian hair and in particular encouraging women of dual and single heritage to embrace their hair (without using hair-straightening chemicals) as part of their rich diasporic roots, influences and identities. Claiming Italian urban landscapes and using visual effects, these women have organised several events, including glamorous photo shoots that showcase the variety and beauty of African European bodies in Europe. These initiatives have encouraged women-led businesses and also contribute to the collective resistance against discrimination through what Frisina and Hawthorne call the 're-appropriation' of important signifiers.[4] These signifiers had previously been used to discard black bodies in the discourse around beauty canons.

The beauty industry, and fashion in particular, has been one of the arenas that has contributed to shaping Afro-Italian identity and by extension Italian understandings of identity and citizenship. Hawthorne's research also provides information about the role of Afro-Italian female designers in that specific industry.[5] AFRO Fashion Association, set up in 2015, has made it its mission to use black designers and promote African fabrics. Their fashion shows are resolutely political. They continue to take place in an environment that is hostile to people of African descent. For decades, Italy has been the first port of entry for people of African descent crossing the Mediterranean in boats illegally piloted by human traffickers. The so-called 'migrant crisis' seemed to scare Europeans, and has led to a brutal series of racially motivated attacks on people of African descent, including Afro-Italians, over the last few years. The fashion shows were aimed at demonstrating how sophisticated, varied and vibrant African cultures are. It was also about showcasing the ingenuity of entrepreneurs whose work could contribute to the Italian economy.

Expanding on the premise of 'Black Geographies', Hawthorne demonstrates how the experiences of Afro-Italian female entrepreneurs can help to challenge racial capitalism. She notes that 1 million children of immigrants born in Italy (making up 10 per cent of the youth population in Italy as a whole) do not have Italian citizenship. With its stagnating economy and high youth unemployment, Italy saw the arrival of over 119,000 refugees in 2017 (a vast majority of them from sub-Saharan Africa) as a threat. Yet these newcomers' arrival further pushed the question of citizenship that has been at the heart of discussions in Afro-Italian communities for decades. The question of birth right became an urgent matter. Entrepreneurship in an environment that views children of African descent as valuable only if they contribute economically to society—the 'Good Immigrant' syndrome—has become an asset that allows these communities to bring about further activism and public debate.[6]

In Italy, however, the boundaries around this discourse remain difficult to shift significantly. Children of immigrants are still posited as outsiders and distrusted. Even their economic contributions seem to reproduce exploitation, or 'a new form of colonial extraction, wherein Black women's bodies and labour are conscripted as the raw materials from which European nations can be (re)built or (re)produced.'[7] Resistance at a national level to conversations about these issues further highlights the exclusionary nature of such forms of exploitation. However, these silences have led Afro-Italian communities to take up new forms of activism. They are determined to claim 'Italianness' through a reappropriation of global 'Good Immigrant' narratives, transforming them into a discourse of resilience and pride whereby they assert belonging to multiple spaces both in and outside Italy, whether the white Italian majority group agrees or not.[8]

The experiences of African Europeans are as varied as there are individual trajectories. There is, however, a commonality of methods when it comes to fighting various forms of discrimination such as racial capitalism—for example, the creative assertions of identity shown by Afro-Italian designers. African European identities also spread beyond Europe and Africa. They encompass a range of diasporic voices, including Afro-Latinx histories. They offer invitations to move beyond male-dominated discourses on identity, as Afro-Italian entrepreneurs have demonstrated. They are also cross-European, as they reflect collective endeavours to examine African European points of convergence and divergence. Exactly these questions have been explored by a series of conferences, workshops and summer schools on topics such as Afro-Europeans, Afropeans and Afro-Europes, as well as a thriving academic and non-academic body of work spanning podcasts, films, music, arts and academic publications over the last decade. From Theodor Michael's story to the teams running *Hijab Elegante* or *Nappytalia*, the notion of home is central to understanding African Europeans. African European thinking celebrates the idea of home, but also states the importance of seeking a home that embraces one's differences. The quest for home has led many African Europeans to return to what they see as their parents' ancestral home.

Afro-Swedish trajectories illustrate the complexity of finding and integrating into a home that is in fact a recreation and an imagined refuge. Several studies have shown how children of immigrants born and bred in Sweden have decided to go and fight in Somaliland. In 2010, for example, twenty young men went to Somalia to fight with militant groups. Some of them had never previously been to Somalia. A sense of otherness in their country of birth and the context of the war on terror are some of the possible explanations for such engagements. Anne Kubai argues that nostalgia passed down from parents who have been rendered stateless plays a key role in the attachment of younger generations to a place they have never set foot in.[9] Marianne Hirsch has put forward the useful notion of postmemory, which could shed light on intergenerational links and memories.[10]

Somalis forced to flee their homes over the last decades of conflict in Somalia became stateless; in the face of traumatic memories of displacement, home became an imagined place where this pain could be soothed. The idea of home was thus reinvented, and these dreams and memories were passed on to the next generation. In addition, constant reminders of being a refugee in a country that is not one's own have also been transmitted to children, thus leading some of them to try to claim a place they have never known. Home is about memories, but also practical intervention to secure the safety of one's clan. As a Swedish Somali in Malmo put it, 'when I receive information that my clan is involved in a conflict with another clan, I feel that I am obliged to assist ... since I cannot join them in the struggle, I can send something small to support them.'[11] Sending money is a way to show one's attachment to home and to honour the trust people back home have put in those who have left and are perceived as financially better off. Trust and support were part of the values and experiences that were transmitted to the next generation of Afro-Swedes.

In the 1970s, the Swedish government, convinced that immigrants from the Horn of Africa would eventually go back home, encouraged them to set up their own associations. Somalis, Eritreans and Ethiopians who arrived in Sweden set up various associations that are said to be apolitical and strive for social justice in Sweden, but some of them have lent support to military agendas in the Horn of Africa. A large number of these groups have also greatly contributed to peacebuilding projects in their own or their parents' homelands. Kubai argues that, beyond the various conflicts within those groups and in Somalia, it is the desire to contribute and the need for ownership that motivates Afro-Swedes from the Horn of Africa.[12] The older generations are refugees because of conflict, yet they have tried to participate in the histories that marginalised and victimised them. They want to feel that they could help to build a present and a future they could be proud of. The desire to create 'roots and routes' should not be disregarded, as Lena Sawyer notes.[13]

The larger transnational dimension, and the desire to play a role in that sphere, does not negate the fact that these groups also want to belong to their local communities and to Sweden; the same applies in other African European geographies. African European communities in Paris, Berlin, London and other places are constantly squaring their migratory journeys with a sense of local belonging. While race and cultural affiliation play a role in shaping African European identities, discourse of colour blindness contributes to exclusion. The notion that hard work and moral integrity will prevail against the spectre of racism is at the basis of Swedish debates on race. As Sawyer argues, the popular narrative of a raceless society is believed to be justified by Sweden's non-participation in transatlantic slavery.[14] One could argue that this partial historical amnesia has been used as a justification for an allegedly neutral, universalising discourse of equality. Sweden was involved in enslavement, and yet this history was not taught to students for centuries.

Sweden's alleged distance from any colonial ties fuels the state of its postcolonial discourse. Swedish exceptionalism operates on colour blindness and the refusal to engage in questions of race, because Sweden supposedly has no guilt to deal with or no pride to take in an imperial past. As Michael McEachrane puts it:

> A widespread self-conception of the Nordic countries is that they were mere bystanders to European colonialism and slavery and are largely unscathed by racial worldviews. Rather, their image is of being egalitarian human rights champions in solidarity with the world's poor and downtrodden ... Yet, the Nordic countries are not without a colonial history nor were they uninvolved in the transatlantic slave trade and they certainly have not been untouched by racial worldviews.[15]

Colour blindness in this instance is about positioning one's nation or oneself as anti-racialist. However, as Goldberg notes, anti-racialism is about the dominant party's decision not to racialise, and yet is a gesture of domination. In other words, anti-racialism 'seeks to remove the condition not indirectly through removal of the category in the name of which the repression is enacted. Rather, it seeks to remove the structure of the condition itself.'[16]

These attempts to circumvent the procedures that name racial hierarchies ignore ideologies that have been prevalent since the fifteenth century, as geographer Katarina Schough shows in her 2008 volume *Hyperborean: Images of Sweden's Place in the World*, which describes medieval Swedish accounts of a superior white Nordic race.[17] As Ylva Habel notes, Swedish people have found ways to talk about race while avoiding the term itself. In fact, defining oneself as 'black' or 'white' disrupts social norms of politeness. The etiquette of euphemisms has allowed people to engage with discussions about inequality that may affect 'non-white people'. Those euphemisms also include terms such as 'culture', 'multiculture' and 'ethnicity'.[18] Similarly, engaging with the privileges and power dynamics around whiteness becomes difficult when attempting to debate with the majority group. When it does appear, the focus of the narrative about colonial engagement is the rationalisation of colonial endeavour. It insists on the civilising mission of the kingdom, and ends its analysis with Sweden's disengagement from the colonial project upon the abolition of slavery in 1847. The perception that Sweden could not possibly have actively participated in debates about the so-called scientific racism of the nineteenth century has persisted. The discrepancy between Sweden's contemporary beliefs and the fascination with black bodies in its art remains, and is an interesting point to further analyse.

One figure remains inscribed into the Swedish collective memory in relation to the perception of black bodies:

Pierre Louis Alexandre, also known as Jean Louis Pierre, P. L. Alexandersson, Svarte Pedro, or, more negatively, Negern Pettersson.[19] He was born in French Guiana in 1844, four years prior to the French abolition of slavery in 1848, and arrived in Stockholm in 1863 when he was nineteen years old. After working at the docks, he became a very popular model for the Swedish Academy of Fine Arts. The striking terracotta head sculpted by Verner Åkerman in 1885 shows a black man in his forties with a slightly receding hairline and a few wrinkles, smiling lightly while looking sideways. Åkerman won a royal medal and a scholarship for this piece of art, which he titled *Zambo*. Pierre Louis was also routinely exoticised in portraits by other artists. He is seen elsewhere carrying a sword or a long knife, wearing a flamboyant yellow turban and baring his chest. He appeared in numerous attires that were supposed to represent Africa, even though it is very unlikely he ever set foot on the continent. We know very little of Pierre Louis and what happened to him after his career modelling for various famous Swedish artists. However, in addition to these representations, nineteenth-century Sweden also saw a proliferation of colonial discourses in historical and geographical writing and education which entrenched racial inequality.[20]

Twentieth- and twenty-first-century Sweden, on the other hand, has been focused on post-war migration and the rise of nationalism and far-right groups. However, a sizeable literature demonstrates that academics have been working on links between nineteenth- and twentieth-century Sweden and have been fighting both colonial amnesia and the Swedish model of 'racial innocence'. Echoing Sawyer, Habel reiterates that debating race in society is frowned upon in Sweden, and that silence has contributed to the normalisation of whiteness as a point of reference.[21] Whiteness and, paradoxically, colour blindness have also been used as a way of focusing almost exclusively on social inequality, thus erasing the links between race and class. Colour does not exist in Sweden, and therefore any racial crime or assault is defined as 'un-Swedish' even when carried out by white Swedes. As Habel puts it, 'just *starting* a very basic critical discussion in public fora such as panel discussions and debates involves Sisyphean labor; and in order to be accepted, it needs to be kept on a markedly low level of problematization to accommodate the pain/knowledge threshold of White organisers, moderators and participants.'[22] In this context, stories of Afro-Swedes dating back centuries have been erased.

Over the last six decades Afro-Swedish organisations have emerged and contributed to knowledge sharing about cultural practices. In music, for example, Afro-Swedes or *Afrosvenskarnas* are welcomed as part of the country's social fabric, but certain areas—politics, for one—remain the preserve of the white majority group. The Swedish conception of blackness and whiteness, with its silences and euphemisms, has given birth to a very specific way of conceptualising blackness and Afro-Swedish identities. The Swedish exceptionalism that appeared at the end of the nineteenth century has led to a very specific model of social democracy. As Monica L. Miller argues, the beliefs that shape Swedishness are based on the notion of sameness. Respect for the law, pride in the figure of the workman and the ideal of progress define the social democratic model in Sweden.[23] Sameness means the exclusion of what does not fit. Consequently, although integration requires the acceptance of all who contribute through their work to society, visible racial differences are still linked to inferiority in many instances. In 2012, a spokesman for the National Association for Afro-Swedes and national coordinator for the European Network Against Racism in Sweden, Jallow Momodou, publicly denounced Swedish culture minister Lena Adelsohn Liljeroth for celebrating Sweden's World Art Day by mocking black women and disrespecting the victims of genital mutilation in a tasteless joke set up in an installation by artist Makode Aj Linde. Momodou also noted that this was not an isolated incident.[24] However, many Afro-Swedes are active in defending themselves against the oppressive narrative of Swedish exceptionalism. They have found ways to celebrate their multiple identities through novels, music and painting. They have also come together to build new initiatives whereby cultural activism has ramifications in the political sphere, as demonstrated by the work of Momodou and his counterparts.

Calling for action and publicly challenging politicians do not seem to be viable options for African Europeans in many Eastern European countries and Russia. Russia has one particularly prominent link with Africa.

> O poet, hold not dear the people's acclamation;
> The eager shouts of praise will quickly die away.
> Cold-hearted crowds will mock, and fools prate condemnation;
> But be thou calm and firm, and proudly keep thy way.[25]

These words were written by one of the greatest Russian writers and poets, Aleksandr Pushkin, in 'To the Poet' (1830), which advises a fellow poet, as a warning as much as an encouragement, to keep writing and stay faithful to their craft while trusting their skills. Pushkin was born into old noble families on both his mother and his father's sides. His links with Africa could have gone unnoticed were it not for a slightly darker complexion and features that differed marginally from those of his fellow Russians. His mother was descended from Scandinavian nobles, but his maternal great-grandfather was General Abram Petrovich Gannibal (or Hannibal), a recognised figure in the history of Russia.

Gannibal was kidnapped from West Africa when he was eight years old. He was enslaved, and ended up in the service of a Serbian count who took him to the court of Tsar Peter the Great. Peter took an interest in young Gannibal and decided to have him as his godson. He then sent him to France to be educated. Many opportunities followed for Gannibal, and he embarked upon a military career, rapidly rising through the ranks. His African ancestry came to be known and valued when, in a letter addressed to the Senate in 1742, he stated that he came from a noble family in Africa. After petitioning the court and the Senate to be granted the status of a nobleman, Gannibal succeeded in reaching the highest social status he could have hoped for. His life was not wholly successful; his first marriage was disastrous. However, his second marriage with Christina Regina Siöberg, a noblewoman whose ancestry encompassed both Brandenburg and Scandinavia, proved to be happier. They had ten children, including a son called Osip who went on to have a daughter named Nadezhda. She was Pushkin's mother. The 1742 letter has prompted a historical investigation to determine from which place in Africa Gannibal originated. In the letter, he had written that he was born in a city called Logone or Lagone and that his father was the monarch of two other cities. Historian Dieudonné Gnammankou followed several trails and eventually found out that Gannibal was born in Logone-Birni, a town located near the Logone River in the far north of Cameroon.[26] The research was supported by several Russian bodies, such as the Russian Academy of Sciences and the Pushkin Museum in Moscow.

Gannibal's great-grandson, Pushkin, never shied away from his family's African heritage. In the first edition of his novel in verse *Eugene Onegin* (1825), he warns his readers that he plans to write a biography of his black ancestor.[27] As Cynthia Green notes, the novel 'contains one of his most famous references to his own mixture of Russian and African heritage' in the passage:

> It's time to drop astern the shape
> of the dull shores of my disfavour,
> and there, beneath your noonday sky,
> my Africa, where waves break high,

to mourn for Russia's gloomy savour,
land where I learned to love and weep,
land where my heart is buried deep.[28]

He had prior to that adopted the moniker *afrikanets* ('the African'), and his unfinished historical novel was based on his great-grandfather. He had entitled it *The Moor of Peter the Great*.[29] Modern Russia is proud of both Pushkin's and Gannibal's achievements. They are commemorated on statues and stamps, and Pushkin's work has been reinterpreted through further literary productions, music, films and so on, in Russia and across the world. Pushkin never visited Africa. Both he and Gannibal were resolute European Russians who embodied several histories and reminded their contemporaries of intellectual crossroads, the legacies of education and the tumultuous and brutal histories of conquest.

Other stories of Afro-Russians very often related to transcultural exchanges, Pan-Africanism and the investments of many African intellectuals and politicians in communist ideology.[30] Cameroon and a few other countries sent students to be educated in Russia during the period that followed the independence of most African nations in the 1960s. The expectation was that those students would return to their countries to help shape policies and initiate social change. Many of those who left belonged to families with strong ties to the government, and they were welcomed back with open arms and enviable positions as civil servants in the upper echelons of society.

What is important here is to connect past and present in order to understand how contemporary Europe, Russia included, deals with these legacies and common histories. It appears that the history of engagements and collaborations has been forgotten, as stories of the former Soviet Union are relegated to the past in public discourse. The rise of ethnonationalism in Eastern European countries, with a dangerous emerging tendency to promote monocultures, does not leave room for African Europeans to embrace and celebrate their multiple heritage. Testimonies of assault and racial discrimination are numerous in twenty-first-century Europe. However, the election of Peter Bossman as the first black mayor in Eastern Europe in 2010 seemed to signal a new departure and brought hope to many. Bossman was born in Ghana, but due to the political situation in the country he had to leave when he was in his twenties. He studied medicine and years later settled in Piran in Slovenia, where he set up his own private practice. Bossman was criticised for not speaking Slovene, the country's official language; language is often a measuring tool for integration as well as part of an exclusionary arsenal wielded by anti-immigrant groups. Nonetheless, Bossman stated that he had never experienced racism and truly believed that Slovenia was on the path to great positive change. Class may blur discriminatory boundaries, as Bossman's experience is in stark and puzzling contrast with the voices of African Europeans across Europe.

For those who were born in Eastern European countries, have dual heritage and only grew up with a European parent, finding one's mark in a society that distrusts difference is a daily fight. From Nina, who grew up in Slovakia and was raised by her Slovak mother, to some of the 5,000 or so Afro-Polish who live in Poland, interaction with the majority group is twofold. It is either a sexualised and exoticised relationship in specific public spaces such as dance clubs and arts centres, mainly between black African men and white Eastern European women, or an exoticisation of dual-heritage women by fellow countrymen and countrywomen, who display both fascination with dual-heritage bodies and unexpected racist attitudes towards people of African descent.[31] Violence in every shape and form is part of these exchanges. The European Commission's reports about racism in Eastern European countries such as Latvia, and its recommendations for combatting the problem, often indicate that the arrival of new migrants has unsettled local populations.[32] In many instances, however, these new arrivals have occurred at a relatively low number and cannot convincingly explain racial harassment and racially motivated attacks. Stories about Russian and Eastern European football fans attacking black supporters during international tournaments continue to dominate the news. Racism against black people in sports is not exclusive to these countries, but threats, bodily harm and even deaths have led several players to advise supporters to avoid Eastern European countries.[33] Life for those who reside there remains difficult in many instances.

Despite the immobility and sense of utter helplessness that seem to characterise black Russian and Eastern European experiences, African Europeans in the rest of Europe have fought racism and promoted their agenda of political and economic equality by systematically and openly challenging private individuals, public figures and institutions for previously accepted discriminatory practices. In the Netherlands, for example, Afro-Dutch identities cannot be thought outside of the history of enslavement and the negative stereotypes that it brought about. Drawing together gender history, the history of sexuality and colonial history, Afro-Surinamese Dutch scholar Gloria Wekker demonstrates that plantation power relations and the domination of masters over black bodies persisted in the Dutch consciousness even after the abolition of the slave trade. The perception remained that black women were sexual objects, for instance. Class segregation, characterised by the economic poverty of people of African descent, has resulted in a simplified equation that is a legacy of enslavement: highly sexualised black bodies, with black women figured as sex workers and black men stereotyped as 'overendowed'.[34] This alleged proximity to sexual instincts and appetite was thought to be accompanied by an irrational mind.

The consequence of these beliefs has persisted and survived past the colonial era. They have cemented postcolonial views of people of African descent. They have also led to the criminalisation of black bodies. Wekker recalls instances of unjustified stop and search practices, based on the assumption that the Afro-Dutch had little economic value and forms of harassment were a justifiable way of policing individuals from this group.[35] She establishes a parallel between W. E. B. Du Bois's work on double consciousness and the very specific ways whiteness and blackness interact, arguing that Dutch double consciousness rested on a 'fascination with the black female body and a specific kind of Dutch whiteness'.[36] She demonstrates that Dutch whiteness either posits itself as anti-racist or fiercely defends its own privilege. Denying that racism exists in Dutch society while oppressing bodies racialised as black is at the core of what she names 'white innocence'.[37]

White Dutch innocence is characterised by a series of contradictions, and debates about the figure of Zwarte Piet embody them. For Wekker, he epitomises what Paul Gilroy defines as 'postcolonial melancholia'.[38] Postcolonial melancholia is characterised by the difficulty for white Western subjects of processing their pain over the loss of empire, along with their belief that they have typically been on the right side of history—from the civilising mission and what Kipling called the 'white man's burden' to their feelings of superiority after fighting and winning against the Nazis. All things imperial—the blood, subjugation and exploitation of human beings and lands—have been consciously forgotten. What remains is a nostalgia for an imperial past that was built on violence and whose legacies are still felt at many levels in postcolonial societies. The figure of Zwarte Piet is therefore of both colonial and postcolonial significance.

Zwarte Piet, or Black Piet, is a very specific kind of African European. A fictional character, he presents us with the transformations that took place in the European psyche during and after colonial expansion. Wekker has looked at the controversy around Piet, which demonstrates how Dutch society wanted and still wants African Europeans to be represented, to some extent expecting them to conform to the role they were assigned centuries ago. Dutch writer Jan Schenkman created the character for a children's book in 1850, while the Netherlands were still involved in slavery. The abolition of slavery in Surinam took place relatively soon after, in 1863. One could argue that the ineluctable march towards abolition was creating anxiety within the population. Domination and confidence in the wealth-building potential of slavery had shaped the Dutch outlook on colonial subjects, but British abolition in 1833 and French abolition in 1848 did not go unnoticed, and the writing was on the wall for the Netherlands. A strong abolition movement had already been unsettling the institution of slavery in the country. By 1850, one could see society wavering between the need to preserve what it viewed as a glorious past and the desire to posit itself as benevolent towards those considered to be less fortunate because of the colour of their skin, and by extension their intellectual abilities.

Zwarte Piet was allegedly a moor from Spain with an accommodating personality. He was loved by children. His childlike intellect, his clownish outlook and sometimes even his inability to speak Dutch properly were part of the appeal. Zwarte Piet dolls have been the companions of generations of white Dutch children. The idea that the character is offensive has provoked anger in many quarters. His physical representation as the helper of Sinterklaas, or Saint Nicholas, in the Dutch Christmas festival that takes place every 5 December demonstrates how important he is to the collective cultural memory. White men and women with blackened faces, thick red lips, big earrings and colourful clothes take to the streets to celebrate the festival in various

Dutch cities every year. This attire, as well as the behaviour attributed to both Saint Nicholas and Black Pete, clearly highlights the power relation that has been established between the two characters. As Wekker notes, jolly Pete often walks, while Saint Nicholas rides a horse.[39] Pete is expected to know his place in society while he is helping and entertaining others. A plethora of debates and research on this topic have demonstrated that children are well aware that Black Pete's social status is lower in Dutch society than that of Saint Nicholas. They recognise the imbalance in the power dynamic; although they do not love him any less, they therefore grow up associating that lower social status with racial stereotypes, equating dark skin with poverty, a carefree character and lower intellectual abilities. They also learn to accept Pete's lack of mastery of the Dutch language and other stereotypes as part of his character. What Stuart Hall and Wekker call 'ritualized degradation' becomes part of the narrative of inferiority.

'Ritualized degradation' is a set of degrading attitudes that have become normalised. For example, in the eighteenth century, slaves would stand while the master was sitting down; overseers would inflict punishment upon and examine enslaved women as though they were animals; enslaved men were expected to shelter white women from the sun with an umbrella, running beside them while they were riding, and so on.[40] Those rituals shaped the way black and white bodies interacted in social contexts long after abolition but they have also been rendered obsolete through centuries of fighting for emancipation and equal rights. However, Black Pete allows such practices to continue in a highly ritualised and celebratory way. Pete is what could have happened if the nineteenth-century social context had not changed, but he also embodies what has been called 'entitlement racism' by Philomena Essed.[41] 'Entitlement racism' entails arguing that one is an anti-racist liberal while claiming that derogatory terms and offensive representations of minority ethnic groups are a matter of free-dom of expression. It also concerns the right to shock through the arts, as demonstrated by the Swedish installation about female genital mutilation. Linde, the artist who set up the instal-lation, is Afro-Swedish, and the glee with which Liljeroth, the culture minister, performed eating the mutilated body parts demonstrates cultural perceptions of race and gender.

Such jokes, triggering for many people of African descent, are markers of everyday racism, and perpetuate forms of exclusion. They also allow the offender to claim innocence and even take the moral high ground on the basis that they value the universal-ist principle of freedom of speech. This argument, used to pro-test accusations of racism, is part of Wekker's 'white innocence', and a reminder of Stuart Hall's 'ritualized degradation'. 'Ritualized degradation' and its progeny 'entitlement racism' take a new form in twenty-first-century Europe. They are embedded in the collective psyche, because they have been transmitted through language, rituals and cultural practices. These postcolo-nial memories take many forms in contemporary Europe—from British member of parliament Diane Abbott photographed drinking alcohol on public transport and ridiculed by the media as mediocre and intellectually inferior; to the mature white woman clutching her purse upon seeing a young black man or woman on the street; to instances of misogynoir in which race and gender collide.

The term misogynoir was first coined in 2008 by Moya Bailey; she further expanded upon it in a 2010 essay.[42] Bailey looks at the ways black women and black girls are negatively represented in media. She has noticed that they are often deemed less desir-able, and are ridiculed for the way they look, dress and speak. Any black woman protesting against those negative depictions is met with further abuse, because they have not conformed to the place they have been assigned in society while, paradoxically, conforming to the image of the unreasonable, angry, violent black woman. Beyond the heteropatriarchal practice of misogynoir, Bailey also notes that black men and white feminist women tend to exclude black women and girls from certain spheres, but then actively target them when they do not lend their support to causes that have failed to take their perspectives into account.[43] Bailey insists that misogynoir does not apply to 'women of colour', a term that encompasses all non-white women. Women of colour are treated in a variety of ways depending on gradation in skin colour and the closeness of their facial features to white European features. In contrast, Bailey has argued that misogynoir is a very specific form of oppression that uniquely targets black-skinned women.

Despite Bailey's strict definition of the term, we have seen over the last few years that certain forms of discrimination against black and dual-heritage women have common features. The vile media attacks against the Duchess of Sussex held similarities to those encountered by supermodel Iman. Both were deemed too far away from either blackness or whiteness. Iman famously confronted the editor-in-chief of the black US magazine *Essence* when she stated that Iman was 'a white woman dipped in chocolate' in 1976. Both women have been criticised for having either not enough or too much of certain attributes. Nonetheless, class is an element that needs to be part of the discussion. Iman and Markle have had access to a kind of wealth that many underprivileged dark-skinned black women can only dream of. They have both held professional posts based on their physical attributes as well as expertise and achievement in their fields.

Misogynoir also leads black women to target other black women, often for the colour of their skin or the texture of their hair. This ranges from criticism about wearing hair extensions or a weave as opposed to one's 'natural hair' to insults about 'natural hair' and dreadlocks or braids deemed unsophisticated and 'fresh from the boat', thus supposedly shedding a negative light on all black women. Misogynoir also occasionally highlights seemingly positive attributes. For example, highly educated black women are congratulated for being 'eloquent' or celebrated in the work-place for being 'honest' when white majority groups in the same environment do not expect black women to possess those attri-butes or skills. The assumption is thus that those who display such qualities are exceptional in contrast to their counterparts. These stereotypes date back to plantation life, and have taken various forms.

Returning to Black Pete, we can see that he makes room for an open celebration of these plantation stereotypes, and offers the opportunity for white people to reminisce about times when the racial order was not challenged. Marianne Hirsch's notion of postmemory can also apply here. Racism is an intergenerational process, transmitted as a legacy of the past. In the figure of Black Pete, the politically incorrect becomes a powerful cultural asset. Both the pressure to remove Pete and resistance to it situate debates around race and Europe in a context of postcolonial mel-ancholia. Pete is seen by many as the last frontier before, it is alleged, culture—often expressed through turns of phrase such as 'our Western values'—slips into the dangerously sanitised waters of a hybrid multiculture.

Afro-Dutch identities were diverse, and several groups have found ways to challenge the practice of blackface during the Sinterklaas celebration. Protests led to national debates that have not stopped since 2011. Divides over racist representations of black people in Dutch society have led to other debates about the legacies of the colonial past, such as the question of reparations and the role of the Rijksmuseum, the Dutch national museum, in telling colonial stories and addressing the issue of repatriation. The Netherlands' relationship with the past tends to dominate debate about Afro-Dutch identities. However, the double consciousness evoked by Du Bois and Gilroy has been transformed by a new generation. Millennials fight against contemporary discrimination without necessarily relating it to the ancestral pain of past victims. They claim their place in Dutch society as descendants of the enslaved and survivors of history, but also as Dutch citizens born in Europe. Afro-Dutch identity is both African and Dutch in some instances, and Afro-Surinamese and Dutch in others.

Those whose grandparents or great-grandparents were born in Surinam have found their own ways to celebrate their heritage. Every 1 July, the Dutch Afro-Surinamese community commemorates and celebrates emancipation with the Keti Koti Festival. The festival marks the 1863 abolition of slavery in Surinam with a day of dance, music and peaceful demonstration. The nature of this commemoration has changed over the years. In fact, until the early 2000s links between the colonial past and the present were documented predominantly by formal historians, and even this was discouraged; they were expected to keep the past in the past, and to carefully avoid mentioning the question of slavery. However, people from the Surinamese and Antillean communities started to demand that the country formally acknowledge the Netherlands' involvement in the history of enslavement with a memorial. As Kwame Nimako, Amy Abdou and Glenn Willemsen note, the discrepancy between the narrative around abolition in the nineteenth century, which presented it as a victory to be celebrated, and the long silence that followed for nearly 130 years demonstrates that Dutch society was not ready to look into its past.[44] In 1993, organisations representing various Afro-Surinamese communities living in major Dutch cities set up a committee whose aim was to plan a commemoration of the abolition of slavery. 30 June was chosen as a day to reflect, and 1 July to publicly commemorate. Between 1993 and 1999, several other Afro-Dutch organisations mounted a similar campaign, petitioning and establishing links with other minority groups in the country. They chose commemoration dates that were close to those of the commemoration of the Second World War. They also talked about reconciling the Jewish community with the Afro-Dutch community, as several Jews had been involved in the slave trade as plantation owners and investors.

In 2001, after the Durban Conference in South Africa, the Dutch government decided to look at the question of the legacies of slavery in Dutch society. The work that had already been accomplished by the Afro-Dutch community served as a solid base for discussions about a monument. In 2002, a monument was unveiled in Amsterdam's Oosterpark. However, strong public support failed to materialise. In fact, anti-immigrant political parties garnered further public support. Nimako, Abdou and Willemsen point out that the monument did not generate a robust conversation about fighting racism and ending discriminatory practices for several reasons. For the Afro-Surinamese Dutch, the monument was an acknowledgement of what their ancestors had endured. It was a national homage paid to those who had contributed to the wealth of the nation. However, for the government in power at the time, and most other politicians, it was just a symbol of a shameful but isolated episode in the history of the country. In other words, it was a marker of a moment in time that supposedly did not represent Dutch values. Distrust and misunderstanding led some members of the Afro-Dutch community to view the monument as an empty gesture.[45] Although a shift has certainly now taken place in public awareness and discussion of multiculturalism, Nimako, Abdou and Willemsen note that at the academic level, major changes have not taken place in the way the history of enslavement is researched. With few exceptions, many scholars, historians in particular, are still reluctant to establish links between the history of enslavement and its legacies in Dutch society today.[46]

The work of scholars like Gloria Wekker has been instrumental in building those bridges. Wekker's scholarship, and that of other Afro-Surinamese Dutch thinkers, has brought historical research together with sociology, political science, psychology and gender studies. These Afro-Dutch intellectuals engage in scholarly activism, using both their experiences as members of a minority group in Dutch society and their academic expertise to shed light on various forms of ritualised violence. Wekker's experience as an African European woman in the twenty-first century also has its place in this study. *White Innocence* is a research work in which she shares her encounters with both African European communities and government representatives. We are invited to follow her journey as a researcher who had the opportunity to work for the government at a policymaking level, as well as her trajectory as an Afro-Dutch woman. In bringing her personal history to her research, Wekker makes room for a shift in perspective and closes the distance between the object and subject of her study. Biographical details are provided only when they are relevant to and inform her work.

However, we know that Wekker was born in Suriname in 1950 and moved to the Netherlands when she was in her twenties. From a Master's degree in cultural anthropology in Amsterdam to a PhD at the University of California on the gender and sexuality of Afro-Surinamese women, Wekker's career is transnational and intersectional. She has looked at the interconnections between gender, sexuality, race and class in various postcolonial settings. Her work for the Dutch government, especially in the area of health and social care, has helped shape policies in the Netherlands. In a conversation with Rivke Jaffe, Wekker invites scholars to look at the genealogies of their disciplines in order to understand how they are embedded in colonial structures. For example, she points out that it has become acceptable to centre white women in gender studies, while black

and minority ethnic women's experiences and history are relegated to the discipline of ethnic studies. This division, Wekker
argues, does not allow us to interrogate the way race, class and
gender shape the lives of groups that nonetheless coexist in the
Global North. It is equally telling that so-called 'primitive' societies are relegated to anthropology, while sociology considers
more 'complex' societies. These hierarchies reflect thought processes that are part of colonial legacies.[47]

Examining the work of Afro-European women scholars provides us with perspectives that are cruelly lacking in public
debate about people of African descent in Europe. Black female
scholars make up a shockingly small number of academics in
European universities. The perspectives of black women in
Europe have thus often appeared in the context of testimonies,
or interviews conducted by academics. However, black female
academics have, as we have seen, shaped various intellectual
debates and brought unique insights into a world that many
deem both prestigious and opaque. For example, they continue
to challenge universities' assumptions about notions such as
inclusion and diversity. Numerous debates about equality in
which no black women are to be seen take place in academia.
In addition, it is often assumed that black academics are only
able to discuss the history and stories of people of African
descent and other minority groups, with black and minority
ethnic academics as activists on the one side and the white
majority group as scholars on the other. African European
women scholars have been able to redirect the debate in ways
that challenge those damaging binary structures. They have
also raised questions about the low number of black female
academics in European universities, and the hiring processes
that reproduce race, gender and class divisions and discourage
young black female undergraduates from pursuing a career in
academia, or exclude African European early career researchers.

Minority women, and black women such as Gloria Wekker in particular, have also helped to shape debates outside of academia, amongst activists from various professional backgrounds.

7

IDENTITY AND LIBERATION

AFRICAN EUROPEANS TODAY

In France, the remarkable work done by a generation of young black activists has shaken the self-congratulatory French feminist arena. Since Simone de Beauvoir's famous statement in *The Second Sex* (1949) that 'one is not born but rather becomes a woman', generations of French women have identified with her feminist plight and assertion of her bisexuality. These women were followed by several feminist organisations, such as *Mouvement de libération des femmes* (Women's Liberation Movement), which was set up in 1970. Five years later, the adoption of the Veil Law, named after French Jewish female politician Simone Veil, shifted the debate about women's rights, and in particular their reproductive and health rights, in France.

In the midst of these developments, the fight of African European feminists continued but was not given public prominence. In 2014, younger generations of French Afrofeminists set up an organisation called Mwasi.[1] It is a collective of women and non-binary people of African descent. They argued that their voices were not represented in French society; in fact, their views had been erased by the dominant, universalising white feminist discourse that is very specifically affiliated to French ideas of citizenship and social cohesion. The organisation angered numerous bodies and individuals when, in 2017, it established a festival called Nyansapo Festival, open to 'black women only'. A far-right group attacked them as being exclusionary and working against French values. This criticism was echoed by LICRA, the *Ligue internationale contre le racisme et l'antisémitisme* (International League Against Racism and Antisemitism) and *SOS Racisme*, both major anti-racist groups supported by the French state. Mayor of Paris Anne Hidalgo followed suit and tried to prevent the festival from going ahead. However, she eventually found out that it was taking place on privately owned premises, meaning she had no say in the matter.

The objection raised was that the festival did not make room for all women. Instead, it offered a space that allowed black women to speak freely about the many ways in which racial discrimination, alongside other discriminations such as gender, class, age and religion, was harming their self-worth. The events of 2017 and subsequent controversies are particularly revealing. French feminist groups are open to all women, and yet the glaring absence of minority ethnic women and black women in particular has gone largely unnoticed. Questions such as the working conditions of minority ethnic women in certain jobs, such as cleaning or childcare, are not discussed by most mainstream French feminists. Those causes are generally taken up by unions, when in fact they relate to the specific living and working environments of black French women. Other issues, such as the lack of queer women's voices in debates about the LGBT community in France, highlight the blatant erasure of experiences which is at play within French society. In fact, in a situation which Gloria Wekker has observed in the Netherlands, a sizeable portion of the gay community has been supporting and voting for anti-immigrant and far-right political parties across Europe, France being no exception.[2]

Mwasi offers a space for queer women to discuss these issues, and the interplay of multiple forms of exclusion. The group stance when it comes to creating spaces is very clear:

> this collective is non-mixed because we believe that we are best equipped to seize the tools for our own emancipation. Mwasi is neither against men, nor against other racial and ethnic groups. In fact, they will be able to join us as allies after a consultation has taken place amongst members of the collective.[3]

Mwasi has tackled very practical issues that affect black women, as well as reflecting on scholarly material and questions. The group acknowledges that it was born from the conjunction of several events, including violence against women in the Democratic Republic of the Congo over the last decades and the emergence of new critical race and gender theories from African American scholars and activists. Several high-profile black French feminists have participated in workshops organised by Mwasi or publicly given their support to the group. Amongst such individuals are scholar and activist Françoise Vergès and filmmaker, author, journalist and activist Rokhaya Diallo. Both women have been in the public eye for decades and are regularly targeted by both far-right and mainstream media in France.

Diallo's work as a journalist in mainstream media has been a thorn in the side of anti-immigration and far-right groups. Beyond her support for black women's rights in France, she has fiercely defended Muslim women, LGBT people and Roma, gypsy and traveller communities. However, a significant difference is apparent between her treatment by the French media and that of Vergès. An acclaimed political scientist, Vergès was born in Paris in 1952. She has written widely on French colonial and postcolonial issues. In 2009, she succeeded novelist Maryse Condé to become president of the National Committee for the

Memory and History of Slavery. The committee was established in 2005 under French president Jacques Chirac and marked a significant shift in the way France dealt with the memory of enslavement. Diallo was born in 1978 in Paris. From setting up a non-governmental organisation in 2006 to writing about racism in France and becoming a sought-after public commentator, she has been a constant presence in French media. However, she has also been the target of misogynoir both from the very media who invite her to speak and from French audiences. Vergès and Diallo are both outspoken feminists, but one has to ponder the discrepancy in their treatment. Academic Vergès has benefitted from the support of a number of media outlets, while Diallo constantly has to defend her own position and that of other black French women. There is a perceptible respect for academic work, in contrast with disdain for what many perceive as non-scholarly activism. Diallo has spoken and written about colourism and published a cartoon about afro hair, as French society views natural hair as unprofessional. However, both women continue to contribute to debates about French identities, tackling questions of race and racial discrimination in a country that continues to claim colour blindness.

One of many unspoken preoccupations in French society is colourism and dual-heritage bodies. The problematic word *métis*, which could be translated as 'dual-heritage person', aligns with the exoticisation of black and dual-heritage female bodies in France. The nation's supposed colour blindness is contradicted by examples of racial branding. Scholar Myriam Cottias has shown how dual-heritage women in plantations used and circumvented power as a technique for resistance and survival.[4] In twentieth- and twenty-first-century France, the figure of the *métis* remains an object of desire, pitching black and brown women against each other. From blatant hierarchisation in Afro-Caribbean communities between light- and dark-skinned women to skin-lightening products widely used by black African European women, light skin is a currency that has enabled many instances of socio-economic advancement both within and outside of the black community. The *métis* crosses borders which alleviate the colour anxiety that is embedded into French society.

Overall, French Afrofeminism has challenged perceptions about the power of the majority group in defining identities. People thought to be on the margins have redefined the contours of Frenchness and feminism at both social and political levels. This was exemplified by the atrocious campaign against member of parliament Christiane Taubira, the first black woman to be appointed Minister of Justice in France, who was subjected to racist abuse by far-right groups.[5]

Race and gender stereotypes also, paradoxically, play a role in the superficial social cohesion of French society. In 2008, the French football team counted African European superstars such as Zinedine Zidane and Lilian Thuram among its players. However, Zidane's African roots are never discussed. His parents are of Algerian descent, but like most members of the North African community in France, his identity is defined as 'Arab', a term that has become both an insult and a source of pride for young French men and women of North African descent. Rarely do children of North African heritage claim their African roots. Instead, they often specifically emphasise their parents' or grand-parents' country of origin. They are French Algerians, French Moroccans or French Tunisians, or they identify as 'Marseillais', 'Lyonnais', 'Bordelais' or 'Parisiens'. Africa is viewed as an abstract concept, and does not clearly appear in the way they define themselves. Well-known French football player Lilian Thuram's connections to Africa seem more obvious. He was born in Guadeloupe, a French overseas territory, and grew up in France. A football prodigy, Thuram played for a series of increas-ingly prestigious clubs.

Numerous studies have demonstrated the unifying aspects of football and various other collective sports. However, football in France, the 1998 World Cup in particular, has brought to the surface aspects of French society's relationship with race and gender that are not often debated openly. The hyper-visibility of black bodies was and still is articulated around a series of stereotypes. The dark-skinned black man is seen as a 'natural' at tasks that require physical strength. In France, questions of race, identity and citizenship have recurred in sports. Notable incidents range from attacks by Jean-Marie Le Pen, founder of the far-right National Front, on French black football players in the 1990s to blatantly racist comments from newspapers and television programmes about black French figure skating champion Surya Bonaly.

Bonaly's outstanding performances led her to win national, European and world championships. Yet many were more preoccupied by the fact that she represented France as a black woman. The underlying insinuation was that a French person could not be black, and that if he or she was that information needed to stay within the confines of the Hexagon or in French overseas territories. Bonaly's nationality was difficult to dispute. She was born in Nice, in the south of France, and was adopted by a white French family. For a very long time it was believed that she was born in La Réunion, a French territory, but this story had been made up by her coach so that she would appear more exotic. French society had difficulty accepting that one could be both born in France and black. Exoticising Bonaly through her place of birth was a way to gain acceptance and support from those who were nostalgic about the French colonial empire. As Félix Germain and Silyane Larcher have noted, black French citizens are often referred to as people *issus de l'immigration* ('from an immigrant background') 'as if white French citizens were not also issus de l'immigration', with the implication that 'whites are natives, but people of African descent are not'.[6]

The eroticisation and exoticisation of black women are also part of the racial identifiers that shape interactions in French society. These two markers function as a cement for particularly toxic forms of social cohesion. Over the last decades, the televised election of Miss France has further highlighted the way they are reproduced. A vast majority of young women crowned Miss France have come from overseas territories. According to French society, women can be black and beautiful as long as they conform to an aspect of 'Frenchness' that could be defined as colonially and geographically 'other'. France accepts its 'exotic' citizens as long as they can be placed in French territories away from mainland France. In the last five years or so, there has been an increase in the number of criticisms and abuses directed at Miss France candidates who are black or of dual heritage and born in mainland France. Along with race, the anger has been about the fact that these young women and their families cannot be relegated to overseas territories. Large numbers of white French citizens have expressed their views on social media, claiming that they feel 'invaded' by these families.

This sense of anxiety is reflected in the rising numbers of young men and women who have joined the far right to defend what they see as 'indigenous Europeans'. The group *Les Identitaires* ('The Identitarians') has gathered momentum in various European cities and has managed to raise funds to sail across the Mediterranean, allegedly to protect European borders from illegal vessels carrying African migrants. There was, however, some respite from French racial anxiety when the national football team demonstrated that it could win major championships. In 2018, the recurrent comments from far-right leaders about the French national team were expected, and came. However, the young team won the World Cup and players such as Kylian Mbappé, whose parents are of Algerian and Cameroonian descent, or Paul Pogba, whose parents are Guinean, suddenly became French and nothing else. In fact, there were even displays of anger when their origins were mentioned in the French media. Some of the players saw themselves as French first and foremost, while African supporters insisted that their talents had origins in Africa. However, the essentialisation of identity through citizenship is an old trope that does not remove racism from the equation. The black players had performed the assigned racist role of physically capable black bodies, as well as fulfilling society's expectations of 'good immigrants'.

Although those stereotypes permeate French society, a pushback is nevertheless visible in the way young Afro-French individuals claim their Frenchness. From Mwasi to the seven women who spoke to academic Mame-Fatou Niang and filmmaker Kaytie Nielsen in their documentary film *Mariannes noires* (2015), change is on its way. The seven interviewees in *Mariannes noires* shared with Niang their experiences as black women in France, as well as their fears, their hopes and how they defined themselves. They all felt French and refused to be relegated to the roles of second-class citizens or exotic beings that were sometimes assigned to them. They also all fought against stereotypes on a regular basis, and had learnt or were trying to learn to deal with the strain of challenging the boundaries set for them. When I asked Niang at an event in 2018 to explain how these experiences related to her own trajectory, she stated that the idea for the film was born out of frustration. The lack of representations of black women's experiences in twenty-first-century literature, media, academia and so on incited the need to tell their stories, and by extension her story. These women came from very different backgrounds, and yet they had all reached their goals and were incredibly successful in their fields. They troubled the misconceptions held by many about black women's role in and contribution to French society. They had refused to be silenced and continued to push discriminatory boundaries at all levels and in different settings.

Niang is an associate professor at Carnegie Mellon University in Pittsburgh, USA. France's inability to support many talented black men and women has led a noticeable number of them to immigrate elsewhere in the last twenty years—in particular to the United States, where a vibrant community of researchers is working on the history of people of African descent as well as critical race theory and the intersection of race, class, gender and religion. The work of black French feminists, however, is studied by scholars whose research relates to their experiences. From academic Audrey Celestine's beautifully interwoven colonial and postcolonial family history, spanning three different continents from the 1930s to the present day, to the books for children by writer Laura Nsafou, to writing by young poet and activist Kiyémis and many others, a new generation of powerful Afrofeminist voices has emerged. These women want the experiences, publications and intellectual journeys of previous Afrofeminists to be acknowledged and widely taught. They also want to narrate their own stories as twenty-first-century citizens, mothers, daughters, sisters and aunts, working in various professions and studying in various environments, in ways they deem relevant. Nsafou and illustrator Barbara Brun have chosen to focus on an area that encapsulates the challenges of difference and the ways othering can break black women's spirits: afro hair. This starts at a very young age, which is why Nsafou chose to write a book for children about a young girl's hair, *Comme un million de papillons noirs* (*Like a Million Black Butterflies*). The book is about dealing with other children's cruelty, but also the way the women in the child's family support her and help her to accept and love herself. It is a story of solidarity between black girls and women.

Body shape, colour and hair are part of the personal realm. They relate to our intimate sense of self, and yet, as Audre Lorde and many others have stated, 'the personal is political'. Afro hair is political. In 2015, five Afro-Finns set up the Good Hair Day, an annual day of celebration of black hair in a country that is failing to properly support and protect its population of African descent against discrimination and racial violence. The architects of the event also wanted to better equip families with the tools to look after their children's hair. Educational and celebratory, the occasion has grown in strength in a context where racist harassment still prevails. Finland is often presented as a model for innovative and successful educational practices. It also has a reputation for strong and efficient policies with regards to gender and sexual violence. However, the 2018 report of the European Union Agency for Fundamental Rights established that Finland had the highest rate of racist harassment within the EU. 63 per cent of respondents in Finland, all people of African descent, stated that they had been harassed in the five years preceding the survey.[7] The report also established that skin colour was the main reason for discrimination in housing and employment. In addition, some people were discriminated against because of the way they dressed, and what their clothes conveyed about their religion. Finland then Ireland were at the top of the list when it came to discrimination based on skin colour and physical attributes.

The issue of hair recurs in all EU member states. *Don't Touch My Hair*, a 2019 book by dual-heritage broadcaster Emma Dabiri, moves from the personal experience of Dabiri's upbringing in Ireland and the pain of having to define and defend herself because of the nature of her hair to the history and social and cultural ramifications of afro hair. Dabiri's inquiry is a valuable addition to a long line of scholarship on afro hair, and in particular the way it has been used by black activists, from Angela Davis and the Black Panthers in America to Olive Morris in Britain. Visibly wearing one's hair in an afro style connotes a refusal to conform to Western beauty standards and a celebration of one's heritage. Similarly to skin lightening products, however, afro hair is also a multi-billion-pound industry. The politics of representation have economic implications. Afro hair is also the battleground for debates about colourism within the African diaspora. Curly dual-heritage hair faces discrimination from the white community, but many within the black community deem it more appealing than the hair of single-heritage individuals. Attraction and repulsion regarding afro hair vary within communities, but when the personal becomes political then afro hair becomes a tool to fight prejudice and exclusion, as shown by Michelle De Leon, who founded World Afro Day in 2017. De Leon's work also informs discussions about cases of discrimination against afro hair in British schools. She and others have shown that beneath school hair policies lie several discriminatory practices. Schoolchildren are routinely denied the right to wear braids, locks or other hairstyles that are common in African-Caribbean communities, which has posed a number of problems for parents and guardians of African descent.[8]

Afro hair is one of many areas that have been the focus of pan-European and global collaborations between various groups of African descent. The experiences of African Europeans vary greatly, and reflect both the societies they live in and the legacies of the European colonial past. The way these communities approach questions related to their heritage also vary. However, the commonality of their experiences and their sense of belonging to communities located beyond national borders has brought them together and prompted a call for action. A transnational body, the European Network of People of African Descent (ENPAD), has been gathering information on initiatives and reports about African Europeans in twenty-first-century Europe. It is an important platform for information sharing, as well as discussion about coordinated actions to be taken at national and European levels. One of its stated aims is 'support, empowerment and enabling black people to organise in self defined spaces throughout Europe'.[9] ENPAD also supports policymakers by ensuring that they have access to a number of relevant reports, especially in countries where reporting about discriminatory practices is inconsistent.

For example, a report on stop and search police practices in Spain corroborates word of mouth stories about the relationship of the Spanish police with minority ethnic communities. The harrowing reports demonstrate that stop and search for no valid reason is widely accepted by the majority group. In fact, it is one of many ways the police force shows that it values white bodies above all else. The report found that, according to the police, racial profiling reassures the majority group even when there is no evidence of danger. Yet the practice also propagates the idea that there must be a need to profile specific communities. In 2015, the last year that police data about stop and search in Spain is available, 6,550,422 police identifications were conducted. To put things into perspective, the report argues, this needs to be compared with 1.2 million stop and searches conducted in England and Wales in 2011–12.[10] Police impunity in public spaces has rendered these places unsafe for most minority ethnic groups in Spain. Abuses are often left unreported, even when there are testimonies. Reporting abuse from the police often means reporting to the very same unit that one is complaining about. Constant stop and search also leads to anxiety in public spaces. The communities targeted experience constant fear, leading to changes in the way they apprehend certain places. For example, the recurrent theme in interviews is that one has to avoid train and bus stations and that public transport, generally speaking, is unsafe.

The scale of stop and search policing in Spain amounts to public harassment. Stop and searches are always conducted in public, and the humiliation of those targeted is enhanced by the lack of support from the majority group. They can last from ten to thirty minutes and one is expected to fully collaborate, unpacking and displaying one's belongings. Afro-Spanish groups do not simply denounce those practices, but have also advocated a number of solutions and alternative good practices that could improve the situation. For example, the report mentions initiatives such as 'evidence-led policing' which aim to identify stop and search practices. For example, police officers are asked to fill out a stop form in order to identify bias, and to undertake various forms of training. Such proposals were successful in several places in the country, including the city of Madrid. Yet a new coalition government came into power in 2019 and decided to discontinue the project.

The discrimination faced by the Afro-Spanish is by no means uncommon in the rest of Europe. In Greece, for example, people of African descent are often believed to be part of a new wave of migrants who are crossing the Mediterranean. The appalling treatment of these populations has gone unrecorded for many years. The narratives of those who are not newcomers, with parents who have been in Greece for a long time, are little known outside the country. Figures such as Christos, the black man who was a model for several Greek painters in the nineteenth century, have been forgotten. Greece has other stories to tell about African Europeans.

The experiences of many Afro-Greeks who have been living in the country for centuries came to be known by the Greek population and by other African Europeans when Alexandra Tzavella interviewed black Greeks from Avato, a village in the Xanthi region in north-east Greece, in 2014. The oldest interviewee was eighty-five years old. The origins of Avato's inhabitants are unclear, but it is likely that their ancestors were the servants of the Ottoman beys, or governors, and were left behind when the Ottoman Empire was defeated. These populations became Greek citizens in 1923. Later, a new wave of black soldiers or mercenaries from Sudan may have come to the region and settled in the village after the First World War. 85-year-old Hakic Mehmetoglu recalled what he was told about his ancestors' origins and Ottoman connections. Dual-heritage Rasim Raim talked about his grandfather from Sudan and his mother from the Caucasus. Others, such as 41-year-old Ogun Sabri, the father of dual-heritage daughter Merve Sabri, also shared their stories. Ogun had married and had children with a Moldavian woman. Many black Greeks who have ventured away from Avato have been mistaken for immigrants and asked to provide identification, or have ended up in police stations before being released after demonstrating that they were Greek. The village was not mixed for centuries because beys chose their servants' spouses and only allowed them to marry people who looked like them. Avato's first mixed marriage took place in the 1990s.

Beyond the village, the idea of black Greece really entered the minds of ordinary Greeks when the story of basketball player Giannis Antetokounmpo came to be widely known both in and outside Greece.[11] He was born in 1994 in Athens, to Nigerian parents who had immigrated to Greece in search of a better life. Without legal documents to stay in the country, they lived under the radar of Greek authorities for decades and had four sons there. They had been forced to leave their oldest child in Nigeria when they moved to Europe. Parents and children lent a hand bringing in food for the table. The boys would sell various accessories on the street, while both parents accepted every job opportunity that arose. For eighteen years Giannis and his brothers were officially stateless, even though at the age of twelve Giannis had been spotted by a talent coach and trained as a basketball player in Greece. Young Giannis was an outstanding player courted by NBA clubs in the USA, but he could not travel. After years of petitioning, he was granted a passport and the Greek citizenship that allowed him to play for the NBA. Giannis thrived in the USA and came back to Athens as a hero. He is still a top player for the Milwaukee Bucks. Giannis's trajectory encompasses a strong family unit and work ethic whereby two boys—Giannis and his older brother Thanasis—trained together and motivated each other for years. Thanasis is a well-known basketball player himself, and is also playing for the Milwaukee Bucks in the NBA.

Afro-Greeks whose parents immigrated to the country have founded several organisations to support those who often live at the margins of Greek society and yet have contributed to it economically, socially and culturally. Racism and discrimination are rife in Greece, much as they are in the rest of Europe. To fight these problems, Generation 2.0 was set up, a non-profit organisation led by 'second-generation' immigrants in Greece. Through campaigning, hosting cultural activities and debates and informing policymakers and the general public about issues of citizenship, immigration, discrimination and integration, the organisation has played a crucial role in supporting generations of immigrants. It is the result of combined efforts by the children of immigrants who initially established the organisation in 2006. The impact of such organisations on the daily lives of African Europeans is difficult to measure, but they remain an important point of contact and provide information and answers to questions or controversies that regularly emerge in popular debates. For example, in April 2018 Generation 2.0 debunked myths and fears about the 'Greekization' of migrants, reminding the media that a term usually applied to food was not meant to be used for people.[12] The organisation also publicised Afro-Greeks' experiences of attacks and discrimination, their aspirations, and simply their daily lives. For instance, in sharing Giannis's response to verbal and racially motivated abuses from a Greek journalist who was targeting his older brother Thanasis in

November 2018, Generation 2.0 wanted to demonstrate that fame and a successful career did not erase racism and flawed perceptions about what it means to be Greek.[13]

Racism is not simply a popularly debated issue within the realm of the spoken and written word, however; it also kills. In 2017, nine men were arrested for beating a young African American named Bakari Henderson to death. Henderson, a college graduate from Texas, had gone to Greece to work on a photography shoot for a clothing line. A selfie with a female bartender had resulted in a number of men attacking, chasing and ultimately murdering him. An extraordinarily disappointing judgement and subsequent sentencing charges showed that racism was still at play. Five of the Serbian men arrested received five to ten years in prison. The bar's bouncer, a British citizen of Serbian origin, received fifteen years for causing Henderson's death. However, the Greek bartender and two other men were released, even though they had been convicted for assault. Bakari Henderson never stood a chance of survival. His parents were devastated and warned African Americans and black people in general against travel to Greece.

Stories of assaults on black people travelling across Europe are not unusual, particularly in Eastern European countries. The Twitter hashtag #travellingwhileblack is used to document such experiences, a reference to the *Green Book* first published in 1936 by the National Association for the Advancement of Colored People (NAACP) to help African Americans avoid places that were dangerous for them after the passage of the Jim Crow laws. Racism has often been attributed in part to a lack of education about the history of people of African descent.

Afrophobia in many countries cannot be erased simply through training and education. However, its impact can be mitigated by awareness about questions of diversity. African Europeans are not demanding to be loved by their employers, but to be respected for the work they provide and for their contributions to various companies and institutions. A few organisations have set out to provide solutions to endemic problems such as a lack of diversity in the workplace. In 2019, Generation 2.0 published a comprehensive document titled 'Employer's Guide'. The aim was to provide employers with tools to look at the issue of diversity. However, before going into what is required from employers, the organisation started from migrants' point of view by looking at the reasons they were in the country and the legal framework that allowed or denied them citizenship or employment. Documents about diversity have often focused on cultural differences and on how to overcome them to make the workplace a more inclusive place. This document proposes to define briefly concepts of diversity, acculturation and so on, but it also focuses on the historical, social and psychological reasons for migration and their implications for those who chose or were forced to travel to Greece.[14] These issues are not specific to African Europeans but they inform their experiences. African Europeans are also part of a broader network of migration narratives and histories of settlement and integration. In this context, intercommunity collaborations are vital. Partnerships and comparisons can capture commonalities and differences in the treatment and perception of minority ethnic groups across Europe.

Stories of intercultural collaboration are at the heart of the history of African Europeans in Britain. The terminology used in Britain, such as 'black British', encapsulates a shift in emphasis from people's country of origin to their Britishness. In France, one is French of X or Y country of origin. In Britain one is black, Asian, white, and so on, British. Ethnicity rather than country of origin is foregrounded. It means that people of African descent are grouped under the racialised term 'black'. The wording of such classification has been widely accepted but not necessarily approved by most of the population. Challenging this terminology and reimagining ways of telling the history of black Britons necessitates an understanding of the history of black presence on the island.

The notion of 'black presence' needs to be briefly analysed. Seemingly unobtrusive and pertaining to racialist discourse, it appears to acknowledge visible biological differences without bringing to the surface any idea of inequality. However, the number of research volumes that map out black presence in given spaces across several periods often acknowledge the existence and the contributions of black people in those settings. They open the door to stories that have been considered unimportant in national or local narratives. In this sense, such research is resolutely anti-racist, drawing on a long anti-racist tradition of storytelling. From oral histories of resistance from the sixteenth to the nineteenth centuries to organised activism and scholarly production, anti-racists have worked to fight against discrimination and all forms of oppression, whether they were acknowledged or not in European national histories. Those national silences strongly suggest a hierarchisation of histories and a prioritisation of those deemed worthy of attention. They also suggest that racialism has failed to fight against racism, as have those opposed to racialism. As Goldberg asks:

> Is antiracialism a counter to claims about biology, or a counter to a social/cultural set of articulations, a mode of expression or its lack, a sense of naturalized entitlement or historically ordered incapacity? Antiracism, by contrast, conjures a stance against an imposed condition, or set of conditions, an explicit refusal or a living of one's life in such a way one refuses the imposition, whether one is a member of the subjugated population or the subjugating one.[15]

The absence of black stories in most British history books prior to the Second World War sheds some light on the question of racism by omission. Utilitarian views on the usefulness of imperial subjects and black and brown bodies demonstrate that they were not seen as part of the national experience. They were useful, and then they were forgotten. One could argue that given the low number of black Britons, they were likely to be excluded from grand narratives. Yet one could also argue that there was a relatively low number of white Britons in comparison to indigenous populations across the British Empire, and yet their stories have been widely researched and shared.[16]

The historical amnesia of these omissions is in fact a blanket which hides a history of violence. The destruction of the collective history and memories of the other is part of a racial war that never truly ended. As Goldberg notes, 'Race ... has been an enduring occupation of modernity. Its structural legacy, institutional articulation, and social implications have lingered despite racial conception becoming less pressed or formally elaborated ... In short, race is now circulated more readily and openly in private spheres than in formal public ones.'[17]

Post-war Britain, however, has remedied these lacks in its national historiography. The multicultural project of the 1980s and 1990s, influenced by anti-apartheid movements, presented several countries with the opportunity to redefine racial discrimination. A series of race-related riots, and subsequent race relations acts, provided the terrain for a new racial contract. Britain abandoned claims of colour blindness for a stronger stance on racial inequality.

Numerous books have been dedicated to aspects of the black presence in Britain. From the stories of Roman soldiers defending Hadrian's Wall in the third century BCE to post-war migration narratives, Peter Fryer has covered an array of topics centred on the experiences of people of African descent. Other outputs, such as the pioneering scholarship of Onyeka Nubia, James Walvin's *longue durée* study, Miranda Kaufman's engaging work and the reinterpretation of the fascinating John Blanke by Michael Ohajuru, have looked extensively at black Tudors in England.[18]

From Eric Williams, S. I. Martin, Arthur Torrington, Gretchen Gerzina, Kennetta Hammond Perry and Marc Matera, who have looked at black presence in specific places such as London, to the extensive work of Stuart Hall and Paul Gilroy, scholars of post-slavery societies have examined the interactions, social changes and race relations of post-war Britain. A particularly interesting approach to black presence in twentieth- and twenty-first-century Britain is demonstrated by testimonies which start with personal experiences in the form of autobiography and shift to salient questions about identity and the sense of alienation or belonging in Britain today. In *Black and British: A Forgotten History* (2017), David Olusoga places his research in the context of his own family and their roots in Nigeria and the north of England. Writer and musician Akala's *Natives: Race and Class in the Ruins of Empire* and journalist Afua Hirsch's *Brit(ish): On Race, Identity and Belonging*, both published in 2018, offer deeply insightful analysis of a contemporary Britain fascinated by far-right ideology and unaware of its history of subjugation and discrimination, despite key markers such as the 1980s riots and subsequent reports, Stephen Lawrence's tragic death, the struggle for justice of Baroness Doreen Lawrence, and the Stephen Lawrence Report, with its ramifications for policing.

Twenty-first-century debates about racism seem to follow a pattern of justification, guilt and ahistorical mythmaking about a glorious past. The debate has become incredibly polarised, with historians, sociologists, activists and social commentators attempting to explain the past and include these histories in the school curriculum on one side, and on the other politicians and social commentators, with sympathy for far-right movements in some cases, determined to present a whitewashed past that centres around the Second World War and aims to incite nostalgia for empire in the majority population. The media input from black British journalists has been crucial in debunking certain myths and exploring the issues that lie at the heart of inequality. From far-right interactions with black communities to the Grenfell tragedy, the Windrush scandal and the pay gap for British women academics from minority ethnic backgrounds, Gary Younge, Rianna Croxford, Nadine White, Seren Jones, Charlie Brinkhurst-Cuff and many others have been quick to bring to the surface stories that would not have usually reached the general public.

Beyond written and broadcast media, one of the most effective ways of telling the evolving story of black British identities has been music and the visual arts. The contemporary black British cultural scene is highly visual and almost tactile. The 2017 Turner Prize winner, artist Lubaina Himid, uses deceptively festive characters to tell the complex stories of African Europeans, presenting us with human beings interacting, travelling, going about their daily lives and surviving. Himid has the ability to convey joy and movement, and establishes the history of African Europeans in ways that leave the viewer free to interpret the artist's vision as they see fit. Moving away from the academy to represent beauty and fashion in extra-academic communities, encompassing both the mundanity and the pain of human experience, Himid has blurred several boundaries while reinterpreting the story of the nation. Her ability to generate discussions at workshops and consciously listen to what audiences have to say, sometimes letting silences settle, allowing timid audience members to take the time and space they need, have shown how a visual dialogue can be established between artist and viewer beyond the art object or installation. It is almost as though Himid uses conversations about her projects to guide the creative process for subsequent pieces. A professor of contemporary arts at the University of Central Lancashire, the scholar and artist has masterfully brought together scholarly production, art and education.

AFRICAN EUROPEANS

A younger generation of artists have taken matters into their own hands when it comes to telling the various stories of Britain's past and present. In Bristol, artist Michele Curtis wanted the community of St Paul's to remember the elders who founded St Paul's Carnival in 1968. Over the last decades, funding for the carnival has dramatically decreased and some deprived areas in Bristol have seen residents leaving to settle in more affluent parts of the city once they have climbed the social ladder. However, the heart of that particular community has been shaped by the stories of key figures such as the Honourable Owen Henry, Delores Campbell, Carmen Beckford, Roy Hackett, Audley Evans, Clifford Drummond and Barbara Dettering. Curtis decided to paint their portraits on a grand scale, on the side of several buildings in St. Paul's. The project has been met with enthusiasm and widely applauded across the city. It is an homage to black elders who settled in Bristol and made an outstanding contribution to the city while sharing their multiple identities through the carnival. Beyond celebration and recognition, Curtis's work situates the history of black Britons in an urban landscape while further adding to Bristol's reputation as a creative hub. Curtis represents a generation of black British artists who claim urban spaces and are able to reach audiences that might not usually be interested in art or think that their voices matter. *The Seven Saints of St. Paul's* (#SevenSaintsofStPauls) is an engaged and powerful artwork that establishes a dialogue between Bristol's inhabitants away from the city's recognised museum. It is an invitation to search for new ways and opportunities to tell the histories of black Britons, and by extension African Europeans.

While the intergenerational projects of visual artists such as Curtis have appealed to a broad community, within and outside of Bristol, musicians in Britain have also been able to attract a wide audience. A specific genre of music called grime has been in the limelight over the last few years. Grime music was born in the 2000s. It combines electronic music with hip hop and the use of four beats to a bar. Sociologist Monique Charles looks at the crafting of its beats, its lyrics, and the experiences it shares.[19] Charles has also studied how grime has shifted racial boundaries as a marker of urban youth identities, and how grime artists and audiences are reacting to the criminalisation of both grime music and young people racialised as black.[20] grime music describes the experiences of young Britons living in deprived areas, and the means many find to survive. Injunctions banning grime artists from performing in Britain in 2019 have had an impact on those whose main artistic expression takes place through music. Rather than protecting communities from gang-related offences and gun and knife crime, the criminalisation of Drill music, a sub-genre of grime, can be interpreted as part of an arsenal that further marginalises young black Britons and in some instances pushes them back into a lifestyle that they are trying to escape through their music. Artists such as Krept and Konan have utilised these barriers to facilitate their creativity. Krept and Konan's song 'Ban Drill' clearly demonstrates how one's life can be changed through music, and the missed opportunities and waste of potential that these bans can cause.

From pioneers such as Wiley, Skepta, JME and Dizzee Rascal to a new generation of award-winning artists such as Stormzy and Dave, the grime scene remains open to talent from across the country. Artists such as Bugzy Malone and Aitch from Manchester or JayKae and Lady Leshurr from Birmingham have shown how grime musicians transcend regional boundaries while telling regional stories. These artists have reached national fame, while others such as Ocean Wisdom have attained a large fanbase both in the UK and across Europe. It is important to note that the grime scene remains overwhelmingly male-dominated, with notable exceptions such as Little Simz, Ms Banks and Stefflon

Don. Pressure to sexualise themselves might be a strong deterrent for young female artists.

Intergenerational musical collaborations have enhanced the genre. Pioneer Skepta supported young artist AJ Tracey by releasing a song with him, showing a continuity and unity that often goes unnoticed by many within the majority group who see grime as simply an expression of youth anger. Some grime artists have also appeared in acclaimed UK television series *Top Boy*. The series gained a large audience for two seasons and was aired on one of the main national television broadcasters, Channel 4. After its second season in 2013 it was cancelled, much to the disappointment of Canadian rapper Drake. He was instrumental in the revival of the show for a third season on Netflix, becoming its executive producer and demonstrating that despite a lack of support for black British artists, their creativity does not go unnoticed at the international level.

In fact, Britain has provided Hollywood with a number of black British actors who have changed the way Britain is perceived, tearing down the classic image of an exclusively white upper-class Britain. These actors range from well-known names such as Idris Elba, Oscar nominee Chiwetel Ejiofor, David Oyelowo, *Star Wars* actor John Boyega and Daniel Kaluuya from the Academy Award-winning film *Get Out* to the up-and-coming *Top Boy* and *Blue Story* star Micheal Ward. Few black female actors from Britain have reached international fame. However, young actresses such as Naomie Harris, who starred in Oscar-winning movie *Moonlight*, and Letitia Wright of *Top Boy* and *Black Panther* have received international recognition.

Black British artists have contributed to the creative industry in various ways. Over the last few years, some of them have crossed the boundaries of their disciplines. Rapman was a storyteller and an MC before moving into filmmaking and becoming a national sensation when he created the three-part YouTube series *Shiro's Story* in 2018. He then went on to make his debut feature film *Blue Story*, which stirred controversy due to reports of violence at Vue screenings. Negative perceptions about young black Brits led the chain to remove the film from their cinemas. However, a national outcry forced Vue to bring *Blue Story* back to some of their screens.

Beyond the artistic arena, black Britons have also made significant contributions to debate about social issues, with a strong impact on the way social movements are envisaged. From the Rhodes Must Fall movement in Oxford, which started in South Africa, to protests about decolonising the curriculum and debates around the question of academic representation in the classroom, black Britons have forced certain institutions in the country to rethink how they deal with questions of diversity within and outside the academic arena. These debates were further enhanced by high-profile developments such as the appointment of the first black professor of history in the UK, Hakim Adi. Adi has written extensively on Pan-Africanism, Caribbean and Asian histories and black Britons. Collaborative work within and outside the academy has shaped his intellectual engagement, but recognition was slow to come in British academia despite his internationally recognised scholarship.

Student protests, demands for a change in national mentality and the refusal to accept a history that does not fully represent Britain have been at the core of recent black British activism. Yet the last ten years have seen significant political changes. Support for multiculturalism and a desire to rewrite the 'island story' have led to stronger resistance from various communities, including the African Caribbean community in Britain. The 2012 Olympic Games opening ceremony in London showcased Britain as a beautifully diverse country, but the Grenfell Tower tragedy, the Windrush scandal, the bitter debate about Brexit, and media narratives of a white working class that have been left behind in opposition to their black and Asian counterparts show that Britain in 2020 has challenges to overcome.[21] However, what is certain for black and African European British communities is that turning back the wheel of time and relinquishing the rights Darcus Howe, Altheia Jones-LeCointe, Toyin Agbetu and many others, fought to achieve is not an acceptable option.

The extent of the Windrush scandal's impact on British society continues to surprise the nation. In 2018, it was revealed that people had been detained and deported at a national scale, sometimes to countries they had never set foot in, by the UK Home Office. Most of those people had arrived before 1973 and were British subjects at the time of their birth. They were part of what was named the Windrush Generation, in reference to the Empire Windrush, the ship that brought African Caribbean men and women to Britain to help rebuild the country after the Second World War.[22] In 2020, the scale of the scandal is still being uncovered, and even though a compensation scheme was set up by the government the small numbers of those who have been able to access it, and the irreparable damage done to generations of people who have suffered economic and social hardship and ongoing mental illness, continue to be minimised and at times dismissed by the UK government.

At the time of the scandal the home secretary Amber Rudd, appointed by then prime minister Theresa May, resigned, but the 'hostile environment' policy that characterised the approach of successive Conservative governments is still being enforced by May's successor Boris Johnson.[23] New scandals have emerged related to Home Office practices, such as the regular deportation of young people who came to the country as children or teenagers, with many left in limbo over the question of citizenship. These experiences are illustrated by the poignant story of 28-year-old Chadwick Jackson, who arrived in Britain at the age of ten. A talented young filmmaker with a promising career,

Chadwick has been unable to work and forced to report to the Home Office on a weekly basis while struggling to find funds to support his legal case against deportation.[24]

For many people from Black British communities, the way forward is to continue demanding a clearer stance from the government about the practices of the hostile environment, and to push for a more comprehensive and rigorous presentation of the country's past and present which includes the histories of people of African descent in the overall narrative of British history, as well as target measures to fight against poverty and exclusion in all communities. Should governments fail to meet these demands, the African-Caribbean community will continue to work towards them regardless, with strong intercommunity support. Contemporary Britain's outlook on intercommunity collaboration has shifted. Minority groups such as British Asians and black Britons, amongst many others, have been working together on issues that are dear to them for decades. This has been the case in multiple areas, with artists, academics and activists finding creative and engaging means to produce and share knowledge while fighting against social inequalities and discrimination, and advocating for reforms of the prison and sentencing system. In addition, various members of these minority communities have asked successive governments to address mental health issues and provide greater support to young people and single parents.

Black British communities have also been working with other African Europeans over the last few years. Sociologists such as Kehinde Andrews, Camilla Hawthorne and Stephen Small, working in Britain, Europe and America, have organised annual summer schools with a focus on black Europeans for many years. Small has also written widely on the black presence in Europe. Scholar and activist Nathaniel Adam Tobias Coleman has brought together European and African diasporic voices in a series of powerful conversations at UCL, Oxford and Bristol. Artist Johny

Pitts's recent book *Afropean* is a beautiful invitation to acknowledge and share the life stories of several African Europeans in various cities. Black female contributions to social and cultural issues and academic debates have also been remarkably rich. A 2020 exhibition of portraits of academics from the Black Female Professors Forum at London's City Hall, curated by Nicola Rollock and photographed by Bill Knight, encompassed outstanding thinkers such as Heidi S. Mirza, Stella Dadzie and the first black woman to receive the prestigious Man Booker Prize, Bernardine Evaristo. From the literary to the academic world, black women continue to bring their unique experiences to the table.[25] Black British women are standing on the shoulders of those who paved the way for black female voices in the UK, including Claudia Jones, Olive Morris, Baroness Doreen Lawrence and politicians Baroness Valerie Amos, Diane Abbott and Dawn Butler at a national level, and women doing outstanding work at regional and local levels such as Asher Craig, Cleo Lake, Jendayi Serwah, Sado Jirde, Marti Burgess, Marie-Annick Gournet, Peaches Golding, Latoya McAllister, Rebecca Scott and many others.[26]

These women and many others are celebrated and acknowledged in the remarkable work, both high profile and smaller scale, carried out by black activists, scholars, artists, hairdressers, business owners, mothers, sisters, daughters and grandmothers, from all walks of life and all across the country. All of these women are constantly reshaping the narratives of isolation, single parenthood and pain that people may associate with black women. Black women in Britain are taking up space, as exemplified by the popular self-help guidebook of that name for black girls and women published in 2019 by Chelsea Kwankye and Ore Ogunbiyi, or the scholarly work produced by Denise Noble, Lisa Palmer or Akwugo Emejulu. Black women have also been at the forefront of debates on issues that have not been tackled within the black community in Britain, as typified by the interventions of black feminist Jade Bentil on the subject of working class black women's activism.[27] Others, like psychologist Guilaine Kinouani and actress, entrepreneur and dancer Kelechi Okafor, use social media to share ideas and challenge everyday racism. These women speak at festivals and write about gender and equality, community activism, sexual orientation and discrimination. Phyllis Akua Opoku-Gyimah (or Lady Phyll) cofounded UK Black Pride, and Paula Akpan and Nicole Krystal founded the first Black Girl Festival in London in 2017.

Black European women can therefore be found in all arenas, as activists and as scholars. These women are refusing to talk about race in apologetic ways when they are often on the receiving end of racial harassment. They are occupying places that were not assigned to them, in some instances leaving areas in which they thrived to become social and political commentators. One example is Bonnie Greer, who was born in the USA and made Britain her home over three decades ago.[28] Black British identity is multiple. It is not constructed solely around the heritage of one's ancestors or parents, but is also intertwined with one's partner, one's home and the effects of resettling and building a new life. It is about the notion of home and a sense of belonging. One can feel both African American and Black British, as demonstrated by the lives of women such as Greer. A notable number of African Americans settled in Europe and were able to reach fame in Paris through their connections to the world of entertainment. Other men and women found a propitious terrain in Europe for mobilising groups to fight for social justice and against racism. Ollie Harrington, William Gardner Smith, James Baldwin, Audre Lorde and Jean Sindab have spent years in Paris, London, Berlin, Switzerland and elsewhere.

Other African American women came to the attention of the media because of their political engagement. Such was the case for North Carolina-born Jean McNair. Following in the footsteps of Black Panthers Roger Holder and Catherine Kerkow, 25-year-old Jean and her husband Melvin, accompanied by their two young children and four other Americans, hijacked a Delta Air Lines plane in Detroit in 1972 with the aim of reaching Algeria, where the Black Panthers had established their headquarters. They arrived in Algeria and obtained ransom money from Delta, but the collaboration with Algerian authorities turned out to be disappointing for the couple, and for all Panthers who had moved to the country. Eventually they all left, and the McNairs took the difficult decision to send their children to their family in the United States while they moved to France. Tyler Stovall contends that post-1968 France was a place of activism, close-knit collaborations and practical support for people from all backgrounds and various political factions. He writes: 'The McNairs' clandestine move to Paris had been facilitated in part by the French organization Solidarity, a small and diverse group of left-wing activists founded by the dynamic and mercurial Henri Curiel.'[29] Curiel was instrumental in Jean's early intellectual journey with regards to political engagement and theory.

Eventually the couple and a few other hijackers were arrested. The United States asked for an extradition; the French court refused but they had to trial them in France, as required by international law. The hijackers were sentenced to five years in prison, but the two women, Jean McNair and Joyce Tillerson, were released on the grounds that they had to look after their children. The McNairs eventually moved to Normandy and Jean continued her life of social engagement, working with young people. Tyler Stovall's encounters with Jean McNair provide us with precious information about her life, and reveal her extraordinary commitment to social justice. They also show how Jean transformed from an African American expatriate to a Frenchwoman. Stovall has studied the transnational dimension of Jean's story, and notes that 'to write about McNair as a black

Frenchwoman is to take seriously a transnational perspective on French history and contemporary life.'[30] Her life clearly brings to the surface the wide network of post-slavery transnational collaborations that had their roots in Pan-Africanism, interwar anti-imperialism movements and black radicalism.[31]

The lives of these well-known African American women and men should not, however, obscure those of many others who travelled to Europe as enslaved servants or free black men and women over centuries. Some spent just a few years there, while others made it their home. Some were soldiers who had children and left to return to the United States after the First or Second World War. Many never knew they were parents, and left dual-heritage children who were raised in multicultural cities and communities in London, Cardiff and other places. Black and dual-heritage girls and boys of African American descent are also part of the British history of migration, identity and citizenship. Some of them have been living in multicultural, marginalised enclaves, and have redefined the identity of these places.

Tiger Bay, now known as Butetown or Cardiff Bay, is a vibrant hub where many people from across the globe settled. The place is a palimpsest of histories. These histories have never been forgotten, but they made the national headlines when thousands of people voted in a BBC Wales poll to have a statue of Betty Campbell erected in Cardiff city centre. Betty Campbell passed away at the age of eighty-seven in 2017. She was Wales's first black headteacher. Her firm, fair and warm approach to teaching, as well as her extraordinary dedication to her community and to teaching children from all walks of life, has been the pride and joy of many in Wales. Betty was a committed educator, a music lover and an incredible activist whose background reflected the history of multicultural Wales, black Britain and African Europe. She was born in Cardiff in 1934 to a working-class Welsh Barbadian mother and Jamaican father. Betty grew up, was educated and taught in Cardiff. She was fiercely in love with the city, but was not blind to its inequalities and to the work that needed to be done to improve children's lives. Concerned with education for all children as well as the representation of minority ethnic groups, she believed that one had to be part of advisory or policymaking boards in order to make a positive change. She was a councillor for her ward and became a member of the Race Relations Board (1972–76) and the Home Office Race Advisory Committee. Betty's story is a black Welsh story. There are many other black Welsh, black Scottish and black Northern Irish men and women whose stories are known and whose lives and contributions are yet to be widely shared. Those dedicated black community members are still alive, and have been relentlessly working towards a better present and future for their families and their communities. They have been working to improve the lives of all black men and women in Britain.

EPILOGUE

The history of African Europeans is vibrant and complex, just as it is brutal. It is a collection of experiences that vary greatly from one place to another and across time. All of these histories have shaped the social practices and identities of European communities and continue to do so today. The trajectories of African Europeans are embedded in local architecture, as well as in national and international visual, literary and other cultural productions. From religious artefacts to representations of the magi; from an intellectual in fifteenth-century Granada to the young grime artists of twenty-first-century Britain, African European identities have continuously evolved. While most eighteenth-century African Europeans had to tiptoe around their spaces, reluctant to assert their presence, twenty-first-century French Afrofeminists and other African Europeans are claiming their rights to self-define, reshaping discourses around race, feminism, and their own lives.

This book has attempted to look at a variety of stories across time, while bearing in mind that the term African European cannot encompass or convey all aspects of black and brown people's experiences. The people in this book did not always view themselves within the context of imperialist and capitalist histories of oppression, and the possibilities of defining oneself or analysing one's attempts at self-liberation through writing—while using 'the master's tools', to quote Audre Lorde—could be illusory in understanding the lives presented in this volume. Examining these experiences has demonstrated that for African Europeans to navigate the requirements of the societies in which they were living, the private sphere often remained a mystery. We rarely know, for example, what Olaudah Equiano or Mary Prince truly thought about their fellow abolitionists. We have a better sense of the hopes, and even the exhaustion, of the Nardal sisters through records of their work in various salons and their writings. In contrast, Senegalese-born boxer Battling Siki's tragic life remains difficult to apprehend because we only know what has been written about him. A working-class boxer from a fishing village in Saint Louis was not inclined, or did not have the tools, to teach us about his experiences in the boxing world of the 1920s, whereas we know far more through the media about the twenty-first-century life story of UK and world boxing champion Anthony Joshua. It is important to be well-equipped to share one's life story so that future generations can learn, but the tools used by African Europeans to share knowledge are also highly significant. African Europeans have been creating and sharing knowledge for centuries. They have been transmitting their various cultures in environments that were hostile to them and in ways that were not recognised as valuable by scholars from the Global North.

These trajectories must also be placed in the broader context of both European and African history. The history of Africa is presented here in an oblique way, as most of the stories in this book are about people who left the continent. It is therefore not just about Africa, but about the influence Africa has exerted abroad for several millennia. It is about the impact of a continent on the societies that colonised it and that used its resources and its people to build wealth. This brings us to the question of the legacies of the past, and in this case of European occupation. Africa's mark on Europe was, alongside its raw material, artefacts and plants, mainly visible and long-lasting through its people. Several outstanding histories have been left aside in this volume, but they also need to be remembered. These include, for example, African-born Angelo Soliman, who died an Austrian free-mason in the eighteenth century;[1] Nathaniel Wells, born in Saint Kitts, who became Britain's first black sheriff in Monmouth, Wales in the nineteenth century and died a wealthy man at his residence in the English city of Bath; and the extraordinary life and activism of Newport nurse Vernester Cyril OBE.[2]

The stories of migratory movement from Africa to the Americas and to Europe educate us about the forced contributions of people of African descent. Even 'voluntary' migrations are also forced in many ways, as economic migrants leave their families and culture in search of better lives. What to make of all these histories colliding, and contributing to anxiety amongst some contemporary groups while they are deeply valued by others? These stories should be taught, widely analysed, and valued. They bring us back to our human nature, while also serving as reminders that 'humanity' itself is a shifting concept.

Each section in this book establishes a link between the past and the present. Some individual or collective decisions shape communities' futures, but the bigger story is ultimately what we make of these experiences. The most consistent and longstanding threat to the human species has always been, beside environmental changes, human beings themselves. Yet these human stories have shown that we can also live in a non-exploitative way that diminishes suffering and even increases wellbeing. The decision is ours to make—whether to learn from these experiences, or to ignore them and continue to reproduce destructive patterns of violence and subjugation. The question of race and racial discrimination is central to the lives explored in this book. Twenty-first-century Europe is characterised by a mutation of the concept of race, and of its impact on those whose lives are transformed by various forms of racial oppression. Present-day European societies often see and understand racism as a physically violent act designed to harm the visibly different other. Small acts of violence are often ignored, and yet emerge under the cover of one's private circle, or behind attitudes of 'civility'. As Goldberg concludes:

> Racisms without racism, then, is the peculiar expression of neoliberalizing globalization ... It is the (re-)institutionalizing of racism gone private, the privatizing of institutionalized racisms. Racisms cut off from their historical fertilizer. Racisms born again, renewed. But shorn of the referential language. The wolf in sheep's clothing, speaking of sheep while deeply ambivalent about defanging the wolf.[3]

This volume is an invitation to analyse these experiences and see how one can lead one's life differently. The liberating stories it contains show that collaboration and support will ultimately prevail. As Ornette D. Clennon brilliantly demonstrates, there is power in all forms of black collaboration, from grassroots organisations to scholarly activism.[4] Complete erasure of the past is illusory, because residues lurking in the outskirts of memory and history always resurface. They do so because the histories of marginalised communities have found ways, be it through music, dance, food, arts or sports, to permeate the societies in which they live and have lived. Lived experiences have also been transmitted by these groups through successive generations. However, simply remembering is not the ultimate goal. Triumph against institutionalised brutality, everyday forms of racism and microaggression, poverty, exclusion and marginalisation requires a radical way of using transmitted experience of resistance. It demands a collective degree of consciousness that runs across social, economic, gender and cultural barriers. It entails a renewed and adaptable practice of kinship. It means engaging with black radicalism.

Black radicalism includes movements that have shifted perceptions around definitions of whiteness, white supremacy and notions of white fragility. The movement that best exemplifies those changes is Black Lives Matter. In February 2012, 17-year-old Trayvon Martin was shot while he was visiting his relatives in a gated community in Florida. George Zimmerman, the neighbourhood manager who killed Trayvon, was acquitted after he claimed that he had acted in self-defence. Martin was not armed. Following accounts of the arrest, trial and acquittal, several demonstrations started. The Black Lives Matter movement was created in 2013. Its aim was to fight police and vigilante violence and white supremacy in the United States and to support local black communities.[5] The movement's aims resonated with people of African descent in other European capitals such as Paris, London, Amsterdam and Berlin. However, shifting methods of social and political engagement have reflected the changing nature of white supremacy groups and rhetoric. Black Lives Matter has been portrayed as a disruptive and even a dangerous group on social media, by so-called alt-right or far-right movements, and at times by the conservative media. These counter-narratives highlight the ways that racism and identitarianism work in conjunction when it comes to defining whiteness and the alleged exclusiveness of a European identity.[6]

As we have seen, there is a constant pushback against narratives of exclusion and against self-congratulatory posturing about supposedly post-racial societies. In a 'post-truth' era, social media has played a crucial role in exposing instances of discrimination and killings of black people by ordinary citizens or by the police.[7] Several scholars have dedicated volumes to demonstrating that black people's real lived experiences in America and Europe put paid to claims that racism is characterised only by the killings of black people and that other forms of racial discrimination should be dismissed.[8]

Another development that warrants our attention is the Me Too movement, initiated by African American activist Tarana Burke. Burke had already been working for many years to support victims of sexual violence when she launched the Me Too initiative on MySpace in 2006. She was still working for and with survivors when in 2017 actress Alyssa Milano turned Me Too into the hashtag #MeToo in response to allegations of sexual abuse against film producer Harvey Weinstein. Several articles have been written about the appropriation by white feminists of a movement that was started by a black woman.[9] The erasure of black women's work in the discourse of contemporary feminism was once again at the forefront of debates. When Burke was made aware that her initiative had been used to create the hashtag, she nevertheless offered to support the movement. It gained a global reach that went far beyond the world of entertainment.

In France, the #MeToo hashtag was translated as #balanceton-porc ('denounce your pig'), yet the racial dimension that implicitly accompanied the American movement through Burke's pioneering work had seemingly disappeared from its French counterpart. In light of the history of exoticisation and sexualisation of black women in France, as we have seen in previous chapters, it is hardly surprising that the intersection of race and gender, and the nature of sexual violence directed against black French women, seemed to be absent in French debates about #MeToo. Afrofeminists have bridged that gap and offered a space for black French women to share experiences and attempt to heal. Referring to the 'third wave of feminism', Bibia Pavard notes that 'the development of feminist groups that identify as queer, inclusive, Afrofeminist or Muslim reinforce the idea that the third wave is about a movement that is more interested in having social, racial, sexual and religious differences recognized.'[10] It is about acknowledging that there are multiple feminisms.

We should also examine the movements embodied by young people and students and the role they play in bringing about political, social and cultural changes through education. From the Rhodes Must Fall movement, both in South Africa and the UK, to the British National Union of Students (NUS) initiatives 'Why Is My Curriculum White?', 'Why Isn't My Professor Black', 'Dismantling the Master's House' (#DTMH), and 'Decolonising the Curriculum', several campaigns have proven that the mobilisation of large numbers of students could be instrumental in forcing institutions to reconsider both their curriculum and the staff that teach it.[11] The success of these campaigns has come from within and outside the universities. Grassroots groups and community work have also brought about change. Yet what these campaigns have demonstrated is that fee-paying students do have the means to pressure institutions into rethinking their courses, as historians Meleisa Ono-George and Patrick Vernon have reiterated.[12]

Attempts have also been made by these movements in recent years to tap into community expertise and make full use of local and national community archives.[13] In other European countries, students' mobilisation and activism have taken various forms, and so have the local community houses passionately maintained by black activists.[14] For example, in the Netherlands the Black Archives, an initiative founded by Jessica de Abreu, Mitchell Esajas, Miguel Heilbron and Thiemo Heilbron, is aimed at bringing people of Surinamese and African descent together, along with other communities, to explore and enjoy unique archival material such as the Heilbron and Huiswoud collections or Keti Koti program booklets from 1948 to 1960.[15] The Black Archives are managed by New Urban Collective, a network that brings together students, young professionals and other young people in order to foster dynamic collaborations.

Building on a long history of resistance and black radical thinking, as well as contributing to or initiating campaigns and movements for economic and social justice, African Europeans continue to carve out their place in African and European history and to build new bridges, as we have seen through intergenerational and intercultural collaborations that reach across gender, cultural, and even political, economic and social boundaries. The path to equality needs to be facilitated by access to political power and meaningful representation in all disciplines, industries and institutions. It is a path that we must pave together.

NOTES

INTRODUCTION

1. Some of these are Allison Blakely, *Blacks in the Dutch World: The Evolution of Racial Imagery in a Modern Society*, Indiana University Press, 1993; Hakim Adi (ed.), *Black British History: New Perspectives*, Zed Books, 2019; Stephen Small, *20 Questions and Answers on Black Europe*, Amrit, 2017; Sara Lennox (ed.), *Remapping Black Germany: New Perspectives on Afro-German History, Politics, and Culture*, University of Massachusetts Press, 2016; Trica Danielle Keaton, T. Denean Sharpley-Whiting and Tyler Stovall (eds), *Black France/France Noire: The History and Politics of Blackness*, Duke University Press, 2012; Tiffany N. Florvil and Vanessa D. Plumly (eds), *Rethinking Black German Studies: Approaches, Interventions and Histories*, Peter Lang, 2018; Darlene Clark Hine, Tricia Keaton and Stephen Small (eds), *Black Europe and the African Diaspora*, University of Illinois Press, 2009; Mischa Honeck, Martin Klimke and Anne Kuhlmann (eds), *Germany and the Black Diaspora: Points of Contact, 1250–1914*, Berghahn, 2013; Michael McEachrane (ed.), *Afro-Nordic Landscapes: Equality and Race in Northern Europe*, Routledge, 2014; Dominic Thomas, *Black France: Colonialism, Immigration and Transnationalism*, Indiana University Press, 2007; Dominic Thomas (ed.), *Afroeuropean Cartographies*, Cambridge Scholars Publishing, 2014; Akwugo Emejulu and Francesca Sobande (eds), *To Exist is to Resist: Black Feminism in Europe*, Pluto Press, 2019; and Felipe

Espinoza Garrido et al., *Locating African European Studies: Interventions, Intersections, Conversations*, Routledge, 2019.

2. Examples range from volumes such as Thomas F. Earle and Kate J. P. Lowe (eds), *Black Africans in Renaissance Europe*, Cambridge University Press, 2005, which examine various countries' black presence, to books that delve into the black presence at a regional level, such as Alan Llwyd and Glenn Jordan, *Cymru Ddu/Black Wales: A History: A History of Black Welsh People*, Hughes & Son, 2005.

3. Cedric J. Robinson, *Black Marxism: The Making of The Black Radical Tradition*, University of North Carolina Press, 2000, p. 72.

4. Ibid., p. 83.

5. Robinson notes that the process of erasure did not only concern Africans. 'The tendency of European civilization through capitalism was thus not to homogenize but to differentiate—to exaggerate regional, subcultural, and dialectical differences into "racial" ones. As the Slavs became the natural slaves, the racially inferior stock for domination and exploitation during the early Middle Ages, as the Tartars came to occupy a similar position in the Italian cities of the late Middle Ages, so at the systemic interlocking of capitalism in the sixteenth century, the peoples of the Third World began to fill this expanding category of a civilization reproduced by capitalism.' Ibid., p. 26.

6. Ibid., p. 81.

7. Ibid.

8. Philippa Levine, 'Is Comparative History Possible?' in *History and Theory*, vol. 53, no. 3 (2014), pp. 331–47.

9. Ibid., p. 342.

10. Dienke Hondius, *Blackness in Western Europe: Racial Patterns of Paternalism and Exclusion*, Routledge, 2017, p. 2.

11. Paternalism was the subject of productive debates between leading scholars of the history of slavery in the United States, such as Stanley Elkins, Eugene Genovese and John Blassingame. They demonstrated how paternalism transpired and evolved within slave societies, and how its implementation was redeployed and shaped by African Americans.

12. Hondius, *Blackness in Western Europe*, p. 2.

13. The British Prime Minister Theresa May stated at a Conservative Party

conference in Birmingham on 5 October 2016 that 'if you believe you're a citizen of the world, you're a citizen of nowhere. You don't understand what the very word "citizenship" means.' 'Theresa May's conference speech in full', *The Telegraph*, 5 October 2016, https://www.telegraph.co.uk/news/2016/10/05/theresa-mays-conference-speech-in-full/, last accessed 26 May 2020.

14. David Theo Goldberg, *The Threat of Race: Reflections on Racial Neoliberalism*, Wiley-Blackwell, 2009, p. 21.

1. EARLY ENCOUNTERS: FROM PIONEERS TO AFRICAN ROMANS

1. Academic and artist Shawn Sobers has produced a valuable body of work about Selassie, Fairfield House and the surrounding community. Shawn Naphtali Sobers, 'Fairfield House Rastafari Graphics', http://www.shawnsobers.com/portfolio/uncategorized/fairfield-house-rastafari-graphics/, last accessed 27 May 2020. A five-year project titled 'Rastafari in Motion' also examined Selassie's impact in Britain, on the Rastafari movement in particular. 'Rastafari in Motion', http://www.rastafari-in-motion.org/, last accessed 27 May 2020.

2. Strabo, *Geography*, 17.1.54, trans. H. C. Hamilton and W. Falconer, George Bell and Sons, 1903, pp. 267–69; D. M. Dixon, 'The Origin of the Kingdom of Kush (Napata-Meroë)' in *The Journal of Egyptian Archaeology*, vol. 50, no. 1 (1964), pp. 121–32.

3. Dio Cassius, *Roman History*, vol. 7, 54.5.4, trans. Earnest Cary, Harvard University Press, 1917, pp. 293–95; *The Greek Alexander Romance*, trans. Richard Stoneman, Penguin, 1991, pp. 135–42.

4. Geraldine Heng, *The Invention of Race in the European Middle Ages*, Cambridge University Press, 2018, p. 111.

5. Ibid.

6. Ibid., p. 116.

7. Heng cites Brian A. Catlos, who writes: 'This trend can be seen from the earliest Christian ideological engagements with Islam, whether by the likes of the Syrian Christian functionary, John of Damascus (676–749) in the eastern Mediterranean, or the eighth-century Mozarab

chroniclers of Spain in the west, or the author of the apocryphal ninth-century *Risālat al-Kindī* at the Abbasid court. Latin thinkers from Baetica to Britain portrayed Islam as a Christian heresy, pagan idolatry, or a herald of the Apocalypse, and the Prophet Muhammad as a fraud, the Antichrist, a false prophet, magician, hypocrite, and letch'. Catlos, *Muslims of Medieval Latin Christendom, c. 1050–1614*, Cambridge University Press, 2014, p. 327.

8. Heng, *The Invention of Race in the European Middle Ages*, p. 118.

9. Ibid., p. 138. Heng provides other examples of this kind of romance, including the *Roman de Saladin*, the final instalment of an Old French trilogy, and the Man of Law's Tale in Chaucer's *Canterbury Tales*.

10. Ibid., pp. 142–43.

11. Ibid., p. 143.

12. Ibid., pp. 146–47.

13. Ibid., p. 149.

14. Eckhard Breitinger, 'African Presences and Representations in the Principality/Markgrafschaft of Bayreuth' in *Exit: Endings and New Beginnings in Literature and Life*, ed. Stefan Helgesson, Rodopi, 2011, pp. 107–45.

15. David Woods, 'The Origin of the Legend of Maurice and the Theban Legion' in *The Journal of Ecclesiastical History*, vol. 45, no. 3 (1994), pp. 385–95.

16. Denis van Berchem, *Le martyre de la légion Thébaine: essai sur la formation d'une légende*, Basel, 1956, pp. 42–43.

17. Dietrich Hoffmann, *Das spätrömische Bewegungsheer und die Notitia Dignitatum*, Dusseldorf, 1969, p. 238.

18. Woods, 'The Origin of the Legend of Maurice', p. 392.

19. Breitinger, 'African Presences and Representations', p. 119.

20. Reinhold Grimm, 'Two African Saints in Medieval Germany' in *Die Unterrichtspraxis / Teaching German*, vol. 25, no. 2, Focus on Diversity (1992), p. 129.

21. Effrosyni Zacharopoulou, 'The Black Saint Maurice of Magdeburg and the African Christian Kingdoms in Nubia and Ethiopia in the Thirteenth Century' in *The Southern African Journal of Medieval and Renaissance Studies*, vol. 25 (2015), pp. 77–110.

22. See Zacharopoulou, 'The Black Saint Maurice of Magdeburg' and Breitinger, 'African Presences and Representations'.
23. Breitinger, 'African Presences and Representations', p. 112.
24. David Theo Goldberg, *The Threat of Race: Reflections on Racial Neoliberalism*, Wiley-Blackwell, 2009, p. 2.
25. E.159 membranes 10, 12, 4 dorse, Public Record Office, thirteenth century. Reproduced in Geraldine Heng, 'The Invention of Race in the European Middle Ages II: Locations of Medieval Race' in *Literature Compass*, vol. 8, no. 5 (2011), p. 334.
26. Heng, *The Invention of Race in the European Middle Ages*, pp. 33–35.
27. Ibid., p. 38.
28. Erin Kathleen Rowe, *Black Saints in Early Modern Global Catholicism*, Cambridge University Press, 2019.
29. Ibid., pp. 16–19.
30. Ibid., p. 22.
31. Ibid., p. 25.
32. Ibid., p. 38.
33. Ibid., p. 35.
34. Ibid., pp. 35–36.
35. Ibid., p. 6.
36. Peter Biller, 'The Black in Medieval Science: What Significance?', Proceedings of the Fifth Annual Gilder Lehrman Center International Conference at Yale University, Collective Degradation: Slavery and the Construction of Race, 7–8 November 2003, https://glc.yale.edu/sites/default/files/files/events/race/Biller.pdf, last accessed 31 May 2020.
37. Manuel Joao Ramos and Isabel Boavida, 'Ambiguous Legitimacy: The Legend of the Queen of Sheba in Popular Ethiopian Painting' in *Annales d'Éthiopie*, vol. 21 (2005), pp. 85–92.
38. Alice Ogden Bellis, 'The Queen of Sheba: A Gender-Sensitive Reading' in *Journal of Religious Thought*, vol. 51, no. 2 (1994–95), pp. 17–28.
39. For one medieval depiction of the Queen of Sheba's beauty, see Conrad Kyeser's fifteenth-century manuscript *Bellifortis*. Jeff Bowersox and Astrid Khoo, 'Blackening the Queen of Sheba (ca. 1402–1405)', Black Central Europe, https://blackcentraleurope.com/sources/1000–1500/blackening-the-queen-of-sheba-before-1405/, last accessed 24 June 2020.

40. Rowe, *Black Saints in Early Modern Global Catholicism*, p. 52.

41. Ibid., pp. 61–62.

42. Dio Cassius, *Roman History*, vol. 9, trans. Earnest Cary, Harvard University Press, 1927, pp. 151–277; Herodian, *Herodian of Antioch's History of the Roman Empire from the Death of Marcus Aurelius to the Accession of Gordian III*, trans. Edward C. Echols, University of California Press, 1961, pp. 62–108.

43. Dio, *Roman History*, vol. 9, 74.1.5, p. 163.

44. Herodian, *History of the Roman Empire*, 3.10.6, p. 97.

45. Jo-Marie Claassen, 'Cornelius Fronto: A "Libyan Nomad" at Rome', *Acta Classica*, vol. 52 (2009), p. 49.

46. Ibid., p. 47.

47. Ibid., p. 50; Edward Champlin, *Fronto and Antonine Rome*, Harvard University Press, 1980, p. 16.

48. Claassen, 'Cornelius Fronto', p. 63.

49. Ibid., p. 64.

50. Ibid., p. 63.

51. Wytse Keulen, 'Fronto and Apuleius: Two African Careers in the Roman Empire' in *Apuleius and Africa*, eds Benjamin Todd Lee, Ellen Finkelpearl and Luca Graverini, Routledge, 2014, p. 131.

52. Jacques Maquet, *Africanity: The Cultural Unity of Black Africa*, Oxford University Press, 1972.

53. Keulen, 'Fronto and Apuleius', p. 134.

54. Ibid., p. 135.

55. Ibid., p. 136.

2. BLACK MEDITERRANEANS: SLAVERY AND THE RENAISSANCE

1. John K. Brackett, 'Race and Rulership: Alessandro de' Medici, First Medici Duke of Florence, 1529–1537' in *Black Africans in Renaissance Europe*, eds T. F. Earle and K. J. P. Lowe, Cambridge University Press, 2005, pp. 303–25.

2. Ibid., p. 303.

3. Ibid., p. 305.

4. Ibid., p. 325.
5. Nicholas Scott Baker, 'Writing the Wrongs of the Past: Vengeance, Humanism, and the Assassination of Alessandro de' Medici' in *The Sixteenth Century Journal*, vol. 38, no. 2 (2007), pp. 307–27.
6. Nicholas Scott Baker, 'Power and Passion in Sixteenth-Century Florence: The Sexual and Political Reputations of Alessandro and Cosimo I de' Medici' in *Journal of the History of Sexuality*, vol. 19, no. 3 (2010), p. 441.
7. Ibid., p. 447.
8. Catherine Fletcher, *The Black Prince of Florence: The Spectacular Life and Treacherous World of Alessandro de' Medici*, Oxford University Press, 2016, p. 252.
9. Ibid., p. 251.
10. Ibid., p. 255.
11. Ibid., p. 258.
12. Georges-Henri Dumont, *Marguerite de Parme: Bâtarde de Charles Quint (1522–1586): Biographie*, Le Cri, 1999, p. 19; quoted in Fletcher, *The Black Prince of Florence*, p. 260.
13. David Theo Goldberg, *The Threat of Race: Reflections on Racial Neoliberalism*, Wiley-Blackwell, 2009, p. 5.
14. Nelson H. Minnich, 'The Catholic Church and the Pastoral Care of Black Africans in Renaissance Italy' in *Black Africans in Renaissance Europe*, eds T. F. Earle and K. J. P. Lowe, Cambridge University Press, 2005, pp. 280–300.
15. Ibid., p. 281.
16. Debra Blumenthal, *Enemies and Familiars: Slavery and Mastery in Fifteenth-Century Valencia*, Cornell University Press, 2009, p. 55.
17. Ibid., p. 57.
18. Ibid., p. 64.
19. Ibid., pp. 94–95.
20. Goldberg, *The Threat of Race*, p. 4.
21. Ibid., pp. 4–5. See Kwame Anthony Appiah, 'Racisms' in *Anatomy of Racism*, ed. David Theo Goldberg, University of Minnesota Press, 1990, pp. 3–18.
22. Goldberg, *The Threat of Race*, p. 5. See George Fredrickson, *Racism: A Short History*, Princeton University Press, 2002.

23. Goldberg, *The Threat of Race*, p. 5; Goldberg outlines his definition of 'racial historicism' in *The Racial State*, Wiley-Blackwell, 2001.

24. Goldberg, *The Threat of Race*, p. 5.

25. Sergio Tognetti, 'The Trade in Black African Slaves in Fifteenth-Century Florence' in *Black Africans in Renaissance Europe*, eds T. F. Earle and K. J. P. Lowe, Cambridge University Press, 2005, pp. 213–24.

26. Ibid., p. 217.

27. Ibid., p. 222.

28. Cedric J. Robinson, *Black Marxism: The Making of The Black Radical Tradition*, University of North Carolina Press, 2000, pp. 88–89.

29. Andrew Lemons, 'Juan Latino's Worldly Poetics: Lepanto, Lucretius and Literary Tradition' in *Calíope: Journal of the Society for Renaissance and Baroque Hispanic Poetry*, vol. 21, no. 1 (2016), p. 58.

30. Ibid.

31. Michael A. Gomez, 'Juan Latino and the Dawn of Modernity', lecture delivered at the University of Chapel Hill, 20 March 2014, http://as.nyu.edu/content/dam/nyu-as/asSilverDialogues/documents/M%20Gomez%20May%2020171.pdf, last accessed 4 June 2020, pp. 8, 19.

32. Baltasar Fra-Molinero, 'Juan Latino and His Racial Difference' in *Black Africans in Renaissance Europe*, eds T. F. Earle and K. J. P. Lowe, Cambridge University Press, 2005, pp. 336–37.

33. Ibid., p. 337.

34. Ibid., p. 338.

35. Ibid., pp. 239–44.

36. Aurélia Martín Casares and Marga G. Barranco, 'Popular Literary Depictions of Black African Weddings in Early Modern Spain' in *Renaissance and Reformation*, vol. 31, no. 2 (2008), pp. 111–12.

37. Gomez, 'Juan Latino and the Dawn of Modernity', p. 5.

38. Aurélia Martín Casares, 'A Review of Sources for the Study of Juan Latino: The First Afro-Spanish Poet in Renaissance Europe' in *eHumanista*, vol. 39 (2018), pp. 297–99.

39. Ibid., pp. 299–301.

40. Elizabeth R. Wright, 'Narrating the Ineffable Lepanto: The Austrias Carmen of Joannes Latinus (Juan Latino)' in *Hispanic Review*, vol. 77, no. 1 (2009), p. 73.

41. Ibid., pp. 74–75.

42. Ibid., p. 88.
43. Henry Louis Gates, Jr. and Maria Wolff, 'An Overview of Sources on the Life and Work of Juan Latino, the "Ethiopian Humanist"' in *Research in African Literatures*, vol. 29, no. 4 (1998), p. 43; Antonio Gonzaléz Garbín, 'Glorias de la Universidad Granadina: El Negro Juan Latino' in *Boletin del Centro Artistico de Granada*, vol. 56 (1886).
44. Fra-Molinero, 'Juan Latino and His Racial Difference', p. 327.
45. Ibid., pp. 329, 331.
46. Ibid., pp. 331–32.
47. Lemons, 'Juan Latino's Worldly Politics', p. 62.
48. Ibid., p. 65.
49. Ibid., p. 62.
50. Ibid., p. 83.
51. Gomez, 'Juan Latino and the Dawn of Modernity', p. 3.
52. Ibid., p. 16.
53. Emily Weissbourd, '"I Have Done the State Some Service": Reading Slavery in *Othello* through *Juan Latino*' in *Comparative Drama*, vol. 47, no. 4 (2013), p. 531.
54. Gomez, 'Juan Latino and the Dawn of Modernity', p. 13.
55. Annette Ivory, 'Juan Latino: The Struggle of Blacks, Jews, and Moors in Golden Age Spain' in *Hispania*, vol. 62, no. 4 (1979), p. 613.
56. Weissbourd, 'Reading Slavery in Othello through Juan Latino', p. 532.
57. Ibid.
58. Nicholas R. Jones, *Staging* Habla de Negros: *Radical Performances of the African Diaspora in Early Modern Spain*, Penn State University Press, 2019, p. 119.
59. Ibid.
60. Ibid., p. 120.
61. Ibid., p. 124.
62. Ivory, 'Juan Latino', p. 614.
63. Ibid., p. 615.
64. Ibid., p. 616.
65. Ibid., p. 617.
66. Gomez, 'Juan Latino and the Dawn of Modernity', p. 19.
67. Weissbourd, 'Reading Slavery in Othello through Juan Latino', p. 539.
68. Ibid., pp. 539–40.

3. THE TRANSATLANTIC SLAVE TRADE AND THE INVENTION OF RACE

1. Michael A. Gomez, 'Juan Latino and the Dawn of Modernity', lecture delivered at the University of Chapel Hill, 20 March 2014, http://as.nyu.edu/content/dam/nyu-as/asSilverDialogues/documents/M%20Gomez%20May%2020171.pdf, last accessed 4 June 2020, p. 21.
2. Eugene D. Genovese, *Roll, Jordan, Roll: The World the Slaves Made*, Vintage, 1974; Stanley M. Elkins, *Slavery: A Problem in American Institutional and Intellectual Life*, University of Chicago Press, 1959.
3. Olivette Otele, *Histoire de l'esclavage britannique: Des origines de la traite transatlantique aux prémisses de la colonisation*, Michel Houdiard Éditeur, 2008, pp. 42–56.
4. Dienke Hondius, 'Access to the Netherlands of Enslaved and Free Black Africans: Exploring Legal and Social Historical Practices in the Sixteenth–Nineteenth Centuries' in *Slavery & Abolition*, vol. 32, no. 3 (2011), p. 380.
5. Ibid., p. 381.
6. Christine Levecq, 'Jacobus Capitein: Dutch Calvinist and Black Cosmopolitan' in *Research in African Literatures*, vol. 44, no. 4 (2013), p. 150.
7. Jos Damen, 'Dutch Letters from Ghana' in *History Today*, vol. 62, no. 8 (2012), p. 51.
8. Levecq, 'Jacobus Capitein', p. 152.
9. Gerald H. Anderson (ed.), *Biographical Dictionary of Christian Missions*, William B. Eerdmans Publishing Co., 1999, p. 352.
10. David Nii Anum Kpobi, *Mission in Chains: The Life, Theology, and Ministry of the Ex-Slave Jacobus E.J. Capitein (1717–1747) with a Translation of His Major Publications*, Uitgeverij Boekencentrum, 1993, p. 234; quoted in Levecq, 'Jacobus Capitein', p. 158.
11. Levecq, 'Jacobus Capitein', p. 159.
12. Ibid., p. 163.
13. Dienke Hondius, *Blackness in Western Europe: Racial Patterns of Paternalism and Exclusion*, Routledge, 2017, p. 20.
14. Hondius, 'Access to the Netherlands', p. 384.

15. Jan Nederveen Pieterse, *White on Black: Images of Africa and Blacks in Western Popular Culture*, Yale University Press, 1992, pp. 46–47.

16. Sadiah Qureshi, *Peoples on Parade: Exhibitions, Empire, and Anthropology in Nineteenth-Century Britain*, University of Chicago Press, 2011.

17. 'Meghan Markle: I'm More than an "Other"', *ELLE*, 22 December 2016, https://www.elle.com/uk/life-and-culture/news/a26855/more-than-an-other/, last accessed 8 June 2020.

18. Nora Fakim, 'The Documentary Podcast: My Mixed Up World', BBC Sounds, 13 May 2018.

19. Olivia Woldemikael, 'Why Barack is black and Meghan is biracial', Media Diversified, 28 June 2018, https://mediadiversified.org/2018/06/28/why-barack-is-black-and-megan-is-biracial/, last accessed 24 June 2020.

20. Karis Campion, '"You Think You're Black?" Exploring Black Mixed-Race Experiences of Black Rejection' in *Ethnic and Racial Studies*, vol. 42, no. 16 (2019), pp. 196–213.

21. Trevor Noah, 'The Racist', BBC Radio 4, 10 June 2017. Noah writes about his experiences as a dual-heritage South African in *Born a Crime*, John Murray, 2016.

22. Sue Peabody, *'There Are No Slaves in France': The Political Culture of Race and Slavery in the Ancien Régime*, Oxford University Press, 1996, p. 24.

23. Pierre H. Boulle, 'Racial Purity or Legal Clarity? The Status of Black Residents in Eighteenth-Century France' in *Journal of The Historical Society*, vol. 6, no. 1 (2006), pp. 19–46.

24. Ibid., p. 20.

25. Peabody, *'There Are No Slaves in France'*, p. 123.

26. Ibid., p. 126.

27. Boulle, 'Racial Purity or Legal Clarity?', p. 29.

28. Jennifer L. Palmer, 'What's in a Name? Mixed-Race Families and Resistance to Racial Codification in Eighteenth-Century France' in *French Historical Studies*, vol. 33, no. 3 (2010), p. 357.

29. Ibid., pp. 366–67.

30. Ibid., p. 360.

31. Ibid., p. 367.

32. Ibid., pp. 372–73.

33. Alain Guédé, *Monsieur de Saint-George: Virtuoso, Swordsman, Revolutionary: A Legendary Life Rediscovered*, trans. Gilda M. Roberts, Picador, 2003; Claude Ribbe, *Le Chevalier de Saint-George*, Éditions Perrin, 2004; Emil F. Smidak, *Joseph Boulogne, Called Chevalier de Saint-Georges*, Avenira Foundation, 1996.

34. M. La Boëssière, *Traité de l'art des armes: à l'usage des professeurs et des amateurs*, Didot, 1818, pp. xv–xxii.

35. Lionel de La Laurencie and Frederick H. Martens, 'The Chevalier de Saint-George: Violinist' in *The Musical Quarterly*, vol. 5, no. 1 (1919), pp. 74–75.

36. Ibid., p. 75.

37. Ibid., p. 78.

38. Crystal M. Fleming, *Resurrecting Slavery: Racial Legacies and White Supremacy in France*, Temple University Press, 2017.

4. NEITHER HERE NOR THERE: DUAL HERITAGES AND GENDER ROLES

1. Siep Stuurman, 'François Bernier and the Invention of Racial Classification' in *History Workshop Journal*, no. 50 (2000), pp. 4–5.

2. Erick Noël, *Être noir en France au XVIIIe siècle*, Tallandier, 2006, p. 32.

3. Naïl Ver-Ndoye and Grégoire Fauconnier, *Noir: Entre peinture et histoire*, Omniscience, 2018, pp. 20–23.

4. Marla Harris, 'Not Black and/or White: Reading Racial Difference in Heliodorus's *Ethiopica* and Pauline Hopkins's *Of One Blood*' in *African American Review*, vol. 35, no. 3 (2001), p. 375.

5. Elaine K. Ginsberg (ed.), *Passing and the Fictions of Identity*, Duke University Press, 1996, p. 16; quoted in Harris, 'Not Black and/or White', p. 375.

6. Pierre H. Boulle, 'Racial Purity or Legal Clarity? The Status of Black Residents in Eighteenth-Century France' in *Journal of The Historical Society*, vol. 6, no. 1 (2006), p. 21.

7. Olivette Otele, '"Liberté, Egalité, Fraternité": Debunking the myth of egalitarianism in French education' in *Unsettling Eurocentrism in the*

Westernized University, eds Julie Cupples and Ramón Grosfoguel, Routledge, 2019, p. 223.

8. Noël, *Être noir en France*, p. 29.

9. Ibid., pp. 223–25.

10. Ver-Ndoye and Fauconnier, *Noir*, pp. 8–10.

11. Robin Mitchell, *Vénus Noire: Black Women and Colonial Fantasies in Nineteenth-Century France*, University of Georgia Press, 2020, p. 30.

12. Ibid., p. 79.

13. Ibid., p. 133.

14. For Gilroy's work on double consciousness see Paul Gilroy, *The Black Atlantic: Modernity and Double Consciousness*, Verso, 1993.

15. Marie-Hélène Knight-Baylac, 'Gorée au XVIIIe siècle: l'appropriation du sol' in *Revue française d'histoire d'outre-mer*, vol. 64, no. 234 (1977), pp. 33–34.

16. Ibid., p. 35.

17. Ibid., pp. 44–45.

18. Ibid., p. 46.

19. Bronwen Everill, '"All the baubles that they needed": "Industriousness" and Slavery in Saint-Louis and Gorée' in *Early American Studies*, vol. 15, no. 4 (2017), p. 721.

20. Ibid., p. 731.

21. Yvon Bouquillon and Robert Cornevin, *David Boilat, 1814–1901: Le précurseur*, Les Nouvelles Éditions Africaines, 1981, pp. 25–28.

22. Aissata Kane Lo, *De la Signare à la Diriyanké sénégalaise: Trajectoires féminines et visions partagées*, L'Harmattan Sénégal, 2014, p. 66.

23. Ibid., p. 63.

24. Jean Boulègue, 'Bathily (Abdoulaye): *Les portes de l'or: Le royaume de Galam (Sénégal) de l'ère au temps des négriers (VIIIe-XVIIIe s.)*' in *Outre-Mers. Revue d'histoire*, vol. 78, no. 291 (1991), pp. 291–92.

25. Bouquillon and Cornevin, *David Boilat*, pp. 33–36.

26. Christopher R. DeCorse, 'The Danes on the Gold Coast: Culture Change and the European Presence', *The African Archaeological Review*, vol. 11, Papers in Honour of Merrick Posnansky (1993), p. 153.

27. Ibid., p. 154.

28. Ibid., pp. 154–56.

29. Ibid., p. 155.

30. Pernille Ipsen, '"The Christened Mulatresses": Euro-African Families in a Slave-Trading Town' in *The William and Mary Quarterly*, vol. 70, no. 2, Centering Families in Atlantic Histories (2013), pp. 371–98.

31. Ibid., p. 373.

32. Pernille Ipsen, *Daughters of the Trade: Atlantic Slavers and Interracial Marriage on the Gold Coast*, University of Pennsylvania Press, 2015, p. 29.

33. Ibid., pp. 32–33.

34. Irene Odotei, 'External Influences on Ga Society and Culture' in *Research Review NS*, vol. 7, nos 1–2 (1991), p. 62.

35. The Akwamu were part of the gold-mining group referred to as the Akans.

36. Odotei, 'External Influences on Ga Society and Culture', p. 64.

37. Ipsen, 'Euro-African Families in a Slave-Trading Town', p. 386.

38. Ipsen, *Daughters of the Trade*, pp. 52–53.

39. Ipsen, 'Euro-African Families in a Slave-Trading Town', p. 397.

40. Ipsen, *Daughters of the Trade*, p. 95.

41. Ibid., pp. 1–17.

42. Ibid., p. 175.

43. Ibid., p. 176.

44. David Theo Goldberg, *The Threat of Race: Reflections on Racial Neoliberalism*, Wiley-Blackwell, 2009, p. 6.

45. Ibid.

46. Maj Bach Madsen, 'Denmark cannot apologise for slave trade', ScienceNordic, 27 August 2012, http://sciencenordic.com/denmark-cannot-apologise-slave-trade, last accessed 11 June 2020.

47. Scholars such as Hilary McD. Beckles (*Britain's Black Debt: Reparations for Caribbean Slavery and Native Genocide*, University of West Indies Press, 2013), Ana Lucia Araujo (*Reparations for Slavery and the Slave Trade: A Transnational and Comparative History*, Bloomsbury Academic, 2017) and many others have argued that claims for reparations for the slave trade and slavery have often been initiated by activists of African descent in the Caribbean, Africa and Europe.

48. Astrid Nonbo Andersen, 'The Reparations Movement in the United

States Virgin Islands' in *The Journal of African American History*, vol. 103, nos 1–2 (2018), p. 105.

49. Ibid., p. 106.
50. Ibid., pp. 131–32.
51. Mathias Danbolt and Michael K. Wilson, 'A Monumental Challenge to Danish History', Kunstkritikk, https://kunstkritikk.com/a-monumental-challenge-to-danish-history/, last accessed 11 June 2020.
52. I am Queen Mary, https://www.iamqueenmary.com/, last accessed 11 June 2020.
53. 'Trans-Atlantic Slave Trade: Estimates', Slave Voyages, https://www.slavevoyages.org/assessment/estimates, last accessed 11 June 2020.

5. FLEETING MEMORIES: COLONIAL AMNESIA
   AND FORGOTTEN FIGURES

1. I am using the term 'double jeopardy' in reference to the theoretical work done by black feminists to analyse the lives and experiences of black women and to fight against the double discrimination that is directed specifically against them. Although the term relates to the memory of slavery and the questions of obscuring, remembering and forgetting, it is also concerned with the way that this memory of slavery is gendered and male-centric, as demonstrated in the first part of this chapter related to Brandenburg.
2. Adam Jones, 'Archival Materials on the Brandenburg African Company (1682–1721)' in *History in Africa*, vol. 11 (1984), p. 379.
3. Ibid., p. 383.
4. Daniel Purdy, 'Mobilizing the Archive in Support of Colonialism during the Kaiserreich' in *Journal of Germanic Studies*, vol. 53, no. 3 (2017), pp. 219–33.
5. Ibid., p. 220.
6. Ibid., p. 221.
7. Ibid., p. 228.
8. Douala is also spelt Duala or Dualla.
9. Genevoix Nana, 'Language Ideology and the Colonial Legacy in Cameroon Schools: A Historical Perspective' in *Journal of Education and Training Studies*, vol. 4, no. 4 (2016), p. 173.
10. Marc Michel, 'Les plantations allemandes du mont Cameroun (1885–

1914)' in *Outre-mers. Revue d'histoire*, vol. 57, no. 207 (1970), pp. 183–213.

11. Eloise A. Brière, 'Writing in Cameroon, the First Hundred Years' in *Tydskrif vir Letterkunde*, vol. 53, no. 51 (2016), pp. 52, 62 (note 5).

12. Ibid., p. 52.

13. 'The Last of the Cameroons' Kings', *The Times*, 5 March 1898, no. 35456, p. 10.

14. Robbie Aitken, 'Education and Migration: Cameroonian Schoolchildren and Apprentices in Germany, 1884–1914' in *Germany and the Black Diaspora: Points of Contact, 1250–1914*, eds Mischa Honeck, Martin Klimke and Anne Kuhlmann, Berghahn, 2013, pp. 213–30; see also Robbie Aitken and Eve Rosenhaft, *Black Germany: The Making and Unmaking of a Diaspora Community, 1884–1960*, Cambridge University Press, 2013, pp. 30–37.

15. Aitken, 'Education and Migration', p. 215.

16. Ibid., p. 219.

17. Brière, 'Writing in Cameroon', pp. 52–53.

18. 'Prince's Dishonoured Cheque', *The Times*, 29 July 1921, no. 42785, p. 9.

19. Richard Joseph, 'The Royal Pretender: Prince Douala Manga Bell in Paris, 1919–1922' in *Cahiers d'études africaines*, vol. 14, no. 54 (1974), p. 341.

20. Ibid., p. 346.

21. Aitken and Rosenhaft, *Black Germany*, pp. 114–15.

22. One example is Joseph Bilé; an insightful account of his life and activism can be found in Robbie Aitken, 'From Cameroon to Germany and Back via Moscow and Paris: The Political Career of Joseph Bilé (1892–1959)' in *Journal of Contemporary History*, vol. 43, no. 4 (2008), pp. 597–616.

23. Michael Goebel, 'Spokesmen, Spies, and Spouses: Anticolonialism, Surveillance, and Intimacy in Interwar France' in *The Journal of Modern History*, vol. 91, no. 2 (2019), pp. 380–414.

24. Ibid., p. 390.

25. Ibid.

26. Michael C. Lambert, 'From Citizenship to Negritude: "Making a Difference" in Elite Ideologies of Colonized Francophone West Africa'

in *Comparative Studies in Society and History*, vol. 35, no. 2 (1993), pp. 245–46.

27. Jennifer A. Boittin, 'In Black and White: Gender, Race Relations, and the Nardal Sisters in Interwar Paris' in *French Colonial History*, vol. 6, 2005, p. 121.

28. Ibid., p. 124.

29. Claire Oberon Garcia, 'Remapping the Metropolis: Theorizing Black Women's Subjectivities in Interwar Paris' in *Black French Women and the Struggle for Equality, 1848–2016*, eds Félix Germain and Silyane Larcher, University of Nebraska Press, 2018, p. 215.

30. Paulette Nardal, *Beyond Negritude: Essays from Woman in the City*, ed. and trans. T. Denean Sharpley-Whiting, State University of New York Press, 2009, p. 18.

31. Peter Benson, *Battling Siki: A Tale of Ring Fixes, Race, and Murder in the 1920s*, University of Arkansas Press, 2006.

32. Ibid., p. 147.

33. Gerald Early, 'Battling Siki: The Boxer as Natural Man' in *The Massachusetts Review*, vol. 29, no. 3 (1988), p. 469.

34. Benson, *Battling Siki*, p. 278.

35. Ryan Hanley's volume *Beyond Slavery and Abolition: Black British Writing, c. 1770–1830*, Cambridge University Press, 2018, presents striking and detailed accounts of the lives and influence of these African Europeans.

36. Theodor Michael, *Black German: An Afro-German Life in the Twentieth Century*, trans. Eve Rosenhaft, Liverpool University Press, 2017, p. 56.

37. Ibid., p. 64.

38. Ibid., p. 184.

39. Ibid., p. 186.

40. Tiffany Florvil, 'Rethinking Black History Month in Germany', Black Perspectives, 20 February 2019, https://www.aaihs.org/rethinking-black-history-month-in-germany/, last accessed 16 June 2020.

6. CLAIMING A PAST, NAVIGATING THE PRESENT

1. Annalisa Frisina and Camilla Hawthorne, 'Italians with Veils and Afros: Gender, Beauty, and the Everyday Anti-Racism of the Daughters of

Immigrants in Italy' in *Journal of Ethnic and Migration Studies*, vol. 44, no. 5 (2018), p. 718.

2. Ibid., pp. 719–20.

3. Ibid., p. 721.

4. Ibid., p. 729.

5. Camilla Hawthorne, 'Making Italy: Afro-Italian Entrepreneurs and the Racial Boundaries of Citizenship' in *Social & Cultural Geography* (2019), pp. 1–21.

6. Nikesh Shukla, *The Good Immigrant*, Unbound, 2016.

7. Hawthorne, 'Making Italy', p. 14.

8. The idea of the good immigrant who 'gets the job done' is itself a global narrative, as exemplified by Lin Manuel Miranda's music video for 'Immigrants (We Get the Job Done)', originally from the musical *Hamilton*. 'The Hamilton Mixtape: Immigrants (We Get the Job Done)', YouTube, 28 June 2017, https://www.youtube.com/watch?v=6_35a7sn6ds, last accessed 16 June 2020.

9. Anne Kubai, 'Being Here and There: Migrant Communities in Sweden and the Conflicts in the Horn of Africa' in *African and Black Diaspora: An International Journal*, vol. 6, no. 2 (2013), pp. 174–88.

10. Marianne Hirsch, *The Generation of Postmemory: Writing and Visual Culture After the Holocaust*, Columbia University Press, 2012.

11. Kubai, 'Being Here and There', p. 183.

12. Ibid., p. 186.

13. Lena Sawyer, 'Routings: "Race," African Diasporas, and Swedish Belonging' in *Transforming Anthropology*, vol. 11, no. 1 (2008), pp. 13–35.

14. Ibid., p. 16.

15. Michael McEachrane (ed.), *Afro-Nordic Landscapes: Equality and Race in Northern Europe*, Routledge, 2014, p. 1.

16. David Theo Goldberg, *The Threat of Race: Reflections on Racial Neoliberalism*, Wiley-Blackwell, 2009, p. 22.

17. Cited in Ylva Habel, 'Challenging Swedish Exceptionalism? Teaching While Black' in *Education in the Black Diaspora: Perspectives, Challenges, and Prospects*, eds Kassie Freeman and Ethan Johnson, Routledge, 2012, pp. 100–1.

18. Ibid., p. 102.

19. Monica L. Miller, 'Figuring Blackness in a Place Without Race: Sweden, Recently' in *ELH*, vol. 84, no. 2 (2017), pp. 377–97, p. 379.

20. Allan Pred, *Even in Sweden: Racisms, Racialized Spaces and the Popular Geographical Imagination*, University of California Press, 2000, p. 266.

21. Habel, 'Challenging Swedish Exceptionalism?', p. 101.

22. Ibid., p. 106.

23. Miller, 'Figuring Blackness In A Place Without Race', pp. 381–82.

24. Jallow Momodou, 'Sweden: the country where racism is just a joke', *The Guardian*, 8 April 2012, https://www.theguardian.com/commentisfree/2012/apr/18/racism-becoming-the-norm-sweden, last accessed 16 June 2020.

25. Aleksandr Pushkin, 'To the Poet', trans. Donald MacAlister in *The Slavonic Review*, vol. 4, no. 12 (1926), p. 691.

26. Dieudonné Gnammankou and Ruthmarie H. Mitsch, 'New Research on Pushkin's Africa: Hanibal's Homeland' in *Research in African Literatures*, vol. 28, no. 4 (1997), pp. 220–23.

27. Boniface Mongo-Mboussa, 'Débat autour du livre de Dieudonné Gnammankou: *Abraham Hanibal, l'aïeul noir de Pouchkine*' in *Présence Africaine*, no. 157 (1998), p. 240.

28. Cynthia Green, 'How Alexander Pushkin Was Inspired By His African Heritage', JSTOR Daily, 1 February 2018, https://daily.jstor.org/how-alexander-pushkin-was-inspired-by-his-african-heritage/, last accessed 16 June 2020.

29. Anne Lounsbery, 'Russia's Literary Genius Alexander Pushkin: The Great-Grandson of an African Slave' in *The Journal of Blacks in Higher Education*, no. 27 (2000), pp. 105–8.

30. Hakim Adi, Pan-Africanism: A History, Bloomsbury, 2018, pp. 61–79.

31. Sonti Ramirez, 'What it's like being black in Poland', Gal-dem, 13 January 2018, http://gal-dem.com/being-black-in-poland/, last accessed 16 June 2020; Nina, 'Lost in Otherness: Growing Up as a Mixed Raced Child in Eastern Europe', Afropean, 12 December 2016, http://afropean.com/lost-in-otherness-growing-up-as-a-mixed-raced-child-in-eastern-europe/, last accessed 16 June 2020.

32. European Commission Against Racism and Intolerance, 'ECRI Report on Latvia', 5 March 2019, https://rm.coe.int/fifth-report-on-latvia/1680934a9f, last accessed 16 June 2020, p. 15.

33. 'Sol Campbell warns fans to stay away from Euro 2012', BBC, 28 May 2012, https://www.bbc.co.uk/news/uk-18192375, last accessed 16 June 2020.

34. Gloria Wekker, *White Innocence: Paradoxes of Colonialism and Race*, Duke University Press, 2016, p. 47.

35. Ibid., p. 38.

36. Ibid., p. 49.

37. Ibid., p. 2.

38. Ibid., p. 143; see Paul Gilroy, *Postcolonial Melancholia*, Columbia University Press, 2008.

39. Wekker, *White Innocence*, p. 140.

40. Stuart Hall, 'The Spectacle of the Other' in *Representation: Cultural Representations and Signifying Practices*, ed. Hall, Sage Publications, 1997, p. 245.

41. Wekker, *White Innocence*, p. 141; see Philomena Essed, 'Entitlement Racism: License to Humiliate' in *Recycling Hatred: Racism(s) in Europe Today*, European Network Against Racism, 2013, pp. 62–76.

42. Moya Bailey, 'They aren't talking about me...', Crunk Feminist Collective, 14 March 2010, http://www.crunkfeministcollective. com/2010/03/14/they-arent-talking-about-me/, last accessed 16 June 2020.

43. Moya Bailey and Trudy, 'On Misogynoir: Citation, Erasure and Plagiarism', *Feminist Media Studies*, vol. 18, no. 4 (2018), pp. 762–68.

44. Kwame Nimako, Amy Abdou and Glenn Willemsen, 'Chattel Slavery and Racism: A Reflection on the Dutch Experience' in *Dutch Racism*, eds Philomena Essed and Isabel Hoving, Rodopi, 2014, p. 44.

45. Ibid., pp. 46–47.

46. Ibid., p. 48.

47. Gloria Wekker and Rivke Jaffe, 'Reflections: A Conversation with Gloria Wekker' in *Development and Change*, vol. 49, no. 2 (2018), pp. 553–54.

7. IDENTITY AND LIBERATION: AFRICAN EUROPEANS TODAY

1. Mwasi Collectif Afroféministe, *Afrofem*, Éditions Syllepse, 2018.

2. Gloria Wekker, *White Innocence: Paradoxes of Colonialism and Race*, Duke University Press, 2016, p. 109.

3. Mwasi, 'Qui peut nous rejoindre?', https://mwasicollectif.com/portfolio/qui-peut-nous-rejoindre/, last accessed 16 June 2020.

4. Myriam Cottias, 'Free but Minor: Slave Women, Citizenship, Respectability, and Social Antagonism in the French Antilles, 1830–90' in *Women and Slavery, Volume Two: The Modern Atlantic*, eds Gwyn Campbell, Suzanne Miers and Joseph C. Miller, Ohio University Press, 2008, pp. 186–206.

5. Stéphanie Guyon, 'Christiane Taubira, a Black Woman in Politics in French Guiana and in France' in *Black French Women and the Struggle for Equality, 1848–2016*, eds Félix Germain and Silyane Larcher, University of Nebraska Press, 2018, pp. 19–36; Olivette Otele, 'Re-Branding the Trauma of Slavery, or How to Pacify the Masses with Sites of Memory', Discover Society, 3 June 2015, https://discoversociety.org/2015/06/03/re-branding-the-trauma-of-slavery-or-how-to-pacify-the-masses-with-sites-of-memory/, last accessed 16 June 2020.

6. Félix Germain and Silyane Larcher (eds), *Black French Women and the Struggle for Equality, 1848–2016*, University of Nebraska Press, 2018, p. xiii.

7. European Union Agency for Fundamental Rights, 'Being Black in the EU: Second European Union Minorities and Discrimination Survey—Summary', 15 November 2019, https://fra.europa.eu/sites/default/files/fra_uploads/fra-2019-being-black-in-the-eu-summary_en.pdf, last accessed 16 June 2020.

8. Michelle De Leon, 'World Afro Day', Office of the United Nations High Commissioner for Human Rights, https://www.ohchr.org/Documents/Issues/Racism/IWG/Session16/MichelleDeLeon.pdf, last accessed 17 June 2020.

9. ENPAD, 'Our Mission', https://enpad.eu/our-mission/, last accessed 17 June 2020.

10. Open Society Foundations, 'Under Suspicion: The Impact of Discriminatory Policing in Spain', 2019, https://enpad.eu/wp-content/uploads/2019/12/UNDER-SUSPICION-OSF-RIS-1.pdf, last accessed 17 June 2020.

11. Mike Henson, 'Giannis Antetokounmpo: NBA star's rise from "hustling" on Athens streets to MVP award', BBC Sport, https://www.bbc.co.uk/sport/basketball/48832050, last accessed 17 June 2020.

12. '5+1 myths about Greek citizenship', Generation 2.0, 18 April 2018, https://g2red.org/51-myths-about-greek-citizenship/, last accessed 17 June 2020.

13. 'We are here. Whether you like it or not.', Generation 2.0, 16 November 2018, https://g2red.org/we-are-here-whether-you-like-it-or-not/, last accessed 17 June 2020.

14. 'Diversity 2.0: An Employer's Guide', Generation 2.0, 28 February 2019, https://g2red.org/wp-content/uploads/2019/03/Diversity_Guide_Website.pdf, last accessed 17 June 2020.

15. David Theo Goldberg, *The Threat of Race: Reflections on Racial Neoliberalism*, Wiley-Blackwell, 2009, p. 10.

16. Catherine Hall's extensive work on men and women of the empire, and their relationship with racialised populations, remains an invaluable reference.

17. Goldberg, *The Threat of Race*, pp. 355–56.

18. Onyeka, *Blackamoores: Africans in Tudor England, Their Presence, Status and Origins*, Narrative Eye, 2013; James Walvin, *Black and White: The Negro and English Society, 1555–1945*, Allen Lane, 1973; Miranda Kaufmann, *Black Tudors: The Untold Story*, Oneworld Publications, 2017; Michael Ohajuru, The John Blanke Project, https://www.john-blanke.com/, last accessed 17 June 2020.

19. Monique Charles, 'MDA as a Research Method of Generic Musical Analysis for the Social Sciences: Sifting through Grime (Music) as an SFT Case Study' in *International Journal of Qualitative Methods*, vol. 17, no. 1 (2018), pp. 1–11.

20. Monique Charles, 'Grime Central! Subterranean Ground-In Grit Engulfing Manicured Mainstream Spaces' in *Blackness in Britain*, eds Kehinde Andrews and Lisa Amanda Palmer, Routledge, 2016, pp. 101–12.

21. Amelia Gentleman, *The Windrush Betrayal: Exposing the Hostile Environment*, Faber & Faber, 2019.

22. David Matthews, *Voices of the Windrush Generation: The Real Story Told by the People Themselves*, Blink Publishing, 2018.

23. Maya Goodfellow, *Hostile Environment: How Immigrants Become Scapegoats*, Verso Books, 2019.

24. Nadine White, 'Chadwick Jackson: Filmmaker Forced To Turn Down Work As Immigration Limbo Drags On', HuffPost, 16 February 2020, https://www.huffingtonpost.co.uk/entry/chadwick-jackson-british-jamaican-filmmaker-immigration-deportation_uk_5e1464aee4b0b25 20d27ad48, last accessed 17 June 2020.

25. Black Female Professors Forum, https://blackfemaleprofessorsforum. org/, last accessed 17 June 2020.

26. Bristol has a long history of political engagement from people of African descent. In the twentieth and twenty-first centuries a few key individuals, such as Peaches Golding and Marvin Rees, have made strong contributions to the life of the city.

27. Paula Akpan, 'Historian Jade Bentil On Black British Feminism & Doing Justice To Everyday Black Women's Lives', Bustle, 18 November 2019, https://www.bustle.com/p/historian-jade-bentil-on-black-british-feminism-doing-justice-to-everyday-black-womens-lives-1935 5482, last accessed 25 June 2020.

28. Bonnie Greer has brought several transnational black stories together in podcast series *In Search of Black History*, Audible, 2020. She also engaged with history, memory and identity in an ongoing series of public conversations which are aimed at understanding and celebrating the lives of people of African descent across Europe. 'Bonnie Greer: Three Journeys', British Museum, 22 April 2020, https://blog.british-museum.org/bonnie-greer-three-journeys/, last accessed 17 June 2020.

29. Tyler Stovall, 'A Black Woman's Life in the Struggle: Jean McNair in France' in *Black French Women and the Struggle for Equality, 1848–2016*, eds Félix Germain and Silyane Larcher, University of Nebraska Press, 2018, p. 115.

30. Ibid., p. 110.

31. See Jennifer A. Boittin, *Colonial Metropolis: The Urban Grounds of Anti-Imperialism and Feminism in Interwar Paris*, University of Nebraska Press, 2010 and Annette K. Joseph-Gabriel, *Reimagining Liberation: How Black Women Transformed Citizenship in the French Empire*, University of Illinois Press, 2019. Extensive research on these networks

is also available in Hakim Adi, *Pan-Africanism: A History*, Bloomsbury, 2018 and Caroline Bressey and Hakim Adi (eds), *Belonging in Europe: The African Diaspora and Work*, Routledge, 2010. Equally valuable is Imaobong D. Umoren, *Race Women Internationalists: Activist-Intellectuals and Global Freedom Struggles*, University of California Press, 2018.

EPILOGUE

1. Heather Morrison, 'Dressing Angelo Soliman' in *Eighteenth Century Studies*, vol. 44, no. 3 (2011), pp. 361–82.
2. I have had the privilege to interview Mrs Cyril for a funded project. Her story (and the stories of many others, such as Roy Grant) deserves to be widely acknowledged and taught. 'Mrs Vernester Cyril OBE as a student nurse outside the Friars Education Centre, Newport, 1966', https://www.peoplescollection.wales/items/485774, last accessed 17 June 2020. The project was funded by the Arts and Humanities Research Council: 'People of African Descent in the 21st Century: Knowledge and Cultural Production in Reluctant Sites of Memory', https://gtr.ukri.org/projects?ref=AH%2FP006760%2F1, last accessed 17 June 2020.
3. David Theo Goldberg, *The Threat of Race: Reflections on Racial Neoliberalism*, Wiley-Blackwell, 2009, p. 362.
4. Ornette D. Clennon, *Black Scholarly Activism between the Academy and Grassroots: A Bridge for Identities and Social Justice*, Palgrave Macmillan, 2018.
5. Black Lives Matter, https://blacklivesmatter.com/about/, last accessed 17 June 2020.
6. As the premise of this book is not to give prominence to whiteness and white supremacy but rather to assess how African European experiences were also shaped by white supremacy, further space will not be dedicated to this matter. It is, however, useful to consider a few volumes that shed light on the notion of whiteness: Steve Garner, *Whiteness, an Introduction*, Routledge, 2007; Cynthia Levine-Rasky, *Whiteness Fractured*, Routledge, 2013; Robin DiAngelo, *White Fragility: Why It's So Hard for White People to Talk About Racism*, Beacon Press, 2018.

7. Body cameras have become compulsory for police offices in certain states, while in France in March 2020 an application aimed at supporting victims of police brutality was launched under the initiative of *Observatoire national des pratiques et des violences policières* (ONVP). Violence against people of African descent has been at the forefront of the work of several organisations and several high profile cases have made the headlines since the 1960s—including, recently, the violent death of young black French man Adama Traoré (see Assa Traore and Elsa Vigoureux, *Lettre à Adama*, Seuil, 2017). However, the social protests led by the Yellow Vests in France in 2019 and 2020 saw a spike in police brutality against protestors from all backgrounds, and forced France to pay closer attention to the question of police brutality.

8. A vast number of volumes have been published about the Black Lives Matter movement. They include Keeanga-Yamahtta Taylor, *From #BlackLivesMatter to Black Liberation*, Haymarket Books, 2016 and Christopher J. Lebron, *The Making of Black Lives Matter: A Brief History of an Idea*, Oxford University Press, 2017. More general studies include Crystal Fleming, *How to Be Less Stupid About Race: On Racism, White Supremacy, and the Racial Divide*, Beacon Press, 2018 and Reni Eddo-Lodge, *Why I'm No Longer Talking to White People About Race*, Bloomsbury, 2017.

9. Lynne Maureen Hurdle, 'The Culture of Appropriating Movements', Psychology Today, 9 August 2019, https://www.psychologytoday.com/us/blog/breaking-culture/201908/the-culture-appropriating-movements, last accessed 25 June 2020; Tanasia Kenney, 'Move Over White Feminists: Black Activist Tarana Burke Created the #MeToo Campaign 10 Years Ago', Atlanta Black Star, 19 October 2017, https://atlantablackstar.com/2017/10/19/black-activist-tarana-burke-created-metoo-campaign-means-connect-sexual-assault-survivors/, last accessed 25 June 2020. For a broader discussion of conflicts between white and black feminisms, see Phyllis Marynick Palmer, 'White Women/Black Women: The Dualism of Female Identity and Experience in the United States' in *Feminist Studies*, vol. 9, no. 1 (1983), pp. 151–70.

10. Bibia Pavard, 'Faire naître et mourir les vagues: comment s'écrit l'histoire des féminismes' in *Itinéraires* (2017/2018), https://journals.

openedition.org/itineraires/3787, last accessed 17 June 2020. 'Le développement de groupes féministes qui se disent queer, inclusifs, afroféministes ou musulmans renforce l'idée que la troisième vague correspond à une mouvance plus soucieuse de la reconnaissance de la diversité sociale, raciale, sexuelle ou religieuse.'

11. A Royal Historical Society report has highlighted the key issues behind the lack of black professors, and in particular the reasons for low numbers of black students and black academics in History departments in the UK. Royal Historical Society, 'Race, Ethnicity and Equality Report', https://royalhistsoc.org/racereport/, last accessed 17 June 2020.

12. Meleisa Ono-George, '"Power in the Telling": Community-Engaged Histories of Black Britain', History Workshop, 18 November 2019, https://www.historyworkshop.org.uk/power-in-the-telling/, last accessed 25 June 2020; Patrick Vernon, 'Where are all the Black historians?', Media Diversified, 30 March 2016, https://mediadiversified. org/2016/03/30/where-are-all-the-black-historians/, last accessed 25 June 2020.

13. The Black Cultural Archives, https://blackculturalarchives.org/, last accessed 17 June 2020.

14. Places such as Malcolm X Community Centre and Easton Community Centre in Bristol or Pillgwenlly Community Centre in Newport were the heart and soul of local community for several decades. Nowadays they are struggling for funding, and yet they still manage to support people and carry out modest intergenerational projects and activities for families and young people.

15. The Black Archives, http://www.theblackarchives.nl/home.html, last accessed 17 June 2020.

BIBLIOGRAPHY

Adi, Hakim (ed.), *Black British History: New Perspectives*, London: Zed Books, 2019.

Adi, Hakim and Caroline Bressey (eds), *Belonging in Europe: The African Diaspora and Work*, Abingdon: Routledge, 2010.

Adi, Hakim (ed.), *Black British History*

———, *Pan-Africanism: A History*, London: Bloomsbury, 2018.

Aitken, Robbie, 'Education and Migration: Cameroonian Schoolchildren and Apprentices in Germany, 1884–1914' in *Germany and the Black Diaspora: Points of Contact, 1250–1914*, eds Mischa Honeck, Martin Klimke and Anne Kuhlmann, Berghahn, 2013, pp. 213–30.

———, 'From Cameroon to Germany and Back via Moscow and Paris: The Political Career of Joseph Bilé (1892–1959)' in *Journal of Contemporary History*, vol. 43, no. 4. (2008), pp. 597–616.

Aitken, Robbie and Eve Rosenhaft, *Black Germany: The Making and Unmaking of a Diaspora Community, 1884–1960*, Cambridge: Cambridge University Press, 2013.

Akala, *Natives: Race and Class in the Ruins of Empire*, London: Two Roads, 2018.

Akpan, Paula, 'Historian Jade Bentil On Black British Feminism & Doing Justice To Everyday Black Women's Lives', Bustle, 18 November 2019, https://www.bustle.com/p/historian-jade-bentil-on-black-british-feminism-doing-justice-to-everyday-black-womens-lives-19355482, last accessed 25 June 2020.

251

BIBLIOGRAPHY

Anderson, Gerald H. (ed.), *Biographical Dictionary of Christian Missions*, Grand Rapids, MI: William B. Eerdmans Publishing Co., 1999.

Appiah, Kwame Anthony, 'Racisms' in *Anatomy of Racism*, ed. David Theo Goldberg, Minneapolis: University of Minnesota Press, 1990, pp. 3–18.

Araujo, Ana Lucia, *Reparations for Slavery and the Slave Trade: A Transnational and Comparative History*, London: Bloomsbury Academic, 2017.

Arts and Humanities Research Council, 'People of African Descent in the 21st Century: Knowledge and Cultural Production in Reluctant Sites of Memory', Principal Investigator Olivette Otele, https://gtr.ukri.org/projects?ref=AH%2FP006760%2F1, last accessed 17 June 2020.

Bailey, Moya, 'They aren't talking about me...', Crunk Feminist Collective, 14 March 2010, http://www.crunkfeministcollective.com/2010/03/14/they-arent-talking-about-me/, last accessed 16 June 2020.

Bailey, Moya and Trudy, 'On Misogynoir: Citation, Erasure and Plagiarism', *Feminist Media Studies*, vol. 18, no. 4 (2018), pp. 762–68.

Baker, Nicholas Scott, 'Power and Passion in Sixteenth-Century Florence: The Sexual and Political Reputations of Alessandro and Cosimo I de' Medici' in *Journal of the History of Sexuality*, vol. 19, no. 3 (2010), pp. 432–57.

———, 'Writing the Wrongs of the Past: Vengeance, Humanism, and the Assassination of Alessandro de' Medici' in *The Sixteenth Century Journal*, vol. 38, no. 2 (2007), pp. 307–27.

BBC, 'Sol Campbell warns fans to stay away from Euro 2012', 28 May 2012, https://www.bbc.co.uk/news/uk-18192375, last accessed 16 June 2020.

Beckles, Hilary McD., *Britain's Black Debt: Reparations for Caribbean Slavery and Native Genocide*, Kingston, Jamaica: University of West Indies Press, 2013.

Bellis, Alice Ogden, 'The Queen of Sheba: A Gender-Sensitive Reading' in *Journal of Religious Thought*, vol. 51, no. 2 (2001), pp. 17–28.

Benson, Peter, *Battling Siki: A Tale of Ring Fixes, Race, and Murder in the 1920s*, Fayetteville: University of Arkansas Press, 2006.

Biller, Peter, 'The Black in Medieval Science: What Significance?', Proceedings of the Fifth Annual Gilder Lehrman Center International

BIBLIOGRAPHY

Conference at Yale University, Collective Degradation: Slavery and the Construction of Race, 7–8 November 2003, https://glc.yale.edu/sites/default/files/files/events/race/Biller.pdf, last accessed 31 May 2020.

Black Female Professors Forum, https://blackfemaleprofessorsforum.org/, last accessed 17 June 2020.

Black Lives Matter, https://blacklivesmatter.com/about/, last accessed 17 June 2020.

Blakely, Allison, *Blacks in the Dutch World: The Evolution of Racial Imagery in a Modern Society*, Bloomington: Indiana University Press, 1993.

Blumenthal, Debra, *Enemies and Familiars: Slavery and Mastery in Fifteenth-Century Valencia*, Ithaca, NY: Cornell University Press, 2009.

Boittin, Jennifer A., *Colonial Metropolis: The Urban Grounds of Anti-Imperialism and Feminism in Interwar Paris*, Lincoln: University of Nebraska Press, 2010.

———, 'In Black and White: Gender, Race Relations, and the Nardal Sisters in Interwar Paris' in *French Colonial History*, vol. 6 (2005), pp. 120–35.

Boulègue, Jean, Review: 'Bathily (Abdoulaye): *Les portes de l'or: Le royaume de Galam (Sénégal) de l'ère au temps des négriers (VIIIe-XVIIIe s.)*' in *Outre-Mers. Revue d'histoire*, vol. 78, no. 291 (1991), pp. 291–92.

Boulle, Pierre H., 'Racial Purity or Legal Clarity? The Status of Black Residents in Eighteenth-Century France' in *Journal of Historical Society*, vol. 6, no. 1 (2006), pp. 19–46.

Bouquillon, Yvon and Robert Cornevin, *David Boilat, 1814–1901: Le précurseur*, Dakar: Les Nouvelles Éditions Africaines, 1981.

Bowersox, Jeff and Astrid Khoo, 'Blackening the Queen of Sheba (ca. 1402–1405)', Black Central Europe, https://blackcentraleurope.com/sources/1000–1500/blackening-the-queen-of-sheba-before-1405/, last accessed 24 June 2020.

Brackett, John K., 'Race and Rulership: Alessandro de' Medici, First Medici Duke of Florence, 1529–1537' in *Black Africans in Renaissance Europe*, eds T. F. Earle and K. J. P. Lowe, Cambridge: Cambridge University Press, 2005, pp. 303–25.

Breitinger, Eckhard, 'African Presences and Representations in the Principality/ Markgrafschaft of Bayreuth' in *Exit: Endings and New*

BIBLIOGRAPHY

Beginnings in Literature and Life, ed. Stefan Helgesson, Amsterdam; New York: Rodopi, 2011, pp. 107–45.

Brière, Eloise A., 'Writing in Cameroon, the First Hundred Years' in *Tydskrif vir Letterkunde*, vol. 53, no. 51 (2016), pp. 51–65.

British Museum, 'Bonnie Greer: Three Journeys', 22 April 2020, https://blog.britishmuseum.org/bonnie-greer-three-journeys/, last accessed 17 June 2020.

Campion, Karis, '"You Think You're Black?" Exploring Black Mixed-Race Experiences of Black Rejection' in *Ethnic and Racial Studies*, vol. 42, no. 16 (2019), pp. 196–213.

Cassius, Dio, *Roman History*, vol. 7, trans. Earnest Cary, Cambridge, MA: Harvard University Press, 1917.

———, *Roman History*, vol. 9, trans. Earnest Cary, Cambridge, MA: Harvard University Press, 1927.

Catlos, Brian A., *Muslims of Medieval Latin Christendom, c. 1050–1614*, Cambridge: Cambridge University Press, 2014.

Champlin, Edward, *Fronto and Antonine Rome*, Cambridge, MA: Harvard University Press, 1980.

Charles, Monique, 'Grime Central! Subterranean Ground-In Grit Engulfing Manicured Mainstream Spaces' in *Blackness in Britain*, eds Kehinde Andrews and Lisa Amanda Palmer, London: Routledge, 2016, pp. 101–12.

———, 'MDA as a Research Method of Generic Musical Analysis for the Social Sciences: Sifting through Grime (Music) as an SFT Case Study' in *International Journal of Qualitative Methods*, vol. 17, no. 1 (2018), pp. 1–11.

Claassen, Jo-Marie, 'Cornelius Fronto: A "Libyan Nomad" at Rome' in *Acta Classica*, vol. 52 (2009), pp. 47–71.

Clennon, Ornette D., *Black Scholarly Activism between the Academy and Grassroots: A Bridge for Identities and Social Justice*, London: Palgrave Macmillan, 2018.

Cottias, Myriam, 'Free but Minor: Slave Women, Citizenship, Respectability, and Social Antagonism in the French Antilles, 1830–90' in *Women and Slavery, Volume Two: The Modern Atlantic*, eds Gwyn

BIBLIOGRAPHY

Campbell, Suzanne Miers and Joseph C. Miller, Athens, OH: Ohio University Press, 2008, pp. 186–206.

Dabiri, Emma, *Don't Touch My Hair*, London: Penguin, 2019.

Damen, Jos, 'Dutch Letters from Ghana' in *History Today*, vol. 62, no. 8 (2012), pp. 47–52.

Danbolt, Mathias, and Michael K. Wilson, 'A Monumental Challenge to Danish History', Kunstkritikk, https://kunstkritikk.com/a-monumental-challenge-to-danish-history/, last accessed 11 June 2020.

de La Laurencie, Lionel and Frederick H. Martens, 'The Chevalier de Saint-George: Violinist' in *The Musical Quarterly*, vol. 5, no. 1 (1919), pp. 74–85.

De Leon, Michelle, 'World Afro Day', Office of the United Nations High Commissioner for Human Rights, https://www.ohchr.org/Documents/Issues/Racism/IWG/Session16/MichelleDeLeon.pdf, last accessed 17 June 2020.

DeCorse, Christopher R., 'The Danes on the Gold Coast: Culture Change and the European Presence' in *The African Archaeological Review*, vol. 11, Papers in Honour of Merrick Posnansky (1993), pp. 149–73.

DiAngelo, Robin, *White Fragility: Why It's So Hard for White People to Talk About Racism*, Boston: Beacon Press, 2018.

Dixon, D. M., 'The Origin of the Kingdom of Kush (Napata-Meroë)' in *The Journal of Egyptian Archaeology*, vol. 50, no. 1 (1964), pp. 121–32.

Dumont, Georges-Henri, *Marguerite de Parme: Bâtarde de Charles Quint (1522–1586): Biographie*, Brussels: Le Cri, 1999.

Earle, T. F. and K. J. P. Lowe (eds), *Black Africans in Renaissance Europe*, Cambridge: Cambridge University Press, 2005.

Early, Gerald, 'Battling Siki: The Boxer as Natural Man' in *The Massachusetts Review*, vol. 29, no. 3 (1988), pp. 451–72.

Eddo-Lodge, Reni, *Why I'm No Longer Talking to White People About Race*, London: Bloomsbury, 2017.

Elkins, Stanley M., *Slavery: A Problem in American Institutional and Intellectual Life*, Chicago: University of Chicago Press, 1959.

Emejulu, Akwugo and Francesca Sobande (eds), *To Exist is to Resist: Black Feminism in Europe*, London: Pluto Press, 2019.

BIBLIOGRAPHY

ENPAD, 'Our Mission', https://enpad.eu/our-mission/, last accessed 17 June 2020.

Espinoza Garrido, Felipe, Caroline Koegler, Deborah Nyangulu and Mark U. Stein (eds), *Locating African European Studies: Interventions, Intersections, Conversations*, London: Routledge, 2020.

Essed, Philomena 'Entitlement Racism: License to Humiliate' in *Recycling Hatred: Racism(s) in Europe Today*, European Network Against Racism, 2013, pp. 62–76.

European Commission Against Racism and Intolerance, 'ECRI Report on Latvia', 5 March 2019, https://rm.coe.int/fifth-report-on-latvia/1680 934a9f, last accessed 16 June 2020.

European Union Agency for Fundamental Rights, 'Being Black in the EU: Second European Union Minorities and Discrimination Survey—Summary', 15 November 2019, https://fra.europa.eu/sites/default/files/fra_uploads/fra-2019-being-black-in-the-eu-summary_en.pdf, last accessed 16 June 2020.

Everill, Bronwen, '"All the baubles that they needed": "Industriousness" and Slavery in Saint-Louis and Gorée' in *Early American Studies*, vol. 15, no. 4 (2017), pp. 714–39.

Fakim, Nora, 'The Documentary Podcast: My Mixed Up World', BBC Sounds, 13 May 2018.

Fleming, Crystal M., *How to Be Less Stupid About Race: On Racism, White Supremacy, and the Racial Divide*, Boston: Beacon Press, 2018.

———, *Resurrecting Slavery: Racial Legacies and White Supremacy in France*, Philadelphia: Temple University Press, 2017.

Fletcher, Catherine, *The Black Prince of Florence: The Spectacular Life and Treacherous World of Alessandro de' Medici*, Oxford: Oxford University Press, 2016.

Florvil, Tiffany, 'Rethinking Black History Month in Germany', Black Perspectives, 20 February 2019, https://www.aaihs.org/rethinking-black-history-month-in-germany/, last accessed 16 June 2020.

Fra-Molinero, Baltasar, 'Juan Latino and His Racial Difference' in *Black Africans in Renaissance Europe*, eds T. F. Earle and K. J. P. Lowe, Cambridge: Cambridge University Press, 2005, pp. 326–44.

Florvil, Tiffany N. and Vanessa D. Plumly (eds), *Rethinking Black German*

Studies: Approaches, Interventions and Histories, Oxford: Peter Lang, 2018.

Fredrickson, George, *Racism: A Short History,* Princeton, NJ: Princeton University Press, 2002.

Frisina, Annalisa and Camilla Hawthorne, 'Italians with Veils and Afros: Gender, Beauty, and the Everyday Anti-Racism of the Daughters of Immigrants in Italy' in *Journal of Ethnic and Migration Studies,* vol. 44, no. 5 (2018), pp. 718–35.

Garner, Steve, *Whiteness, an Introduction,* Abingdon: Routledge, 2007.

Gates, Jr., Henry Louis and Maria Wolff, 'An Overview of Sources on the Life and Work of Juan Latino, the "Ethiopian Humanist"' in *Research in African Literatures,* vol. 29, no. 4 (1998), pp. 14–51.

Generation 2.0, '5+1 myths about Greek citizenship', 18 April 2018, https://g2red.org/51-myths-about-greek-citizenship/, last accessed 17 June 2020.

———, 'Diversity 2.0: An Employer's Guide', 28 February 2019, https://g2red.org/wp-content/uploads/2019/03/Diversity_Guide_Website.pdf, last accessed 17 June 2020.

———, 'We are here. Whether you like it or not.', 16 November 2018, https://g2red.org/we-are-here-whether-you-like-it-or-not/, last accessed 17 June 2020.

Genovese, Eugene D., *Roll, Jordan, Roll: The World the Slaves Made,* New York: Vintage, 1974.

Gentleman, Amelia, *The Windrush Betrayal: Exposing the Hostile Environment,* London: Faber & Faber, 2019.

Germain, Félix and Silyane Larcher, *Black French Women and the Struggle for Equality, 1848–2016,* Lincoln: University of Nebraska Press, 2018.

Gilroy, Paul, *Postcolonial Melancholia,* New York: Columbia University Press, 2008.

———, *The Black Atlantic: Modernity and Double Consciousness,* Verso Books, 1993.

Ginsberg, Elaine K. (ed.), *Passing and the Fictions of Identity,* Durham, NC; London: Duke University Press, 1996.

Gnammankou, Dieudonné, and Ruthmarie H. Mitsch, 'New Research on

BIBLIOGRAPHY

Pushkin's Africa: Hanibal's Homeland' in *Research in African Literatures*, vol. 28, no. 4 (1997), pp. 220–23.

Goebel, Michael, 'Spokesmen, Spies, and Spouses: Anticolonialism, Surveillance, and Intimacy in Interwar France' in *The Journal of Modern History*, vol. 91, no. 2 (2019), pp. 380–414.

Goldberg, David Theo, *The Racial State*, Malden, MA: Blackwell, 2002.

———, *The Threat of Race: Reflections on Racial Neoliberalism*, Oxford: Wiley-Blackwell, 2009.

Gomez, Michael A., 'Juan Latino and the Dawn of Modernity', lecture delivered at the University of Chapel Hill, 20 March 2014, http://as.nyu.edu/content/dam/nyu-as/asSilverDialogues/documents/M%20Gomez%20May%2020171.pdf, last accessed 4 June 2020.

Gonzaléz Garbín, Antonio, 'Glorias de la Universidad Granadina: El Negro Juan Latino' in *Boletin del Centro Artistico de Granada*, vol. 56 (1886).

Goodfellow, Maya, *Hostile Environment: How Immigrants Become Scapegoats*, London: Verso Books, 2019.

Green, Cynthia, 'How Alexander Pushkin Was Inspired By His African Heritage', JSTOR Daily, 1 February 2018, https://daily.jstor.org/how-alexander-pushkin-was-inspired-by-his-african-heritage/, last accessed 16 June 2020.

Greer, Bonnie, *In Search of Black History*, Audible, 2020.

Grimm, Reinhold, 'Two African Saints in Medieval Germany' in *Die Unterrichtspraxis / Teaching German*, vol. 25, no. 2, Focus on Diversity (1992), pp. 127–33.

Guédé, Alain, *Monsieur de Saint-George: Virtuoso, Swordsman, Revolutionary: A Legendary Life Rediscovered*, trans. Gilda M. Roberts, New York: Picador, 2003.

Guyon, Stephanie, 'Christiane Taubira, a Black Woman in Politics in French Guiana and in France' in *Black French Women and the Struggle for Equality, 1848–2016*, eds Félix Germain and Silyane Larcher, Lincoln: University of Nebraska Press, 2018, pp. 19–36.

Habel, Ylva, 'Challenging Swedish Exceptionalism? Teaching While Black' in *Education in the Black Diaspora: Perspectives, Challenges, and Prospects*, eds Kassie Freeman and Ethan Johnson, Abingdon: Routledge, 2012, pp. 99–122.

BIBLIOGRAPHY

Hall, Catherine, *Civilising Subjects: Metropole and Colony in the English Imagination 1830–1867*, Cambridge: Polity, 2002.

———, *White, Male and Middle-Class: Explorations in Feminism and History*, Cambridge: Polity, 1992.

Hall, Stuart, 'The Spectacle of the Other' in *Representation: Cultural Representations and Signifying Practices*, ed. Hall, London: Sage Publications, 1997, pp. 223–90.

Hanley, Ryan, *Beyond Slavery and Abolition: Black British Writing, c. 1770–1830*, Cambridge: Cambridge University Press, 2018.

Harris, Marla, 'Not Black and/or White: Reading Racial Difference in Heliodorus's *Ethiopica* and Pauline Hopkins's *Of One Blood*' in *African American Review*, vol. 35, no. 3 (2001), pp. 375–90.

Hawthorne, Camilla, 'Making Italy: Afro-Italian Entrepreneurs and the Racial Boundaries of Citizenship' in *Social & Cultural Geography*, 2019, pp. 1–21.

Heng, Geraldine, 'The Invention of Race in the European Middle Ages II: Locations of Medieval Race' in *Literature Compass*, vol. 8, no. 5 (2011), pp. 332–50.

———, *The Invention of Race in the European Middle Ages*, Cambridge: Cambridge University Press, 2018.

Henson, Mike, 'Giannis Antetokounmpo: NBA star's rise from "hustling" on Athens streets to MVP award', BBC Sport, https://www.bbc.co.uk/sport/basketball/48832050, last accessed 17 June 2020.

Herodian, *Herodian of Antioch's History of the Roman Empire from the Death of Marcus Aurelius to the Accession of Gordian III*, trans. Edward C. Echols, Berkeley, CA: University of California Press, 1961.

Hine, Darlene Clark, Tricia Keaton and Stephen Small (eds), *Black Europe and the African Diaspora*, Urbana: University of Illinois Press, 2009.

Hirsch, Afua, *Brit(ish): On Race, Identity and Belonging*, London: Jonathan Cape, 2018.

Hirsch, Marianne, *The Generation of Postmemory: Writing and Visual Culture After the Holocaust*, New York: Columbia University Press, 2012.

Hoffmann, Dietrich, *Das spätrömische Bewegungsheer und die Notitia Dignitatum*, Dusseldorf, 1969.

Hondius, Dienke, 'Access to the Netherlands of Enslaved and Free Black

BIBLIOGRAPHY

Africans: Exploring Legal and Social Historical Practices in the Sixteenth–Nineteenth Centuries' in *Slavery & Abolition*, vol. 32, no. 3 (2011), pp. 377–95.

———, *Blackness in Western Europe: Racial Patterns of Paternalism and Exclusion*, Routledge, 2017.

Honeck, Mischa, Martin Klimke and Anne Kuhlmann (eds), *Germany and the Black Diaspora: Points of Contact, 1250–1914*, New York: Berghahn, 2013.

Hurdle, Lynne Maureen, 'The Culture of Appropriating Movements', Psychology Today, 9 August 2019, https://www.psychologytoday.com/us/blog/breaking-culture/201908/the-culture-appropriating-movements, last accessed 25 June 2020.

I am Queen Mary, https://www.iamqueenmary.com/, last accessed 11 June 2020.

Ipsen, Pernille, *Daughters of the Trade: Atlantic Slavers and Interracial Marriage on the Gold Coast*, Philadelphia: University of Pennsylvania Press, 2015.

Ivory, Annette, 'Juan Latino: The Struggle of Blacks, Jews, and Moors in Golden Age Spain' in *Hispania*, vol. 62, no. 4 (1979), pp. 613–18.

———, '"The Christened Mulatresses": Euro-African Families in a Slave-Trading Town' in *The William and Mary Quarterly*, vol. 70, no. 2, Centering Families in Atlantic Histories (2013), pp. 371–98.

Jones, Adam, 'Archival Materials on the Brandenburg African Company (1682–1721)' in *History in Africa*, vol. 11 (1984), pp. 379–89.

Jones, Nicholas R., *Staging* Habla de Negros: *Radical Performances of the African Diaspora in Early Modern Spain*, University Park, PA: Penn State University Press, 2019.

Joseph, Richard, 'The Royal Pretender: Prince Douala Manga Bell in Paris, 1919–1922' in *Cahiers d'études africaines*, vol. 14, no. 54 (1974), pp. 339–58.

Joseph-Gabriel, Annette K., *Reimagining Liberation: How Black Women Transformed Citizenship in the French Empire*, Champaign, IL: University of Illinois Press, 2019.

Kane Lo, Aissata, *De la Signare à la Diriyanké sénégalaise: Trajectoires féminines et visions partagées*, Dakar: L'Harmattan Sénégal, 2014.

Kaufmann, Miranda, *Black Tudors: The Untold Story*, London: Oneworld Publications, 2017.

Keaton, Trica Danielle, T. Denean Sharpley-Whiting and Tyler Edward Stovall (eds), *Black France/France Noire: The History and Politics of Blackness*, Durham, NC: Duke University Press, 2012.

Kenney, Tanasia, 'Move Over White Feminists: Black Activist Tarana Burke Created the #MeToo Campaign 10 Years Ago', Atlanta Black Star, 19 October 2017, https://atlantablackstar.com/2017/10/19/black-activist-tarana-burke-created-metoo-campaign-means-connect-sexual-assault-survivors/, last accessed 25 June 2020.

Knight-Baylac, Marie-Hélène, 'Gorée au XVIIIe siècle: l'appropriation du sol' in *Revue française d'histoire d'outre-mer*, vol. 64, no. 234 (1977), pp. 33–59.

Kpobi, David Nii Anum, *Mission in Chains: The Life, Theology, and Ministry of the Ex-Slave Jacobus E.J. Capitein (1717–1747) with a Translation of His Major Publications*, Zoetermeer: Uitgeverij Boekencentrum, 1993.

Kubai, Anne, 'Being Here and There: Migrant Communities in Sweden and the Conflicts in the Horn of Africa' in *African and Black Diaspora: An International Journal*, vol. 6, no. 2 (2013), pp. 174–88.

La Boëssière, M., *Traité de l'art des armes: à l'usage des professeurs et des amateurs*, Paris: Didot, 1818.

Lambert, Michael C., 'From Citizenship to Negritude: "Making a Difference" in Elite Ideologies of Colonized Francophone West Africa' in *Comparative Studies in Society and History*, vol. 35, no. 2 (1993), pp. 239–62.

Lebron, Christopher J., *The Making of Black Lives Matter: A Brief History of an Idea*, Oxford: Oxford University Press, 2017.

Lemons, Andrew, 'Juan Latino's Worldly Poetics: Lepanto, Lucretius and Literary Tradition' in *Calíope: Journal of the Society for Renaissance and Baroque Hispanic Poetry*, vol. 21, no. 1 (2016), pp. 57–88.

Lennox, Sara (ed.), *Remapping Black Germany: New Perspectives on Afro-German History, Politics, and Culture*, Boston: University of Massachusetts Press, 2016.

Levecq, Christine, 'Jacobus Capitein: Dutch Calvinist and Black

BIBLIOGRAPHY

Cosmopolitan' in *Research in African Literatures*, vol. 44, no. 4 (2013), pp. 145–66.

Levine, Philippa, 'Is Comparative History Possible?' in *History and Theory*, vol. 53, no. 3 (2014), pp. 331–47.

Levine-Rasky, Cynthia, *Whiteness Fractured*, Abingdon: Routledge, 2013.

Llwyd, Alan and Glenn Jordan, *Cymru Ddu/Black Wales: A History: A History of Black Welsh People*, Cardiff: Hughes & Son, 2005.

Lounsbery, Anne, 'Russia's Literary Genius Alexander Pushkin: The Great-Grandson of an African Slave' in *The Journal of Blacks in Higher Education*, no. 27 (2000), pp. 105–8.

Madsen, Maj Bach, 'Denmark cannot apologise for slave trade', ScienceNordic, 27 August 2012, http://sciencenordic.com/denmark-cannot-apologise-slave-trade, last accessed 11 June 2020.

Maquet, Jacques, *Africanity: The Cultural Unity of Black Africa*, Oxford: Oxford University Press, 1972.

Markle, Meghan, 'I'm more than an "Other"', *ELLE*, 22 December 2006, https://www.elle.com/uk/life-and-culture/news/a26855/more-than-an-other/, last accessed 8 June 2020.

Martín Casares, Aurélia, 'A Review of Sources for the Study of Juan Latino: The First Afro-Spanish Poet in Renaissance Europe' in *eHumanista*, vol. 39 (2018), pp. 297–308.

Marynick Palmer, Phyllis, 'White Women/Black Women: The Dualism of Female Identity and Experience in the United States' in *Feminist Studies*, vol. 9, no. 1 (1983), pp. 151–70.

Martín Casares, Aurélia and Marga G. Barranco, 'Popular Depictions of Black African Weddings in Early Modern Spain' in *Renaissance and Reformation*, vol. 31, no. 2 (2008), pp. 107–21.

Matthews, David, *Voices of the Windrush Generation: The Real Story Told by the People Themselves*, London: Blink Publishing, 2018.

McEachrane, Michael (ed.), *Afro-Nordic Landscapes: Equality and Race in Northern Europe*, Abingdon: Routledge, 2014.

Michael, Theodor, *Black German: An Afro-German Life in the Twentieth Century*, trans. Eve Rosenhaft, Liverpool: Liverpool University Press, 2017.

Michel, Marc, 'Les plantations allemandes du mont Cameroun (1885–

1914)' in *Outre-mers. Revue d'histoire*, vol. 57, no. 207 (1970), pp. 183–213.

Miller, Monica L., 'Figuring Blackness in a Place Without Race: Sweden, Recently' in *ELH*, vol. 84, no. 2 (2017), pp. 377–97.

Minnich, Nelson H., 'The Catholic Church and the Pastoral Care of Black Africans in Renaissance Italy' in *Black Africans in Renaissance Europe*, eds T. F. Earle and K. J. P. Lowe, Cambridge: Cambridge University Press, 2005, pp. 280–300.

Miranda, Lin-Manuel, 'The Hamilton Mixtape: Immigrants (We Get the Job Done)', YouTube, 28 June 2017, https://www.youtube.com/watch?v=6_35a7sn6ds, last accessed 16 June 2020.

Mitchell, Robin, *Vénus Noire: Black Women and Colonial Fantasies in Nineteenth-Century France*, Athens, GA: University of Georgia Press, 2020.

Momodou, Jallow, 'Sweden: the country where racism is just a joke', *The Guardian*, 8 April 2012, https://www.theguardian.com/commentis-free/2012/apr/18/racism-becoming-the-norm-sweden, last accessed 16 June 2020.

Mongo-Mboussa, Boniface, 'Débat autour du livre de Dieudonné Gnammankou: *Abraham Hanibal, l'aïeul noir de Pouchkine*' in *Présence Africaine*, no. 157 (1998), pp. 240–48.

Morrison, Heather, 'Dressing Angelo Soliman' in *Eighteenth Century Studies*, vol. 44, no. 3 (2011), pp. 361–82.

Mwasi Collectif Afroféministe, *Afrofem*, Éditions Syllepses, 2018.

———, 'Qui peut nous rejoindre?', https://mwasicollectif.com/portfolio/qui-peut-nous-rejoindre/, last accessed 16 June 2020.

Nana, Genevoix, 'Language Ideology and the Colonial Legacy in Cameroon Schools: A Historical Perspective' in *Journal of Education and Training Studies*, vol. 4, no. 4 (2016), pp. 168–96.

Nardal, Paulette, *Beyond Negritude: Essays from Woman in the City*, ed. and trans. T. Denean Sharpley-Whiting, Albany: State University of New York Press, 2009.

Nederveen Pieterse, Jan, *White on Black: Images of Africa and Blacks in Western Popular Culture*, New Haven, CT; London: Yale University Press, 1992.

BIBLIOGRAPHY

Nimako, Kwame, Amy Abdou and Glenn Willemsen, 'Chattel Slavery and Racism: A Reflection on the Dutch Experience' in *Dutch Racism*, eds Philomena Essed and Isabel Hoving, Amsterdam: Rodopi, 2014, pp. 33–51.

Nina, 'Lost in Otherness: Growing Up as a Mixed Raced Child in Eastern Europe', Afropean, 12 December 2016, http://afropean.com/lost-in-otherness-growing-up-as-a-mixed-raced-child-in-eastern-europe/, last accessed 16 June 2020.

Noah, Trevor *Born a Crime*, London: John Murray, 2016.

Noël, Erick, *Être noir en France au XVIIIe siècle*, Paris: Tallandier, 2006.

———, 'The Racist', BBC Radio 4, 10 June 2017.

Nonbo Andersen, Astrid, 'The Reparations Movement in the United States Virgin Islands' in *The Journal of African American History*, vol. 103, nos 1–2 (2018), pp. 104–32.

Nsafou, Laura and Barbara Brun, *Comme un million de papillons noirs*, Paris: Cambourakis, 2018.

Oberon Garcia, Claire, 'Remapping the Metropolis: Theorizing Black Women's Subjectivities in Interwar Paris' in *Black French Women and the Struggle for Equality, 1848–2016*, eds Félix Germain and Silyane Larcher, Lincoln: University of Nebraska Press, 2018, pp. 215–36.

Odotei, Irene, 'External Influences on Ga Society and Culture' in *Research Review NS*, vol. 7, nos 1–2 (1991), pp. 61–71.

Ohajuru, Michael, The John Blanke Project, https://www.johnblanke.com/, last accessed 17 June 2020.

Olusoga, David, *Black and British: A Forgotten History*, London: Pan Macmillan, 2017.

Ono-George, Meleisa, '"Power in the Telling": Community-Engaged Histories of Black Britain', History Workshop, 18 November 2019, https://www.historyworkshop.org.uk/power-in-the-telling/, last accessed 25 June 2020.

Onyeka, *Blackamoores: Africans in Tudor England, Their Presence, Status and Origins*, London: Narrative Eye, 2013.

Open Society Foundations, 'Under Suspicion: The Impact of Discriminatory Policing in Spain', 2019, https://enpad.eu/wp-content/

uploads/2019/12/UNDER-SUSPICION-OSF-RIS-1.pdf, last accessed 17 June 2020.

Otele, Olivette *Histoire de l'esclavage britannique: Des origines de la traite transatlantique aux prémisses de la colonisation*, Paris: Michel Houdiard Éditeur, 2008.

———, '"Liberté, Egalité, Fraternité": Debunking the myth of egalitarianism in French education' in *Unsettling Eurocentrism in the Westernized University*, eds Julie Cupples and Ramón Grosfoguel, Abingdon: Routledge, 2019, pp. 221–34.

Otele, Olivette, 'Re-Branding the Trauma of Slavery, or How to Pacify the Masses with Sites of Memory', Discover Society, 3 June 2015, https://discoversociety.org/2015/06/03/re-branding-the-trauma-of-slavery-or-how-to-pacify-the-masses-with-sites-of-memory/, last accessed 16 June 2020.

Palmer, Jennifer L., 'What's in a Name? Mixed-Race Families and Resistance to Racial Codification in Eighteenth-Century France' in *French Historical Studies*, vol. 33, no. 3 (2010), pp. 357–85.

Pavard, Bibia, 'Faire naître et mourir les vagues: comment s'écrit l'histoire des féminismes' in *Itinéraires* (2017/2018), https://journals.openedition.org/itineraires/3787, last accessed 17 June 2020.

Peabody, Sue, *'There Are No Slaves in France': The Political Culture of Race and Slavery in the Ancien Régime*, Oxford: Oxford University Press, 1996.

People's Collection Wales, 'Mrs Vernester Cyril OBE as a student nurse outside the Friars Education Centre, Newport, 1966', https://www.peoplescollection.wales/items/485774, last accessed 17 June 2020.

Phillips, Jr., William D., *Slavery from Roman Times to the Early Transatlantic Trade*, Minneapolis: University of Minnesota Press, 1985.

Pitts, Johny, *Afropean: Notes from Black Europe*, London: Penguin, 2019.

Pred, Allan, *Even in Sweden: Racisms, Racialized Spaces and the Popular Geographical Imagination*, Berkeley, CA: University of California Press, 2000.

Purdy, Daniel, 'Mobilizing the Archive in Support of Colonialism during the Kaiserreich' in *Journal of Germanic Studies*, vol. 53, no. 3 (2017), pp. 219–33.

Pushkin, Aleksandr, 'To the Poet', trans. Donald MacAlister in *The Slavonic Review*, vol. 4, no. 12 (1926), p. 691.

Qureshi, Sadiah, *Peoples on Parade: Exhibitions, Empire, and Anthropology in Nineteenth-Century Britain*, Chicago: University of Chicago Press, 2011.

Ramirez, Sonti, 'What it's like being black in Poland', Gal-dem, 13 January 2018, http://gal-dem.com/being-black-in-poland/, last accessed 16 June 2020.

Ramos, Manuel Joao and Isabel Boavida, 'Ambiguous Legitimacy: The Legend of the Queen of Sheba in Popular Ethiopian Painting' in *Annales d'Éthiopie*, vol. 21 (2005), pp. 85–92.

'Rastafari in Motion', http://www.rastafari-in-motion.org/, last accessed 27 May 2020.

Ribbe, Claude, *Le Chevalier de Saint-George*, Paris: Éditions Perrin, 2004.

Robinson, Cedric J., *Black Marxism: The Making of The Black Radical Tradition*, Chapel Hill, NC: University of North Carolina Press, 2000.

Rowe, Erin Kathleen, *Black Saints in Early Modern Global Catholicism*, Cambridge: Cambridge University Press, 2019.

Royal Historical Society, 'Race, Ethnicity and Equality Report', https://royalhistsoc.org/racereport/, last accessed 17 June 2020.

Sawyer, Lena, 'Routings: "Race," African Diasporas, and Swedish Belonging' in *Transforming Anthropology*, vol. 11, no. 1 (2008), pp. 13–35.

Schough, Katarina, *Hyperboré: föreställningen om Sveriges plats i världen*, Stockholm: Carlssons, 2008.

Shukla, Nikesh, *The Good Immigrant*, London: Unbound, 2016.

Small, Stephen, *20 Questions and Answers on Black Europe*, The Hague: Amrit, 2017.

Smidak, Emil F., *Joseph Boulogne, Called Chevalier de Saint-Georges*, Luzern: Avenira Foundation, 1996.

Sobers, Shawn Naphtali, 'Fairfield House Rastafari Graphics', http://www.shawnsobers.com/portfolio/uncategorized/fairfield-house-rastafari-graphics/, last accessed 27 May 2020.

Stovall, Tyler, 'A Black Woman's Life in the Struggle: Jean McNair in France' in *Black French Women and the Struggle for Equality, 1848–2016*, eds Félix Germain and Silyane Larcher, Lincoln: University of Nebraska Press, 2018, pp. 109–27.

Strabo, *Geography*, trans. H. C. Hamilton and W. Falconer, London: George Bell and Sons, 1903.

Stuurman, Siep, 'François Bernier and the Invention of Racial Classification' in *History Workshop Journal*, no. 50 (2000), pp. 1–21.

Taylor, Keeanga-Yamahtta, *From #BlackLivesMatter to Black Liberation*, Chicago: Haymarket Books, 2016.

The Black Archives, http://www.theblackarchives.nl/home.html, last accessed 17 June 2020.

The Black Cultural Archives, https://blackculturalarchives.org/, last accessed 17 June 2020.

The Greek Alexander Romance, trans. Richard Stoneman, London: Penguin, 1991.

The Telegraph, 'Theresa May's conference speech in full', 5 October 2016, https://www.telegraph.co.uk/news/2016/10/05/theresa-mays-conference-speech-in-full/, last accessed 26 May 2020.

The Times, 'Prince's Dishonoured Cheque', 29 July 1921, no. 42785, p. 9.

———, 'The Last of the Cameroons' Kings', 5 March 1898, no. 35456, p. 10.

Thomas, Dominic (ed.), *Afroeuropean Cartographies*, Newcastle upon Tyne: Cambridge Scholars Publishing, 2014.

———, *Black France: Colonialism, Immigration, and Transnationalism*, Bloomington: Indiana University Press, 2007.

Tognetti, Sergio, 'The Trade in Black African Slaves in Fifteenth-Century Florence' in *Black Africans in Renaissance Europe*, eds T. F. Earle and K. J. P. Lowe, Cambridge: Cambridge University Press, 2005, pp. 213–24.

'Trans-Atlantic Slave Trade: Estimates', Slave Voyages, https://www.slave-voyages.org/assessment/estimates, last accessed 11 June 2020.

Traore, Assa and Elsa Vigoureux, *Lettre à Adama*, Paris: Seuil, 2017.

Umoren, Imaobong D., *Race Women Internationalists: Activist-Intellectuals and Global Freedom Struggles*, Berkeley, CA: University of California Press, 2018.

Van Berchem, Denis, *Le martyre de la légion Thébaine: essai sur la formation d'une légende*, Basel, 1956.

BIBLIOGRAPHY

Ver-Ndoye, Naïl and Grégoire Fauconnier, *Noir: Entre peinture et histoire*, Mouans-Sartoux: Omniscience, 2018.

Vernon, Patrick, 'Where are all the Black historians?', Media Diversified, 30 March 2016, https://mediadiversified.org/2016/03/30/where-are-all-the-black-historians/, last accessed 25 June 2020.

Walvin, James, *Black and White: The Negro and English Society, 1555–1945*, London: Allen Lane, 1973.

Weissbourd, Emily, '"I Have Done the State Some Service": Reading Slavery in *Othello* through *Juan Latino*' in *Comparative Drama*, vol. 47, no. 4 (2013), pp. 529–51.

Wekker, Gloria, *White Innocence: Paradoxes of Colonialism and Race*, Durham, NC: Duke University Press, 2016.

White, Nadine, 'Chadwick Jackson: Filmmaker Forced To Turn Down Work As Immigration Limbo Drags On', HuffPost, 16 February 2020, https://www.huffingtonpost.co.uk/entry/chadwick-jackson-british-jamaican-filmmaker-immigration-deportation_uk_5e1464aee4b0b2520d27ad48, last accessed 17 June 2020.

Wekker, Gloria and Rivke Jaffe, 'Reflections: A Conversation with Gloria Wekker' in *Development and Change*, vol. 49, no. 2 (2018), pp. 547–60.

Woldemikael, Olivia, 'Why Barack is black and Meghan is biracial', Media Diversified, 28 June 2018, https://mediadiversified.org/2018/06/28/why-barack-is-black-and-megan-is-biracial/, last accessed 24 June 2020.

Woods, David, 'The Origin of the Legend of Maurice and the Theban Legion' in *The Journal of Ecclesiastical History*, vol. 45, no. 3 (1994), pp. 385–95.

Wright, Elizabeth R., 'Narrating the Ineffable Lepanto: The Austrias Carmen of Joannes Latinus (Juan Latino)' in *Hispanic Review*, vol. 77, no. 1 (2009), pp. 71–91.

Wytse, Keulen, 'Fronto and Apuleius: Two African Careers in the Roman Empire' in *Apuleius and Africa*, eds Benjamin Todd Lee, Ellen Finkelpearl and Luca Graverini, London: Routledge, 2014, pp. 129–53.

Zacharopoulou, Effrosyni, 'The Black Saint Maurice of Magdeburg and the African Christian Kingdoms in Nubia and Ethiopia in the Thirteenth Century' in *The Southern African Journal of Medieval and Renaissance Studies*, vol. 25, (2015), pp. 77–110.

INDEX

INDEX

INDEX

INDEX

INDEX

INDEX

INDEX

INDEX

INDEX

INDEX

INDEX

INDEX

INDEX

INDEX

INDEX

INDEX

Olivette Otele is professor of history and memory of enslavement at the University of Bristol and vice president of the Royal Historical Society. She is the first Black woman to be appointed to a professorial chair in history in the UK, and her writing has appeared in the *Guardian*, *BBC Extra*, and *Times Higher Education*. She lives in the UK.